MOTIVATIONS FOR REFUSAL

Studies in Critical Social Sciences Book Series

Haymarket Books is proud to be working with Brill Academic Publishers (www.brill.nl) to republish the *Studies in Critical Social Sciences* book series in paperback editions. This peer-reviewed book series offers insights into our current reality by exploring the content and consequences of power relationships under capitalism, and by considering the spaces of opposition and resistance to these changes that have been defining our new age. Our full catalog of *SCSS* volumes can be viewed at https://www.haymarketbooks .org/series_collections/4-studies-in-critical-social-sciences.

Series Editor
David Fasenfest (York University)

New Scholarship in Political Economy Book Series

Series Editors
David Fasenfest (York University)
Alfredo Saad-Filho (Queen's University, Belfast)

Editorial Board
Kevin B. Anderson (University of California, Santa Barbara)
Tom Brass (formerly of SPS, University of Cambridge)
Raju Das (York University)
Ben Fine ((emeritus) SOAS University of London)
Jayati Ghosh (Jawaharlal Nehru University)
Elizabeth Hill (University of Sydney)
Dan Krier (Iowa State University)
Lauren Langman (Loyola University Chicago)
Valentine Moghadam (Northeastern University)
David N. Smith (University of Kansas)
Susanne Soederberg (Queen's University)
Aylin Topal (Middle East Technical University)
Fiona Tregenna (University of Johannesburg)
Matt Vidal (Loughborough University London)
Michelle Williams (University of the Witwatersrand)

MOTIVATIONS FOR REFUSAL

Work, Value, and the Limits of Postworkerism

MARK GAWNE

Haymarket Books
Chicago, IL

First published in 2025 by Brill Academic Publishers, The Netherlands
© 2025 Koninklijke Brill NV, Leiden, The Netherlands

Published in paperback in 2026 by
Haymarket Books
P.O. Box 180165
Chicago, IL 60618
773-583-7884
www.haymarketbooks.org

ISBN: 979-8-88890-792-4

Distributed to the trade in the US through Consortium Book Sales and
Distribution (www.cbsd.com) and internationally through Ingram Publisher
Services International (www.ingramcontent.com).

This book was published with the generous support of Lannan Foundation,
Wallace Action Fund, and the Marguerite Casey Foundation.

Special discounts are available for bulk purchases by organizations and
institutions. Please call 773-583-7884 or email info@haymarketbooks.org for more
information.

Cover design by Jamie Kerry and Ragina Johnson.

Printed in the United States.

Library of Congress Cataloging-in-Publication data is available.

Contents

Acknowledgements

This book was written on unceded Dharawal, Yuin, and Gadigal Land. Always Was, Always Will Be Aboriginal Land.

This book has grown out of the PhD I completed in 2014. While a lot of time has passed since then, many of the questions I initially considered have only become more acute. I would like to thank my supervisor and friend Melinda Cooper, for her guidance and support during the years of my PhD, and in the years since. Thank you to my thesis markers, particularly Steve Wright for very useful comments. Thank you to Steve for some extra guidance in updating the manuscript and sharing resources I couldn't find elsewhere. Nate Holdren and Emiliana Armano provided very useful and generous comments in developing the manuscript. Thank you to Brill and David Fasenfest in seeing this project through. Thank you to Elizabeth Humphrys, for being so encouraging as a fellow worker and friend, I probably wouldn't have embarked on the book process without the conversations with you in recent years at UTS. Big thanks to my family – Terry and my siblings, and to Nicky and Tony who we miss dearly. The regional city of Wollongong has played an important part in this book, big thanks to everybody who was involved with RA long ago for teaching me so much about meaningful organisational practice. And thank you to everyone in GC now, for the same and for the novel experiments with compositionist practice in the Illawarra. Thank you to Wollongong Friends of Palestine. Over the past twenty years and more a small cluster of us have probably spent too much time discussing the specific threads of communist thought and practice covered in the book and much more, I would like to thank Nick Southall, Sharon Pusell, Dave Eden, Alexander Brown, and Rachel Rowe for all that has come of it. Thank you to the clusters of friends I've spent time with across recent years in Wollongong, Sydney, Melbourne, and Guangzhou. Thanks to Huck, Yul, Rosie, Peach, Regrette, Sunil, Lou, Claire, Claire, Shane, Eve, Jet and many more friends who have been so pivotal in my life, too many to name you all but thank you. A huge thank you to Rachel Rowe especially, not only for the countless measures in seeing this project through, in time, critique, suggestions, improvements, and all-round amazing generosity, but for always being such an infallible compass as to what really matters in this life we all share. And love to R and Osian, for being brilliant.

CHAPTER 1

Introduction

Work is pervasive yet contested in everyday life, shaping our experiences of the world even when we are excluded from employment. It consumes our time, even when we aren't on the clock, and sits at the heart of some of the most significant contradictions we face. Current, lively debates and discourses of automation, AI, and the changing character of future work arrangements illustrate some of the ways that work is understood as the basis of wider social relations. Utopian, dystopian, and plain moralistic visions of work underpin concerns about how, why, and to what ends we work. Throughout all of this, fundamental truths about the regime of work and the labour-capital relation persist.

If you have ever been unable to afford the things you need in this life, you are aware of the persistence of the disciplinary function and violence of the law of value, and the role of work in expressing the force of that law. Our access to food, shelter, transport, and leisure, among other things, is mediated by money and work remains the primary way that most of us get money. For this fundamental reason, work constitutes a terrain of contestation, struggle, and power relations within contemporary capitalism. The critique of work, waged and unwaged, is therefore central to the critique of capitalist social relations, and the prospects for creating together a different mode of social cooperation.

While continuity in the general structure of the labour-capital relation persists, forms of political, economic, social and cultural reproduction are also subject to contestation and change. One expression of these changes are new techniques of production and labour processes, the character of commodities produced, and the forms of labour subsumed to the imperative of capital accumulation and reproduction. One need only look at the various adjectives prefixed to contemporary capitalism and modes of work, to see how some have grappled with the novelties of the present conjuncture. For example, cognitive capitalism (Moulier-Boutang, 2004), surveillance capitalism (Zuboff, 2019), affective capitalism (Lee, 2023), logistical capitalism (Brennan, 2021), or platform capitalism (Srnicek, 2016), each of these approaches to the analysis of the political economy offer something to the critique of the present conjuncture. They find their counterparts in the figures of the cognitive labourer, the digital and logistics worker, immaterial and affective labour. An attentiveness to the emergence of new forms of work, new modes of management, new iterations of the technological mediation of labour, and forms of class refusal and subversion, is essential to the critique of the labour-capital relation in its specificity and totality. Analysing these concrete dimensions within the organisation of work, production, and reproduction allows us to better understand the contemporary compositions of class and capital as they manifest today.

This book, *Motivations for Refusal: Work, Value, and the Limits of Postworkerism*, contributes to the critical analysis of contemporary work organisation, specifically in its affective dimensions. Throughout *Motivations for Refusal*, the critique of work in its affective dimensions involves four related dynamics. The first is the critique postworkerist theories of labour through an analysis of value-form theory while emphasising the importance of class composition analysis to overcome the limits of value-theory. Second, the book analyses how the production of affect is integrated into modes of labour as an element of commodity production. This component of the book takes place via an interrogation of the theories of affective and immaterial labour. Third, it involves analysing how formations of affective capital have taken shape with the proliferation of immaterial modes of production. This thread of analysis develops via a critique of the integration of the affective sciences into management and workplace technologies as methods to address the challenges of labour intensity in conditions of immaterial production. Finally, the book explores how affective politics emerge in the contestation implied in the relationship between affective labour on the one hand, and affective management and technological mediation on the other. Through the critical analysis of these four aspects of affective production, the book advances the critique of labour in its affective and immaterial expressions.

In pursuing the above lines of inquiry, this book develops an analysis of the affective compositions of class and capital through a sustained critical reading of postworkerism. The postworkerist variant of autonomist Marxism constitutes an important and influential school of thought on contemporary and future work studies. It is characterised by a particularly close and insistent attention to the shifting arrangements of work, and demarcations between work and non-work, or between labour and life. The novelties and innovations in the postworkerist understanding of labour and capital, even in their limitations, provide a rich entry point to outline the persistent antagonism of labour and capital even in their affective modes. In theorising immaterial and affective production, postworkerism has shaped diverse studies into work and politics from care economies, digital labour, creative to cognitive labour (Dowling, 2007; Wissinger, 2007; Christiaens, 2022; Moore, 2018).

However, postworkerism insists that there is no longer a functional distinction between the time when one is at work and when one is outside of work, nor is there any distinction between labour and life: life and labour have merged into a singular productive substance. The anchor of this conflation of labour and life is a productivist ontology of labour-value-affect. For postworkerism, the ongoing struggle between labour and capital, and the real subsumption of labour to capital, realises the complete socialisation of labour, resulting in the merging of labour, life and production. The implication of this argument is an inability to develop a critique of labour in the present or of the commodity. *Motivations for Refusal* identifies this productivist ontology as the fundamental limit of postworkerism's theorisation of labour. Through a sustained critical engagement with the insights and limitations of postworkerism, *Motivations for Refusal* presents an alternative reading of the politics of affect in late capitalist production.

The argument throughout the book draws on value critique and class composition analysis to identify the limitations of theories of affective labour and the specific ways in which the affective sciences have come to constitute an element of the technical composition of class. In reading value-form theory against postworkerism, *Motivations for Refusal* makes two novel contributions and advancements in the critique of capitalist social relations. First, the book illustrates that even in conditions of immaterial production, there is an internalisation of labour to capital and thus a political imperative to retain a critique of labour and value. Second, *Motivations for Refusal* demonstrates that in addition to the critique of value and abstract labour, it is beneficial to retain an attention to class composition analysis in order to navigate the lived contours of class antagonism. Questions that arise in this context include the following, how are productivity and work intensity measured when labour is not producing tangible commodities? If time and motion studies are inadequate for the measure and intensification of work in service economies, what science of management has emerged in its wake? Moreover, what does this mean for the critique of value, the commodity, and class composition in the workplaces of affective and immaterial production? These questions are crucial to understanding the labour-capital relation and its inherent antagonism in conditions of service, immaterial, affective and emotional production today. They call for a reconsideration of the categories and composition of class and capital. This book locates and critically analyses affect theory and the affective sciences as elements within the composition of class and capital, to develop a critique of work in late capitalism.

1 Crisis, Work, Motivation

Economic crises have often provoked a certain fear on the part of bosses and economists that without reward workers will lose the motivation to continue with sufficient effort in their jobs. As management theorist Nadia Steiber puts it, the "concern is that an experience of economic vulnerability during the economic crisis may have long-lasting repercussions for the population's employment commitment" (2013: 195). Steiber's comments draw an interesting connection between the realities of economic downturn and the managerial issues of worker motivation within the job, as well as to the broader question of one's motivation to work at all. Beyond Steiber's worry about the "long-lasting repercussions" for motivation and commitment in general, she also identifies the specificity of these issues within the post-Fordist condition. In other words, the managerial and productivist concern with motivation arises as a key dynamic in contemporary knowledge and service-oriented modes of labour. Steiber argues that "in knowledge-based economies the skilled and motivated employee is an important asset" (2013: 195). The proliferation of service work elevates motivation and affects as variables of management, particularly as earlier modes of productivity management, such as time and motion studies, lose their effectiveness. Steiber is here circling around the limitations of the affective regime of capital. The affective regime of capital is expressed through a concern with motivation, commitment, and attachments to work as a means of managing the labour-capital relation. However, as is implied in the concern expressed by Steiber, commitment is far from given, and the affective regime of employment motivation is anything but absolute. Indeed, it is contested, both individually and socially.

There have been at least two occasions in recent memory that have, for a short time at least, exposed a certain precariousness to the foundation of capitalism as a historic mode of social production, and in turn illustrate the contested character of work and labour. Steiber is reflecting on one of these occasions above, namely the 2008 financial and economic crisis, which brought into question the foundations of the economy and the prospects for its future. The jeopardous condition was attributed to various causes: from the perils of fictitious capital, the flight of finance from the 'real' economy, the anchorless condition of value in the absence of the gold standard, to lack of financial regulation and 'banksters' with too much power. There were, of course, just as many remedies proposed as diagnoses. Amidst the chorus of responses were calls for a return to Keynesian economics, (neo-)social democracies, and anchored currencies, as well as the rise of the political right and theology. Unsurprisingly, the crisis provoked debates about how best to return capitalism to 'normal', whatever that might mean, or to at least reconfigure its reproducibility.

The second more recent occasion has been the impact of the pandemic on capitalism broadly, and the conditions of work more specifically. The upheaval wrought through the pandemic, saw the temporary reversal of fiscal and monetary policies, with massive state expenditure unleashed to keep the economy afloat throughout lockdowns and the closure of large sections of the economy. From the perspective of labour, the experience of the pandemic saw a widespread revaluation of working life. Assessing the situation in China in the early days of the pandemic, Chuang[1] speculated that the lockdowns not only provoked the existential questions of "What will happen to me? My children, family and friends? … Will I get paid? Will I make rent?" (2021: 10). But more broadly, how "the subjective experience [was] somewhat like that of a mass strike … hollowed of its communal features but nonetheless capable of delivering a deep shock to both psyche and economy" (Chuang, 2021: 10). In the years that followed 2020, economic tumult persisted, the cost of living spiralled, and both formal and informal industrial actions proliferated, all seemingly channelled through an affective expression of collective exhaustion, no doubt amplified by the acceleration of the climate breakdown (Chaudhary, 2024). Concerned as always by threats to workplace commitment and motivation, the spokespeople of capital called for evermore motivation and commitment. A wave of exhaustion and refusal rose to meet their calls.

2   Why Work? What Life?

In the politics of everyday life, labour and work continue to be contentious categories. Against the images painted of a workless future by the optimists and pessimists alike, the present remains dominated by the compulsion to work. Mass sackings, unemployment, workfare, precarious work, overwork, unwaged work, and the refusal of work, all turn upon articulations of the condition of labour within the social relation of capital. That is to say, all are manifestations of work.[2] All remain contentious, subject to antagonism and conflict.

---

1   Chuang is a research collective who publish a journal, blog, and books on capitalist development and proletarian struggles in China, and the relationship they have to global capitalism. See https://chuangcn.org/.

2   In navigating the economic, social and political tumult of recent years, movements, critics, and theorists have all sought to identify the primary axes and articulations of social bondage, conflict, and contestation. Some have emphasised the significance of debt as a form of control and a site of contestation (Graeber, 2011; Lazzarato, 2012). The analysis of debt as a mode of social, political and economic regulation has emphasised the debtor-creditor relation as the definitive relation of late capitalism. For others, the return of various forms of rent constitutes the clearest foundation of critique (Vercellone, 2013; Christophers; 2020, Christiaens, 2021). While unavoidably connected to the problem of work and labour, contemporary analyses of debt and rent have tended to approach the question of work as secondary. In this context, the first question I posed above appears somewhat anachronistic: why *work*? Or in other words, if the crisis, the question of the restoration of capitalist reproduction, and the

Work is invoked as a component of the moral order of capitalism. Spending too much time outside of work will provoke calls for disciplinary measures on those so-called 'unproductive' persons. Employment is here cast as a kind of baptism and redemption. Work is thus invoked as both moral stick and redemptive carrot to wield upon the poor and unemployed. We see this, for example, in former Australian Minister for Social Services, Kevin Andrews' comments that "work is the best form of welfare" (quoted in Jabour, 2014: np). In a similar manner, labour is glorified as a necessary social bond. As Ross Douthat worried when observing the decline in full-time, blue-collar work in the US during the wake of the 2008 crisis, "even a grinding job tends to be an important source of social capital, providing everyday structure for people who live alone, a place to meet friends and kindle romances for people who lack other forms of community" (2013: np). Douthat was also concerned that "the decline in work-force participation is of a piece with the broader turn away from community in America – from family breakdown and declining churchgoing to the retreat into the virtual forms of sport and sex and friendship" (2013: np). Douthat's moral concerns align with the rise of theological welfare and the alliances of neoliberals and new social conservatives (Cooper, 2012; Cooper, 2013; Cooper, 2017).

Meanwhile, should workers and the unemployed begin to think that a higher share of wealth should come their way, the disciplinary functions of work return in a flash. During the so-called labour shortage of the pandemic period, the millionaire real estate CEO Tim Gurner, put it plainly,

> I think the problem that we've had is that people decided they didn't really want to work so much anymore through COVID ... They have been paid a lot to do not too much in the last few years, and we need to see that change. We need to see unemployment rise ... Unemployment has to jump 40, 50% in my view. We need to see pain in the economy. We need to remind people that they work for the employer, not the other way around.
>
> cited in JACKSON, 2023: np

In this light, the moral order of capitalism quickly slips into its disciplinary mode. Work and access to money constitute one of the primary levers through which the reproduction of the power of capitalist social relations is wielded.

---

challenges to it have tended to emphasise dynamics of debt and rent as the primary concern, then it may be unclear what is to be gained by posing the issue of work as central to critique.

The contestation of this power, latent or explicit, formal and informal, remains one of the most important socio-political dynamics of late capitalism.

For some, work animates the fantasies and possibilities of the future. The present resounds with the utopian, post-work visions that characterised the nineties. Under the rubric of the new economy and post-industrial capitalism it was seen fit by some, such as 'information revolutionaries' Daniel Bell (2008 [1973]) and Alvin Toffler (1984), to declare the beginning of a workless age. The leftist iteration of this view, captured in the slogan of fully automated luxury communism (Bastani, 2019), casts the same image of the future rooted in the same alleged premises of the present. The alleged condition of a work-free economy was really a celebration of uber-productivity in the new labour-processes of the computerised and so-called creative economy, though still built on the continued extraction of resources necessary for such industries to thrive (Caffentzis, 2003 [1998]). For some these dreams have turned to fears of automation, computerisation and the decline of the middle class, that is, the decline of work (Leonard, 2014). In any case, viewed from each of these perspectives, labour may be unfashionable, but it remains a necessary social relation.

On the other hand, work remains fundamentally mundane. The experience of work and unemployment is often named for how it appears and what it so often is: a pointless activity. David Graeber captured this aptly when he described an amassing of 'bullshit jobs' (2013). The tension between employment, unemployment, and unwaged work are far from new, and the first volume of *Capital* is concerned as much with the question of unemployment as it is with production as such, insofar as they are expressions of the same phenomenon: the relationship between labour and capital. It is not uncommon to read, hear, or indeed experience, the blurring of the distinction between work and life. The various analyses of 'precarity' draw attention to this indistinction. Angela Mitropoulos has argued that

> the search for a life outside work tended to reduce into an escape from the factory and its particular forms of discipline. And so, perhaps paradoxically, this flight triggered an indistinction between work and life commensurate with the movement of exploitation into newer areas.
>
> 2005: np

More importantly, Mitropoulos notes that a condition or relationship of precarity has defined the lives of those historically excluded from the wage, and from the particular exception that was the Keynesian and Fordist compromise (see also Gabin, 1982).

And finally, work is a vehicle of nightmares (Kelly, 2024). Endnotes and Aaron Benanav (2010: 20–51) and Neferti X.M. Tadiar (2012) place the conflation of labour and life in starker terms. Tadiar notes an indistinction between life and labour insofar as "'life' has indeed become productive for capital" but insists that "not all life is valorised or valorisable, that the extraction of value from 'life' takes place through more than one modality" (2012: 787). Indeed, as Tadiar argues, drawing from Endnotes Collective, "concomitant with the new productivity of life … is also the tendency of life toward disposability … absolute redundancy and superfluity", toward "life as waste" (2012: 788–789). As Endnotes and Benanav (2010) argue, this tendency is very much the manifestation of Karl Marx's (1991: 762–870) 'General Law of Capitalist Accumulation': the inherent, inexorable rendering superfluous of workers, of human life, to the imperatives of capital accumulation. 'Superfluity' does not mean exemption from work, evident in the imposition of, for example, workfare or prison labour. Against a valorisation of life as total productivity is the reality of life in catastrophe. The phenomenon of bullshit jobs, workfare, the indistinction between life and work, and the prospect of life as waste, all characterise the contemporary tensions and struggles for a better life. The forms that such struggles might take are another question, but it is clear enough that life, labour and work, all remain contentious and conflicted.

The general question of labour and the contestation of work are thus central to the ongoing critique of capitalist social relations. Within this overall framework, one persistent point of contention in the critique of labour and capital, has been the character of labour, productivity, the commodity, and value in the context of service provision. In particular, the nature of commodity production with intangible outputs, or what has been described as immaterial production, has provoked rich debates about the character of work and its critique in contemporary capitalism. *Motivations for Refusal* locates its argument within this specific debate. Theories of immaterial and affective labour, which canvas a range of service work from care to creative industries, constitute one sustained effort to grapple with these issues. This book critically charts the development and political limitations of these theories, in order to advance the critique of labour in service work contexts. The theoretical frameworks of immaterial and affective labour, once peripheral in both a scholarly and political sense, now hold significant influence across sections of the left to centre political spectrum. They form the foundation for widely publicised demands for a Universal Basic Income (UBI) (Dinerstein and Pitts, 2021), for example, and they have given rise to a range of claims regarding a contemporary "affective capitalism" (Karpi et al., 2016). As such, the scholarly, political, and economic implications arising from analyses of work and affect constitute a key area of interest and debate today.

3   **Preliminary Comments on Postworkerism, Affective Labour, and Immaterial Production**

Postworkerism is most famously associated, outside of Italy, with the publication of *Empire* in 2000 by Michael Hardt and Antonio Negri. However, postworkerism had in fact been developing in different directions throughout the 1970s, 80s and 90s in the work of such theorists as Paolo Virno, Franco Bifo Berardi, Alisa Del Re, Maurizio Lazzarato and Christian Marazzi. All these authors have, in their own way, attempted to come to terms with the new forms and configurations of labour. In doing so, they have theorised and explored emergent relationships between the body, subjectivity and the labour processes of immaterial production (Eden, 2012; 2012a). One primary concern of postworkerism lies in critically analysing the relationship between labour and capital today. The contributions of postworkerism to the theorisation of contemporary labour-capital relations are manifold, evident in the number of theorists drawing from their work to consider contemporary work relations in the digital economy (Christiaens, 2021), the affective economy (Moore, 2018), higher education (Szadowski, 2023), and the creative economy (Stakeheimer and Vishmidt, 2016). Postworkerists have innovated Marxist theory, for better and worse, in such a way that it has reformulated the very foundations of the labour-capital relation.

In 1977, Antonio Negri argued, in a text later wielded against him by the Italian state, that

> we have a method for the destruction of work. We are in search of a *positive measure of non-work*, a measure of our liberation from that disgusting slavery from which the bosses have always profited, and which the official socialist movement has always imposed on us like some sort of title of nobility.
>
> 2005 [1977]: 263

Written in a time of sharp antagonism and innovative political movement, Negri's polemical statement not only captures an ambivalence definitive of *operaismo*, but it also expresses a problem that defines contemporary postworkerism. As such it points to the key problematic of how best to understand the relationship between labour, life and politics.

The ambivalence of *operaismo* is expressed in the divergence between the negationist and the affirmationist approach to understanding the condition of the proletariat. On the one hand, *operaismo* embraced the radical negativity of work refusal, sabotage and proletarian self-negation. On the other, it affirmed the notion of proletarian self-valorisation, the cumulative and immediate practices of meeting working class needs and desires, and the affirmation of class subjectivities and practices as they exist within the framework of struggle. In other words, *operaismo* was as Negri puts it above, both "a method for the destruction of work" and the "search for a positive measure of non-work". It is of course possible to see a complementarity between these perspectives. However, the overwhelming tendency that emerges in the movement from *operaismo* to postworkerism is one that emphasises working-class self-valorisation to such a degree that the cooperative practices of immaterial production allegedly possess an inherent autonomy from capital.

Postworkerism maintains a perspective of antagonism between labour and capital. What is refreshing in this perspective is the refusal to subordinate working-class subjectivity to capital. We are not simply defined by how capital or the state would arrange our lives – the life of the proletariat (now the multitude) is always in some respect in excess and against. However, in theorising the dynamic of antagonism, postworkerism arrives at a perspective characterised by what this book will call a productivist ontology, founded in the construction of labour-value-affect. As we will see throughout the book, the arguments of postworkerism have broken with earlier, narrow conceptions of the productive worker associated with a particular kind of production process. However, their own trajectory which has defined everything as 'productive', not only recapitulates a certain productivism, but undermines the critique of labour in the present. Despite the theoretical innovations of postworkerism, and the rich history from which it emerged, I will argue that the premise of productive life is an untenable position from which to develop a critique of labour today.

Immaterial and affective labour are ways of denoting a form of production in which the output is not a tangible/vendible commodity. Maurizio Lazzarato defines immaterial labour as that "which produces the informational and cultural content of the commodity" (1996: 133). Michael Hardt expands on Lazzarato's definition to include "labour that produces an immaterial good, such as a service, knowledge, or communication" (1999: 94). Continuing, Hardt states that "since the production of services results in no material and durable good, we might define the labour involved as in this production *immaterial labour*" (1999: 94). Affective labour expands Lazzarato's notion of immaterial labour to include forms of caring labour, the production of relationships, "social networks, forms of community, biopower" (Hardt, 1999: 96). Deepening the concept of affective labour, Hardt continues that while affective labour is not new, given that "feminist analyses have long recognised the social value of caring work" (1999: 97), the economic role and significance of affective labour has shifted. According to Hardt, what has changed is the degree to which "affective immaterial labour is now directly productive of capital and the extent to

which it has become generalised throughout wide sections of the economy"
(1999: 97). As a result, for Hardt, "affective labour has achieved a dominant
position of the highest value in the contemporary informational economy"
(1999: 97). *Motivations for Refusal* draws from the insights of postworkerism,
while critiquing the political limitations that arise from the theories of immaterial and affective production.

3.1   *Existing Critiques of Immaterial Production*

Many criticisms have been made since the theory of immaterial labour and production was first developed by postworkerism 30 years ago. It is worth briefly
touching on some of these, in order to situate the argument of *Motivations for
Refusal*. To start with Marx, the forms of work and the relationship to capital
that the postworkerists are analysing are evidently distinct enough from those
of Henri Storch (1823, cited in Marx, 1975: 284–287). Marx derided Storch for
his misunderstanding of material production within capitalism, and for introducing theoretical absurdities into the discussion of "spiritual" or "immaterial"
production (1975: 284–287). Marx argues that for Storch "the physician produces health (but also illness), professors and writers produce enlightenment
(but also obscurantism), poets, painters, etc., produce good taste (but also
bad taste), moralists, etc., produce morals" and so on. That is, Storch presents
an argument of little consequence in terms of understanding the relationship between labour and capital, or the nature of material production. While
Wolfgang Fritz Haug and Joseph Fraccia (2009) take Negri, and by extension
postworkerism, to task for an apparent ignorance of the history of the term
and Marx's rejection of it, I suggest that this is of secondary importance at
best. Moreover, Marx did directly address conditions of immaterial production
in both the *Theories of Surplus Value* and *Capital volume II* in ways that lend
credence to the theory of immaterial production. I come to these in Chapter 2.
In any case, the particular criticisms Marx makes of Storch cannot be made of
the postworkerist use of the term immaterial labour, as Storch and the postworkerists are referring to different phenomena.

Similarly, I put aside those criticisms of immaterial labour that assert that
all labour is material, and so therefore immaterial labour cannot exist (see for
example Caffentzis, 2007). Indeed, as Matteo Pasquinelli has argued, "when
we talk about cognitive capitalism or the hegemony of immaterial labour, we
do not refer to something "'immaterial' but to a very physical *machinic inter-
twining* of our bodies and social relations" (2011: 16). Immaterial production
is a confusing and unfortunate term. However, it is evident enough that all
labour is material, and it is also clear by now that this is not a controversial
statement even insofar as the postworkerist concept of immaterial production

goes: labour is inherently material/corporeal, yet the product of labour is not always a tangible commodity. In any case, the clumsiness of the term aside, the relations that the term immaterial production purports to name are real enough (Szadowski, 2023). It is how these relations are interpreted and theorised politically by postworkerists that is the more important issue to critique. For my part, I approach the critique of immaterial production on the grounds of what it claims to describe, and what the postworkerist analysis implies for the critique of labour.

There are several significant criticisms of the theory of immaterial production that are worth pointing to. Feminist scholarship is often cited as a pivotal source in the development of the theory of immaterial production and affective labour, and in several respects it has been. However, it is important to note the serious criticisms made by feminists of the immaterial production theses. Silvia Federici (2011) has argued that the theory of affective labour effectively marginalises, excludes or ignores the critical insights into the critique of political economy made by feminist scholarship at least since the 1970s. By marginalising feminist insights, the postworkerists smooth over the specific power dynamics and hierarchical divisions that organise the various forms of 'reproductive' labour. I agree with these criticisms, and I address them in greater detail in Chapters 3 and 5.

Another significant criticism, similar to Federici's, has focused upon the disjuncture between the attempt to synthesise the perspective on class through the lens of immaterial production and the global division of labour in late capitalism. Indeed, it is difficult to include within the same composition of labour design workers, fast-food workers, sex-workers, and tertiary workers without addressing the very real distinctions that characterise the class composition of these forms of work and production. George Caffentzis (1987) has made this criticism of Antonio Negri (1991) since at least *Marx Beyond Marx*. Caffentzis then argued that Negri's analysis of class and capitalism was incapable of identifying and expressing the internal divisions of the proletariat, and thus the struggle for workers' autonomy along Negrian lines was always doomed to a neo-Leninism. I address these criticisms in Chapter 3, connecting the postworkerist theory of immaterial production to the problematic idea of the immediately social character of labour.

The alleged hegemony of immaterial production has been criticised, particularly on the grounds that it outweighs in scope the production of material commodities (Henwood, 2003). Hardt and Negri (2004: 109) have countered that they mean immaterial production outweighs, or is hegemonic, in the sense that it has a qualitative effect upon other areas of production. This debate is not directly relevant to the concerns of my argument, as I am not analysing the empirical quantity of service work or asserting the hegemony of immaterial production. Though it is worth noting the significant shifts in employment patterns toward services, digital, education and health care services across many economies of the world. The specific contribution that I make to the critique of contemporary forms of work involves looking at the ways in which affect becomes a contested relation in the context of the material organisation of labour. The criticisms of the hegemony of immaterial production and its failure to consider compositions of class touch upon the question of value. Caffentzis is again instructive here, noting that the crisis of the law of value in postworkerism is at best relevant to only certain industries. In other words, there is in fact no crisis in the law of value, as it does not operate at an industry level, but only at a total level. Thus, the existence of highly technologised industries cannot signal the crisis of value, but instead only points to the need to analyse the movement of value at a global level. Finally, Steve Wright (2005) presents a thorough rebuttal of the thesis of immaterial production and the immeasurability of value. The critique that is developed in this book draws from those made by Federici, Caffentzis, and Wright, among others, but the contribution *Motivations for Refusal* makes lies specifically in its consideration of class composition in relationship to affective production.

4   Motivation, Refusal, and the Affective Compositions of Capital and Class

Motivations for Refusal demonstrates that the affective politics of late capitalism is contested specifically along the labour-capital relationship. In other words, while conditions of affective production define the labour processes of care, relational, cognitive, creative, hospitality and other industries, the character of these types of labour confronts various forms of mediation. The first form of mediation is value, the persistence of exchange as a dynamic of immaterial production challenges the foundations of prominent theories of affective labour. Second, the affective sciences have been drawn into and integrated with techniques of management and affective technologies which modulate and order immaterial labour. Theorising the integration of the affective sciences as a form of affective capital, this book illustrates the implications this holds for contemporary understandings of exploitation, the commodity, and labour in the areas of immaterial production. The analysis of value and the affective sciences carried out in *Motivations for Refusal* advances existing scholarship in the fields of Marxism, affect studies, emotional and affective labour, and class composition analysis.

Part 1, *Labour, Value, Affect* (Chapters 2, 3 and 4), establishes the theoretical foundations of the book. It presents a critical analysis of Marxian theorisations of class, value, profit and rent, and identifies an enduring relevance for class composition analysis in the critique of capitalist work and value. The argument develops via a critical reading of prominent postworkerist theorists emerging from Italian *operaismo*, while engaging with the insights of feminist political economy and value-form theory to problematise the limits of postworkerism (Benanav, 2020; Smith, 2021; Pitts, 2021; Dinerstein and Pitts, 2021; Heinrich, 2014; Hardt and Negri, 2000, 2004, 2009, 2017; Mitropoulos, 2012). Part 1, explores the importance of postworkerism's attentiveness to shifting forms of class composition while critiquing these theorists' construction of the labour theory of value, immeasurability, and immaterial/affective labour. While theories of affective labour point to important conditions of work and exploitation in contemporary service and care economies, *Motivations for Refusal* argues that the increasingly transactional character of forms of affective labour have not led to a decoupling of labour and value or to a crisis of value. Indeed, immaterial commodities and the labour that animates them remain subject to modes of economic measure, which shape labour processes and forms of exploitation in the service sector.

Chapter 2 presents a critical analysis of the key theoretical tenets and concepts that inform the book. The key contribution of this chapter is to demonstrate that reading postworkerism critically through the lens of value-form theory advances the critique of labour and the critical consideration of affective forms of work. The first two sections of the chapter ground the book's perspective on value and labour through a reading of Marx on the value-form and a critical reading of value-form theory. The third section of the chapter provides a detailed and critical overview of prominent theorisations of the categories of value and labour within the field of political economy. It demonstrates that theorisations of value in relation to labour tend to pass through shifting historical iterations, and that each respective iteration comes to inform political questions regarding labour and labour movements (Rubin, 1989; Dooley, 2009; Perrotta, 2018; Mirowski, 1999). This section details how political economy has been characterised by substantialist theories of value, that vary over history according to shifts in the technological arrangements of production. Contemporary theorisations of future work based on the alleged immeasurability of labour, value, and affect, are shown to be the most recent iteration of this historical dynamic. The fourth section critiques the key claims regarding labour and value developed by theorists of postworkerist Marxism. This section outlines how the postworkerist contention that immaterial modes of labour render value immeasurable arises from both a misreading of value theory and an incomplete consideration of contemporary immaterial labour processes.

Chapter 3 traces the development of postworkerism and its key arguments via its immediate historical predecessor, *operaismo*. Here, the argument covers the initial development of the concepts of political and technical class composition, value and labour within *operaismo*. Importantly, this chapter demonstrates that while value-form theory is necessary to critique the valorisation of labour, class composition analysis remains important to understand the lived contours of class antagonism. Workerist-feminism, and the radicalisation and break that it made with classical workerism is analysed as a key moment in the development of the perspective of class composition analysis. The workerist-feminist break retains insights for the analysis of affective labour today, that are explored in this and subsequent chapters. Chapter 3 identifies discrete lines of continuity between *operaismo* and postworkerism, via a consideration of the tension between the affirmation and negation of labour as articulated within each perspective. However, the focus of the chapter is on how the tendency that became known as postworkerism, and its affirmationist politics expressed in the conflation of affective labour and life, set the foundation for the ontological turn of contemporary postworkerism. The chapter also establishes the enduring relevance of class composition analysis, which I return to in Chapter 7.

The fourth chapter traces the limitations that emerge from postworkerism's abandonment of the categories of the technical and political class composition and its construction of the productivist ontology of labour-value-affect. The chapter demonstrates that a defining characteristic of postworkerism is its shift from a foundation in class composition analysis into a political ontology grounded in affect. The ontological turn underpinning postworkerism arises from its analysis of immaterial production, and the cooperative capacities of affective labour. The chapter traces the implications of this shift politically and economically. Politically, the ontological turn via affect renders postworkerism incapable of developing a critique of labour in the present. Economically, the ontological turn leads to the reconstruction of the exploitation of labour into a theory of rent, which reinforces the limitations of postworkerism's critique of work.

Throughout the historical development of capitalism, scientific and social theories have often combined in the shifting managerial techniques of hegemonic forms of production across respective historical periods (Marx, 1991; Tronti, 2018; Panzieri, 1980; Winner, 2020). Labour-processes, economic theories, and forms of managerial and technological discipline are never, in this sense, beyond the science and techniques of their time (Mirowski: 1999). In this regard, the affective turn as an element of labour-capital relations marks a contemporary iteration of a long-established historical dynamic. Part 2, *Contested Terrains of Affect* (Chapters 5, 6 and 7) charts the contemporary iteration of this dynamic process as it is expressed in the affective sciences being put to work. Probing the antagonistic relationship between labour and capital as expressed through management and workplace technologies, it presents a critical analysis of the deployment of the affective sciences in the workplace today. Through an analysis of management, remote sensing, emotion recognition technologies, AI and affective computing models, all informed by theories and sciences of affect, Part 2 explores how the technical composition of capital is shaped in affective production contexts (Moore, 2017; Hudlicka, 2003; Ducey, 2009; Latham, 2012). Each of these mechanisms is shown to influence, modulate and intensify affective forms of labour in conditions when output can no longer be measured in units produced. It first presents an analysis of how the affective sciences have been incorporated into new managerial theory to intensify, measure, and discipline labour. Second, it explores how the affective sciences inform a range of affective technologies used in the workplace to shape the labour performed while on the job. These two lines of inquiry identify the affective sciences as a component of the technical composition of class and capital. *Motivations for Refusal* finds that affect theory and the affective sciences have become increasingly central to the control of labour at the same time as service work has grown as a sector – that is, at the same time as the affective capacities of labour have become increasingly central to labour processes and profitability in deindustrialised economies.

Chapter 5 analyses how theories of affect have been taken up and deployed within the frameworks of new managerial practices. The analysis developed throughout Chapter 5 demonstrates that affect is a heavily contested terrain in the contemporary workplace. While affect has come to characterise many modes of labour in the post-Fordist service economy in terms of what is produced in the act of labour, it is also a key component of how that labour is organised and mobilised from a managerial perspective. Tracing prominent vectors of affect theory into workplace management techniques, Chapter 5 complicates the presence of affect as a dynamic of work today. The chapter focuses on Affective Events Theory and other related aspects of the affective sciences to map out the ways in which affect is integrated into the workplace. This signifies a mode of measure and mobilisation of labour that looks to the affective drives and dynamics of labour. The chapter demonstrates that the integration of the affective sciences into the techniques of management constitute a greater formalisation and specialisation in how labour is managed.

Affective modes of management thus open new, as well as rearticulating old, points of contestation in the organisation of work and the struggle against it.

Chapter 6 analyses the development and deployment of affective technologies in the workplace. The chapter argues that affective technologies, emerging through human-computer interaction design in the workplace, through various types of emotion recognition devices and wearable tech attuned to a worker's mood, motivation and affect, all form part of the technological nexus that characterises the contemporary composition of class. Emotion recognition technologies, affective computing and affect recognition devices illustrate the growing attention to the management and ordering of affect within the workplace. Such examples include smile scans, vocal recognition technology, and productivity sensors attuned to the affective communication of employees. Chapter 6 situates the deployment of affective technologies alongside affective managerial techniques, to argue that the contested nature of affect within the technical composition of class brings with it new political challenges and possibilities for contemporary class struggles. The chapter also considers the inability of affective technologies and managerial practice to address the productivity issues of the service sector.

Informed by the analysis of affect as both a form of production and a component in the composition of capital, the book closes with a reconsideration of class composition analysis. Building on the foundations of class composition analysis as developed within the school of *operaismo*, the final chapter of the book poses a conception of affective composition to name how affective politics are mobilised in worker struggles (Read, 2024) against the techniques of affective management and affective technologies. Taking the contested character of affective politics in contemporary arrangements of work as the point of departure, the final chapter presents affective composition as a lens through which to see the possibilities for class and political struggles emerging from the contemporary forms of affective production. The theorisation of affective composition in the final chapter is articulated through an engagement with the concept of ambivalence as proposed by Romano Alquati (2001). Ambivalence is explored in Chapter 7 through specific workplace articulations of affect as an element of the technical composition of class and within forms of affective class struggle.

PART 1

Labour, Value, Affect

Lineages of Value, Theories of Labour

1   Introduction

Writing in 2003, Antonio Negri stated that "we need to develop an *ontology of immaterial labour*, or rather an *ontology of immaterial being* which has within it a hegemony of immaterial labour" (2008 [2003]: 62, emphases in original). The 'need' to develop this ontology, according to Negri, derives from the ascendency of knowledge and affect as resources, raw materials, and content of production, and by their position as a means of access to, and general wellspring of, wealth. Immaterial labour, as Negri articulates it above, refers to "the ensemble of intellectual, communicative, relational and affective activities which are expressed by subjects and social movements". That is, changes identified in immaterial modes of labour provide a foundation for the ontology of immaterial being. "The ensemble" that characterises immaterial labour must, finally, "lead to production" (Negri, 2008 [2003]: 62). For Negri and postworkerism, the ascendency of immaterial labour has already placed the ensemble of intellectual and affective labour at the centre of contemporary dynamics of capitalist reproduction. As such, the centrality of immaterial labour to the process of capitalist reproduction realises the conditions of a new social and political ontology. Negri thus articulates an explicit connection between the growth of immaterial production, the political relationship between labour and capital, and the living possibility of communism.

Although Negri's comments above are esoteric and expressed in a high philosophical register, they are connected to postworkerism's analysis of shifting forms of work and grounded in a consideration of contemporary labour processes of immaterial production. Paradoxical as it sounds, Negri's emphasis upon the significance of an ontology of immaterial labour is founded upon the postworkerist consideration of what Marx would have called the particularities of concrete labour. The ensemble of immaterial labour that Negri names above denotes a set of specific labour practices that are, at least as far as postworkerism is concerned, definitive in contemporary work arrangements. However, while postworkerists base their claims upon changing arrangements and forms of labour, they do not retain a formal conception of the labour or valorisation process. Rather, postworkerism argues that in the present context, all of social life must be understood as productive, *because of the inherently cooperative character of immaterial production*. Postworkerists thus reconceptualise the labour and valorisation processes of late capitalism. Immaterial production functions as the skeleton key for postworkerism's analysis of labour, value, and the contemporary composition of class.

The following two chapters develop in detail an analysis and critique of the emergence and consolidation of postworkerism as a theoretical and political perspective. The task of this first chapter, however, is to provide an initial commentary on the problems of labour and value, and their relationship to politics. A key claim made throughout the book is that a major limitation of postworkerist thought lies in its critique and rethinking of the concept of value. Specifically, in its attempt to rethink value from below, postworkerism re-inscribes what some theorists (Postone, 1993; Heinrich, 2012; Rubin, 1978 [1927]) have called a substantialist conception of labour and value. Postworkerism's new substantialism is grounded in its ontological trinity of labour-value-affect. The thesis that immaterial and affective labour have become hegemonic in the present context plays a pivotal role in the elaboration of this substantialist conception of value, in that the postworkerists posit affective/immaterial labour as the ontological foundation of value today. This chapter will show why this should be seen as a problem. The argument throughout is elaborated via a critical engagement with postworkerism specifically, however the implications of the argument are wider reaching and bear upon broader contemporary debates concerning labour, value, and measure.

It is not, of course, immediately apparent why a substantialist account of value should be seen as a problem. As one illustration of this, histories of political economy, including various Marxisms, show that the analysis and critique of capitalism has struggled to move forward without reinscribing various foundational accounts of labour and value (Elbe, 2013; Postone, 1993). The precise nature of the foundation has shifted over time, but a reliance upon a foundational substance has remained more or less constant. Indeed, much has been written by various Marxists defending the notion that labour should be celebrated as the foundation and the creator of all wealth, precisely because labour creates value within capitalism. Nonetheless, I contend that not only does the *analysis* of labour and value remain significant for any critical and anti-capitalist politics, but that this analysis must ultimately be expressed as a *critique of* labour as foundational value. To say this another way, the problem that emerges with the return to foundational accounts of labour is that the critique of work, of labour in the present, of the condition of labour as variable capital, and thus our condition as workers however diffuse we might now be, is foreclosed. In my reading, the postworkerists unwittingly reintroduce the transhistorical conception of labour that Marx sought to dispel by relying on a political ontology of labour-value-affect, grounded in affective and immaterial labour.

This chapter first engages with Marx's theorisation of value, demonstrating that he broke with a substantialist account of it, and instead theorised value as a historically specific form of social mediation and domination. The second section of the chapter explores the importance of value-form theory and illustrates the ongoing relevance of the critique of value particularly in terms of destabilising substantialist accounts of value. Following this, the chapter traces the lineages of theories of labour and value in the history of political economy. This section demonstrates that theories of value historically have tended to inscribe a foundational conception of labour upon which broader analyses of social, economic and political questions have depended. The historical outline of political economy provides a background against which to critique the postworkerist theorisation of labour and value. The final section of the chapter argues that even though postworkerists innovate a theory of value, they ultimately reinscribe a substantialist foundation in the trinity of labour-value-affect. While debates about value risk falling into hermeneutics, the argument in this chapter draws attention to the political implications of how the relationship between labour and value is constructed. Specifically, recapitulations of foundational theories of value constituted in specific forms of labour, tend to valorise that form of labour as an agent of politics and thus blunt the capacity for a critique of value as a historically specific form of mediation.

2 Marx on Value: Variations and Ambivalences

There is no doubt as to the numerous and contradictory ways in which Marx can be read. Ingo Elbe (2013), along with the other authors involved in the Neue Marx Lektüre, provide useful analyses of just some of these (see also Heinrich, 2012 and 2013). Elbe traces a lineage of Marxist thought spanning three prominent perspectives: traditional Marxism, Western Marxism, and the Neue Marx Lektüre. Harry Cleaver (1979: 17–47) has similarly developed a schema for categorising various approaches to reading Marx. For Cleaver, these approaches are the philosophic, political-economic and political readings, each of which involves different inflections of interpretation, and different political implications. These categorisations suffice to demonstrate, even though they do not nearly exhaust, the existence of multiple approaches to reading Marx. Insofar as the specific question of value is concerned, we can see that Marx leaves behind various avenues for interpretation, all of which are present in the lineages and perspectives outlined by Elbe and Cleaver respectively. Indeed, it is not difficult to see why and how Marx's analysis of value and other questions has often been read in contradictory ways. As far as value is concerned, Marx certainly was engaged with the problem of the substance of value, and there are numerous references to labour as substance of value, and labour-time as its magnitude, in his work. But as we will see below, the resolution of these iterations of value takes place at the level of a social totality, and not within the specific characteristics of a given labour process. As Elbe and Cleaver show, there is more than one way to read Marx, and it is not clear, in so far as the question of value is concerned, that a neo-Ricardian and substantialist reading is the most adequate. Nonetheless, such readings of Marx persist.

Philip Mirowski (1999) offers a sophisticated critique of Marx's theory of value. Mirowski locates Marx's work within the context of the shifting innovations and insights of the physical sciences. According to Mirowski, Marx represents the 'swan song' of substantialist theories of value, while also acknowledging in Marx a nascent 'field theory' of value. While Mirowski's argument is wide ranging and sophisticated, here I want to draw attention to just one aspect of it.[1] Namely, the fact that Mirowski, aside from the charge of two contradictory theories of value (substance and field theory), consistently argues that for Marx's substance theory, value is simply "reincarnated" or "buried" in each commodity. However, at the very least this argument tends to ignore Marx's considerations of value at the level of totality, which is to say beyond specific production processes (Mattick, 2019: 212), and of value as a historical form. It is precisely Marx's understanding of value as historical form that complicates the neat physicalism of labour and value.

In the first edition of *Capital volume I*, Marx includes a note near the end of the first section of Chapter 1, which provides a significant clue to understanding where and how Marx breaks with classical political economy. Here Marx states that "now we know the *substance* of value. It is *labour*. We know the *measure of its magnitude*. It is *labour-time*. The *form*, which stamps *value* as *exchange-value* remains to be analysed" (1990 [1867]: 131). Later, in another oft-quoted passage, Marx argues that:

> political economy has indeed analysed value and its magnitude ... and has uncovered the content concealed within these forms. But it has never

---

1 One example of an attempt to take up Mirowski's criticisms is George Caffentzis, 'Crystals and Analytic Engines: historical and conceptual preliminaries to a new theory of machines', *Ephemera*, 7:1 2007.

once asked the question why this content has assumed that particular form, that is to say, why labour is expressed in value, and why the measurement of labour by its duration is expressed in the magnitude of the value of the product.

1990 [1867]: 174

I.I. Rubin (1978 [1927]: 114–115) has argued that for Marx, the category of value represents the unity of the substance, magnitude and form of value. He adds that in order to properly understand why value is not a physicalist concept, particular attention must be paid to the form of value: specifically, through an analysis of abstract universal labour. It is Marx's analysis of abstract labour that provides insight into the value form as historically specific to capitalism, and it is the analysis of the commodity that brings this to light.

Marx's opening discussion of the commodity leads us toward an understanding of its dual form of existence. Marx is speaking here of the use-value and the value of a commodity, as well as the more nuanced relationship between value and exchange-value (1990 [1867]: 152). A commodity's use-value is its qualitative character and utility in the world. In this sense, human labour has always produced use-values, regardless of its historically determinate organisation. However, use-value is distinct from value, and it is only with capitalism as a historical formation that value as a social form and relation comes into being. In this respect, it is through exchange-value that value appears, and although use-values, whether these be shoes, a computer or an education, for example, are the "material bearers of exchange value" (1990 [1867]: 126), as "exchange values they do not contain a single atom of use-value" (1990 [1867]: 128). At a certain point in the analysis of value, the concreteness of use-values, that is, their particular sensuous existence, drops behind their role as bearers of exchange-value. It is value that now moves to the forefront of analysis.

What is true for commodities in general is true for the commodity of labour-power, and more specifically for labour-power applied in a given labour-process. For Marx, it is only within the historically determinate form of capitalism that labour assumes an objective quality; that is to say, it is only in capitalism that value as a social relation and form of organisation exists. Labour is subject to the same opposition between use and exchange, the dual character of labour is experienced as a contradiction from the perspective of the worker (Holloway, 2010: 83–99). Concrete labour-processes produce concrete use-values, for example, care, cars, or corn. However, just as exchange-value contains not an atom of use-value, abstract labour, the category that gives expression to value, has no residue of the concrete labour that produced it. As such, it is not sufficient to look to the shifting types of concrete labour throughout capitalism to discover the theory of value; rather one must look to the processes through which given forms of concrete labour appear as abstract labour, that is to say, become expressed as value, and give expression to value.

In particular, the contradictory condition of labour pertains to its various moments of existence as labour-power, variable capital, wage-labour, unwaged labour, and labour as activity. However, across all of these moments it is their actuality within the historically specific context of capitalism that gives them meaning and sets them in motion. It is important to point out, moreover, that the contradictory condition noted above is also expressed in the relationship between concrete and abstract or value-forming labour. Marx argues in *Capital volume III* that "when we have labour as value-forming in mind, we are not considering it in its concrete form as a condition of production, but rather in a social characteristic that is different from wage-labour" (1992 [1894]: 962). Similarly, Marx emphasises that "no producer considered in isolation produces a value or commodity ... His product becomes a value and commodity only in a specific social context ... [and] insofar as it appears as an expression of social labour" (1992 [1894]: 777). Elsewhere, Marx argued that it is social labour, not the specific labour of individuals, that produces value, "the conditions of labour, which creates exchange value ... are *social conditions* of labour or conditions of *social labour*" (1904 [1859]: 26). The incorporation of labour as a component of a production process, as the variable component of capital, represented as wage-labour, shapes the particularity of the labour performed: the worker becomes a component of a specific, concrete labour process. However, labour relates to value only in so far as it is "abstract social labour" and not due to its concrete particularity (Marx, 1990 [1867]: 308).

Marx's emphasis upon abstract labour allows him to move beyond the difficulties other labour theorists have confronted with respect to the tangibility or intangibility of the commodity. Given the emphasis placed upon the vendible commodity in theories of value and labour (see below in section 4), it is not hard to see why it is that services, and immaterial production, pose a theoretical and conceptual challenge to substantialist theories of labour and value. The lack of a physical object within which value could be 'stored' in much of contemporary service work provokes this same problem. Service work disrupts the neat image of the commodity as store of value, as an object that contains value quite literally, and something that can be moved, sold and consumed. However, it is worth emphasising that the particularity of service, communications or transport labour processes do not, as far as Marx is concerned, prove a problem for the theory of value.

For Marx, the production of a vendible commodity is not the condition that determines labour's relationship with capital or value. Marx makes this clear enough in his discussion of productive and unproductive labour. In the first part of *Theories of Surplus Value* (TSV) when looking at material and 'immaterial' forms of production Marx argues that "neither the special kind of labour nor the external form of its product necessarily make it 'productive' or 'unproductive'" (Marx, 1975: 165). Marx argues that the same labour can be productive or unproductive depending upon the context in which it takes place. That is, the use-value produced by a given labour can be productive or unproductive "no matter whether this use-value perishes with the activity of the labour-power itself or materialises and fixes itself in an object (Marx, 1975: 165), that is whether it produces a meal, a car or communication.

In *Capital volume II*, Marx indicates how the analysis of service industries in relationship to value as the organising force of social labour can be developed.[2] Here Marx points out that "there are ... particular branches of industry in which the product of the production process is not a new objective product, a commodity" (1992 [1885]: 133). He goes on to state that at the time of writing the only economically significant example of this is "the communication industry, both the transport industry proper, for moving commodities and people, and the transmission of mere information". In each of these cases, Marx argues, "the useful effect can only be consumed in the production process; it does not exist as a thing of use distinct from this process" (1992 [1885]: 133). In this passage, Marx is commenting on a specific question concerning the appearance of the movement of money capital, but the point here concerning communication is relevant to the present problem. In other words, this point is an opening into thinking through forms of immaterial production, and even labour as relationality, within the context of value's organisation of social labour.

---

2   In a similar manner to the question of the tangibility of a commodity, it is worth emphasising how one further point of contention in Marxian debates concerning service work turns upon the question of whether this labour is productive or unproductive in Marx's meaning of the terms, simply by virtue of the labour being a service. In fact, for Marx, service labour could be productive or unproductive, depending on the conditions in which the labour is employed. For example, a butler or live-in domestic worker, whose wages are paid for out of the personal funds of the capitalist in their immediate, private consumption, would constitute unproductive labour, as it is not engaged in the valorisation of value. However, service labour employed within an enterprise in the pursuit of profit, whether that is education, care, food preparation, transportation, or entertainment, does constitute productive labour, as it is employed for the valorisation of value. Marx explains this point in multiple places in his work, and I explore the issue throughout this chapter.

In both the 'Results on the Immediate Process of Production' and the TSV, Marx rejects the argument that insists that the material content or form of output of a given labour process is the determining factor in the relationship between labour, capital and value. For example, Marx argues that:

> a singer who sings her song for her own account is an *unproductive labourer*. But the same singer commissioned by an entrepreneur to sing in order to make money for him is a *productive labourer*; for she produces capital.
>
> 1975: 401

Elsewhere in *Theories of Surplus Value*, Marx states that:

> an entrepreneur of theatres, concerts, brothels etc, buys the temporary disposal over the labour-power of the actors, musicians, [sex-workers] etc – in fact in a roundabout way that is only of formal economic interest; in its result the process is the same – he buys this so-called 'unproductive' labour, whose services 'perish in the very instant of their performance' and do not fix or realise themselves 'any permanent' ... 'subject of vendible commodity' ... The sale of these to the public provides him with wages and profit. And these services which he has thus bought enable him to buy them again; that is to say, they themselves renew the fund from which they are paid for.
>
> 1975: 166

I refer to these two examples in order to demonstrate that for Marx the particularity of the labour process is not the determining factor in the relationship between labour and value. Services and immaterial labour can be productive of value. Marx thus counters those arguments that insist upon a narrow focus on tangible commodities or industrial labour as necessarily central to capital accumulation.

With the above examples in mind, it is possible to make some sense of Marx's notion of industrial capital as a term that simply names the movement of self-valorising value. Writing in *Capital volume II*, Marx argues that industrial capital is not a name for a concrete form of production, and it does not refer to mass factory production of industrial goods. Rather it is a name for analysing the movement of capital from the perspective of value. In this sense, industrial capital names the process or movement of self-valorising value. As Marx puts it, "industrial capital is the only mode of existence of capital in which not only the appropriation of surplus-value or surplus-product, but also its creation, is

a function of capital" (1975: 135–136). There is nothing in the notion of industrial capital that links it to the material character of the production of tangible
commodities. What matters, rather, are the circumstances in which the work
takes place. As Michael Heinrich has stated, "capital invested in service enter-
prises also belongs to the category of industrial capital", as it is articulated by
Marx. Following Heinrich again,

> the sole difference consists in the fact that that the finished product
> (whether a theatre performance or an act of transportation) is not a
> material object acting as independent commodity-capital; it can only be
> consumed simultaneously with its process of production.
>
> 2012: 134

Thus the circuit of industrial capital as service would look something like:
M-C(mp/l) ... P-M', that is would involve no independent commodity capital.
However, although there is no independent form of commodity capital in this
circuit, this does not change the conditions under which the service occurs,
that is, through exchange for the valorisation of value.

While it is useful to look to Marx's concept of industrial capital and Heinrich's
deployment of it to analyse service work in a critical light, these perspectives
are not without their own shortcomings. In particular, it would be easy to read
into Marx via Heinrich an analysis of service labour that is simply cast on an
industrial scale. Walter Benjamin's (2007: 217–252) reflections on automated,
mass production of entertainment/culture, a form of service on an industrial
scale, resonate here. As we will see in later chapters, the commodification of
services can lead to the fragmentation and hybridisation of labour as well as its
massification. In other words, the contemporary transactional arrangements
of service provision are not simply a mass industrial production of services but
involve an array of novel relationships and management regimes. Nonetheless,
using this perspective to reframe the analysis of service work, and more
broadly immaterial production, provides a nuanced lens through which to
interrogate the relationship between immaterial labour and value, one which
destabilises the assertion of an inherent, cooperative autonomy of immaterial
labour from capital.

A final comment on Marx's approach to the value-form is warranted here.
As indicated above, for Marx, the question of the form of value is one that is
related to but also distinct from the questions of the substance and magnitude
of value. Analysing the question of the form of value implies the more nuanced
problem of the relationship between private and social labour, concrete
and abstract labour, and labour as a historically specific form of mediation and

as a transhistorical capacity or activity. Coming to terms with the dynamics of these relationships can only be achieved through an analysis of the form of value. Insisting on this point, Marx argued in a letter to Kugelman that:

> no natural laws can be done away with. What can change in historically different circumstances is only the *form* in which these laws assert themselves. And the form in which this proportional distribution of labor asserts itself, in the state of society where the interconnection of social labor is manifested in the *private exchange* of the individual products of labor, is precisely the *exchange value* of these products.
>
> 1868

While it is clear then that labour, production and distribution are necessary aspects of human societies, such a general assertion does not tell us anything about the historical specificity of the forms in which these relationships manifest. Regarding the problem of the measure of value, its magnitude and social regulation, it is clear that here too Marx breaks with the perspectives of the classical political economists. Writing to Kugelman again, Marx argued that:

> The vulgar economist has not the faintest idea that the actual everyday exchange relations can*not be directly identical* with the magnitudes of value. The essence of bourgeois society consists precisely in this, that *a priori* there is no conscious social regulation of production. The rational and naturally necessary asserts itself only as a blindly working average.
>
> 1868

The emphasis that Marx places on exchange and the complexity of measure in the above quotes gives a final indication of the significance of the problem of value-form.

Two points are worth emphasising considering this discussion of Marx's perspective on value. The first is that the rule of value, as mediation, domination, and a "mode of sociality" (Best, 2024: 236) does not depend on the particularities of specific labour processes or arrangements of work. Abstract labour is not an aggregation or simple averaging of concrete labour. The implication being transformations in the arrangements of labour, say between manufacturing and services, do not disrupt the value-form. The persistence of the rule of value means that labour remains a mode of expression of capital, and that this condition of labour remains an object of critique. The second is that Marx's theory of value need not be interpreted as a substantialist theory. While it is certainly true that Marx's analyses of labour are open to physicalist interpretations, they are in no way reducible to such interpretations.

3   Value-Form

While Marx's analysis of value is not reducible to a substantialist conception of labour and value, various substantialist readings of Marx persist. In the next section we will see how various theories of value inscribe a foundational conception of labour, before demonstrating how postworkerism, with its emphasis on affective and immaterial production, is a contemporary example of this tendency. Before that, however, it is useful to consider the contributions of value-form theorists who have taken up the question of the form of value to challenge the substantialist iterations of value, and in doing so demonstrate why the critique of capitalist social relations requires the critique of value and abstract labour as historically specific forms of domination and mediation.[3] The engagement with value-form theory is presented as a means to problematise the postworkerist construction of labour-value-affect explored later in the chapter.

I.I. Rubin is notable as an early and key theorist in challenging substantialist readings of Marx. In his book, *Essays on Marx's Theory of Value*, Rubin (1990 [1928]) refutes the idea that Marx's theory of value represents a continuation of the classical labour theory of value and instead develops a circulationist approach to value, where the act of measure is understood to take place through the process of exchange. Drawing on the third volume of Marx's

---

3   It is necessary to acknowledge that it is somewhat difficult to use value-form theory and value-critique as broad umbrella terms. For example, the groups *Wertkritik* and *Krisis* that formed around Robert Kurz have their own unique trajectory, and as Larsen et al. (2014) point out, whilst there are complimentary overlaps between the work of these groups and, for example, Moishe Postone's work, they in fact developed in isolation from each other. Another well-known perspective that is associated with value critique is that of the Neue-Marx-Lekture, and prominently the work of Michael Heinrich. However, there are key differences between Heinrich and the *krisis* group, around, for example, the question of capitalist crisis and collapse. Another lineage can be found in the theorists who came to be associated with Open Marxism, most notable in the work of Georg-Hans Backhaus, Helmut Richelt and others. The work of I.I. Rubin is often an early reference point for the critique of value, as is critical theory and the Frankfurt School, particularly the work of Theodore Adorno; so too has been some of the work of Guy Debord and the Situationist International. Outside of the German speaking world, theorists such as Patrick Murray, Chris Arthur and Anselm Jappe have also contributed to value-critique. It is beyond the scope of my thesis to explore in any detail this field of research, its development and nuances. Such a task would demand another thesis in itself. Nonetheless, I am choosing to use the terms of value-form theory and value-critique in a broad sense to evoke a particular perspective shared by these theorists: specifically, the idea that the critique of value and labour as historically specific, not ontological, categories constitute a pivotal element and beginning point of an anti-capitalist politics.

Theories of Surplus Value, Rubin argues that "the theory of value does not seek an 'external standard' of value, but its 'cause', 'the genesis and immanent nature of value'". Rubin goes on to argue that for Marx, value is not an external standard of measure built through homogenous units of labour time, but rather an immanent standard. "Immanent standard" does not here mean the quantity that is taken as a unit of measure, but a "quantity which is connected with some kind of existence or some kind of quality" (Rubin, 1990 [1928]: 126), and this is value: abstract labour. In other words, abstract labour as substance of value is not measured through an aggregation of units of concrete labour time. As Rubin further argues, "in Marx's theory of value, the transformation of concrete labour into abstract labour is not a theoretical act of abstracting for the purpose of finding a general unit of measurement", as if abstraction were a single step of thinking through which to equalise different concrete forms on the level of the ideal. Rather, "this transformation is a real social event. The theoretical expression of this social event ... is the category of abstract labour" (Rubin, 1989 [1929]: 144). In short, the real social event is value's organisation of labour on the social level through the category of abstract labour, actualised or realised through the process of exchange.

More recently Heinrich (2012) has criticised those who see the theory of value in substantialist terms. Heinrich argues that:

> the 'substance of value' as a figure of speech has frequently been understood in a quasi-physical manner: the worker has expended a specific quantity of abstract labour and this quantity exists *within the individual commodity* and turns the isolated article into an object of value.
>
> 2012: 44

In a similar manner to Rubin, Heinrich emphasises that abstraction is a real event that occurs through exchange, and that moreover, the relationship between exchange, abstraction and value disrupts the substantialist account of value as embodied labour, particularly when understood as a tangible commodity. Heinrich argues that:

> abstract labour cannot be measured in terms of hours of labour: every hour of labour measured by a clock is an hour of a particular concrete act of labour ... abstract labour, on the other hand cannot be expended at all. Abstract labour is a relation of social validation that is constituted in exchange.
>
> 2012: 50

Exchange and abstraction take place and mediate the relation between the individual labour and the total social labour, value is expressed in this process: "only with the act of exchange does value obtain an objective value form" (2012: 50). This does not mean that value originates in exchange. However, at the same time, value is not a reflection of an individual's concrete hours of labour that simply exists or inheres in a commodity at the end of production. Value is not an aggregation of concrete hours. It is, rather, a form of social mediation and domination specific to capitalism, expressed in labour.

Nick Gray (2010) presents a theory of value that claims to overcome both the productivist and circulationist approaches to value. Gray names this approach the capital-theory of value, in which capital is a process that overrides the two spheres of production and circulation. As discussed earlier, the substantialist theory conceives of value in a physicalist sense, in which value is deposited in the individual object/commodity, and subsequently preserved and consumed. According to Gray, the circulationist approach insists that "value inheres in the relation between commodities which are exchanged against the universal equivalent, money" (2010: np). This is evident in Rubin's analysis of exchange as a pivotal organisational process. Gray argues that a capital-theory of value overcomes the opposition between the substantialist and circulationist approach. For Gray, "value subsists only as the movement of its self-expansion ... this movement is the unity of the spheres of production and circulation qua production process of capital" (2010: np). Each sphere presupposes the other.

Patrick Murray (2013) provides some further insights into the complexities of value and form, which also destabilise the substantialist foundations. Murray argues that the price-form is the most adequate expression of the value-form. Murray claims that

> the crux of Marx's value-form theory lies in the proposition that *money is the necessary form of appearance of value*. That means that *the price-form is the value-form*, for only in money can the value of commodities be expressed ... commodities, value, exchange-value, money and prices constitute, for Marx, a whole from which no moment can be extracted.
>
> 2013: 125

Murray's position encapsulates value at the level of totality, expressed across each moment and form of appearance of value. As such, Murray provides a further perspective that destabilises substantialist accounts of value and labour.

Moishe Postone's analysis of abstract labour spends significant time displacing both a substantialist account of value and ontological conceptions of labour. In Postone's account, the rejection of labour as an ontological category follows from Marx's analysis of the dual nature of labour, and its split condition of being. As Postone states: "the categories of Marx's analysis ... are intended not as ontological, transhistorically valid categories, but purportedly grasp social forms that themselves are historically specific" (1993: 146). From the perspective that Postone outlines here, the retreat into an ontologically grounded understanding of labour recapitulates a fundamental analytical error that Marx had sought to dispel.[4]

4   Tracing the Lineages of Theories of Value

Since the historical emergence of political economy as a distinct discipline, much of the controversy concerning the question of value has turned upon the role of labour within a production process in general, and labour in its specific forms. One of the earliest articulations of an emergent labour theory of value is found in the idea that the value of a commodity is equal to the amount of labour embodied in it. This assertion can be considered the crux of substantialist accounts of the labour theory of value, and it continues to inform and limit the critique of value and labour today. Nonetheless, the historical reorientation of the modern concept of value around questions of labour marked a break with Aristotelian theories of value, where value is based in need and demand (Dooley, 2005: 27). With the emergence of classical political economy, the problem of thinking and theorising value is also a problem of how one understands labour: a given perspective on the theory of value will necessarily disclose something about how one understands labour, and vice versa. In this way, the historical development of conceptions of labour occurs alongside or entwined with theorisations of value.

In brief, the above principle is evident in the following examples. For the Physiocrats, agricultural labour was productive; later theorists posited manufacture and heavy industry as the foundational source of value, while some contemporary theorists argue that informational or immaterial labour now constitutes the true source of value rooted in new modes of productivity. Each of these schools of thought have in various ways articulated labour theories of

---

4 For further debates and perspective on these questions see Ben Fine and Alfredo Saad-Filho (2007), Jim Kincaid (2007), Massimo De Angelis (1995), Axel Kicillof and Guido Starosta (2007).

value. A common feature of these variations on the labour theory of value is that each tends to reproduce a substantialist conception of value, particular to the specific form of labour and condition of production that it valorises. In other words, each perspective offers a novel appraisal of the specific form of labour that is thought to produce value. However, the tension introduced is such that while there is an attention to a specific articulation of labour in the form of production, labour itself is rendered transhistorical. In other words, and as Marx (1990: 174n34) pointed out, each fails to question why labour takes the form of value, and how value is a historically specific form of social mediation and domination. In this section of the chapter, I outline the various iterations of substantialist accounts of labour and value in the history of political economy, from the mercantilists through to Ricardo. This overview provides context for the critique of postworkerism made in the following section of the chapter and throughout the book.

4.1 *Recurring Limits of Substantialist Accounts of Value in Political Economy*

Numerous authors have written extensively on the history of the labour theory of value and have identified and criticised its various substantialist foundations (for example Rubin, 1989; Mirowski, 1999; Dooley, 2005). Philip Mirowski has identified and critiqued the limitations of theories of value through a specific analysis of the connection between political economy and the natural and physical sciences of the nineteenth century (1999: 139–192). Mirowski dubs political economy's various considerations of value "substance theories", each of which relies upon the conservation principle of energy. For Mirowski, the fact that political economy and nineteenth century (pre-)physics share the same scientific, social, and cultural horizon, and the same foundation in a particular theorisation of energy, poses a key stumbling block to theorisations of value beyond a substantialist foundation. Within this framework, value, like energy, is understood as a substance that, through production, is deposited and inheres in a commodity, and which must be conserved throughout the process of circulation and distribution, before its exhaustion in consumption.

Adopting a different theoretical approach to Mirowski, Peter Dooley (2005) identifies a similar substantialist premise operating throughout the historical and conceptual development of the labour theory of value. Dooley identifies two fallacies at work here: the materialist fallacy and the retrospective fallacy (2005: 226–227). The materialist fallacy refers to the idea that "production consists of physical things", while the retrospective fallacy insists that "commodities embody the labour of past times" (Dooley, 2005: 226). Value is thus linked to a conception of labour embodied in each object or commodity.

Beyond this, argues Dooley, the classical political economists understand value as something that can only exist in tangible commodities. Interestingly, though perhaps not surprisingly, both Mirowski and Dooley place Marx within the lineage of the classical political economists. Both argue that ultimately Marx did not overcome the substantialist perspective on labour and value. I will trace the defining elements of the substantialist accounts of labour and value in the remainder of this section; however, as illustrated in the previous section, I remove Marx from this lineage.

The mercantilists, in particular William Petty, were among the earliest to move towards a labour or production theory of value. While for the most part mercantilist theory focused upon policy and trade, it remains the case that the foundations of a labour theory of value can be found in mercantilism. As Rubin has shown in *The History of Economic Thought* (1989), the development of capitalist social relations imposed upon the mercantilists the need to engage theoretical political-economic concerns generally, and the question of labour specifically. Thus, the mercantilists articulated elements of a labour theory of value, alongside the usual preoccupation with policy and trade. Marx too, identifies Petty as the first political economist and theorist of a labour theory of value (Marx, 1904 [1859]: 56). Aside from historical curiosity, this fact is of interest insofar as it illustrates the degree to which later debates concerning value and form can be understood to repeat or break with their origins in political economy. Moreover, tracing the development of the debates over value provides a backdrop against which to see how various substantialist notions of labour and value continue to recapitulate earlier incarnations.

Petty's investigation into "natural price", based upon intrinsic qualities of a product, as opposed to the market price determined through external factors, opened the way for the beginnings of a theory of value (Marx, 1975: 355). Petty's analysis reduces the problem of natural price to that of labour expenditure, arguing that corn and silver composed of equal labour time will be equivalent. In this way, Petty grasps the elements for an analysis of the magnitude of a commodity's value by basing it upon the expenditure of labour time. In breaking down the components of the commodity and value into wages and rent of land, Petty also identifies the related problem of the need for a measure of value. However, as Rubin shows, Petty was unable to move beyond a confusion of value and its determination, insofar as his theorisation was at one moment based upon an analysis of use-value and the next upon exchange-value, and thus unable to articulate a contradictory unity of these elements in the form of value (Rubin, 1989 [1929]: 64–76).

Petty's labour theory of value was based on the notion that the origin of all value resided in labour and land, with labour playing the key role. In this perspective, value is the expression of the labour directly expended on a given commodity as well as the labour leading up to the possibility of the production of the commodity in question. Petty thus constructed a theory of value that saw value as originating in past or stored-up labour. As Marx points out, Petty "determines the *value of commodities* by the comparative *quantity of labour they contain*" (1975: 355 emphases in original). Given the emphasis on the idea of stored-up labour, Petty's perspective considered non-perishable commodities as not only superior to perishable commodities, but also the only form of commodity that could act as a store of value, and thus represent wealth. Productive labour, and the accumulation of value and wealth, consisted of those forms of labour that created tangible commodities which outlasted the production period and could retain their exchange-value. More broadly, commodities that added to the stock of a nation's wealth were considered productive, while land offered the material upon which labour worked, and in so doing increased value and wealth.

Later mercantilists such as James Steuart continued unsuccessfully to grapple with the problem of the formation of price, turning around the question of "the real value" of a commodity, and the profit made from a commodity upon alienation (Rubin, 1989 [1929]: 68). The real price of a commodity, for Petty, was the quantity of labour stored up in it. In contrast, Steuart considered the "real value" of a commodity constituted by the quantity of labour contained in a commodity, and "profit from alienation" which emerged in exchange (Marx, 1975: 44). As Marx explains, the emphasis on profit upon alienation is based on the idea that profit comes from the sale of a commodity above its real value (1975: 44). Such a perspective is untenable as an explanation of surplus value and profit, unless the field of economic engagement is considered to be zero-sum. While the mercantilists failed to develop a complete labour theory of value, they did succeed in identifying key elements of the theory, which were reproduced in subsequent formulations, such as distinctions between concrete and social labour, and use and exchange value (Marx, 1904 [1859]: 66–67; Rubin, 1989 [1929]: 75–76). Within these nuances, mercantilists identify labour associated with the production of perishable goods as that which underpins value.

The Physiocrats, most notably François Quesnay, developed a more sophisticated labour theory of value, which offered both a theory of labour as productive of value and a theory of capital (Rubin, 1989 [1929]: 124–139). As Marx argues, "the physiocrats transferred the inquiry into the origin of surplus-value from the spere of circulation into the sphere of direct production" (1975: 45). In doing so, where Petty had placed the origin of value in labour – every tangible commodity being in effect a store of past labour – Quesnay and the

Physiocrats emphasised land over labour as the source of wealth, and held that only agricultural labour, at times including fishing and mining, was productive (Rubin, 1989 [1929]: 124–139). In this sense, it is possible to discern a theory of value-producing labour in the Physiocrats' work, even though they considered land to be the source of all wealth. These forms of labour were considered productive in the sense that they produced an output beyond subsistence, that is labour that produced an embodied surplus constituted productive labour. Connected to their notion of productive labour and surplus is a focus on economic activity as a system of reproduction. The attention to the cycle of reproduction allowed the Physiocrats to develop elements of a theory of capital.

In relation to the notion of productive labour, the Physiocrats developed a distinct system of social classes. Three general social classes emerge in physiocratic thought: the productive class; the sterile class; finally, the landed proprietors. The productive class is composed of those that produce wealth and value. The members of the sterile class may be necessary for circulation, but they do not produce any wealth, and at best participate in its movement and distribution. Proprietors of land do not play a productive function as far as Quesnay was concerned, except insofar as their purchasing and initial investments allowed capitalist farmers to work it (Rubin, 1989 [1929]: 117–122; Mirowski, 1999: 157). Farmers, then, are the productive labourers, whose work 'multiplies' the source of wealth. However, it was not the labourers themselves who were considered productive, given that they themselves produced only an amount sufficient for their own reproduction, but rather the farmers who owned and invested in the farms. Based upon this conception of productive labour, a theory of capital and reproduction also emerges.

Alongside and entwined with the theory of value, the other key contributions from the Physiocrats were a theory of capital, as well as an analysis of reproduction and circulation – in other words, an analysis of capitalism as system and totality. The Physiocrats' focus upon agriculture as productive labour made clear the role of capital. Capital investments in the form of preparing the land for cultivation, logging, draining and fencing, for example, were understood as investments made by proprietors, entitling them to output, or the *net produit*. Movable investments were made by the capitalist farmers in the form of tools and machinery, animals for working and flocks of livestock, for example, to carry out production. The recognition by the Physiocrats of the necessity of these investments, and of the ongoing reinvestments required over time, constituted the basis for their theory of capital. Quesnay's famous *Tableau Economique* put all this together as a totality of circulation and reproduction.

Adam Smith was able to move beyond the perspective of the Physiocrats in certain key respects, but he also reproduced their limitations in others. The most standout progression lies in the fact that Smith dispenses with agriculture as the sole form of productive labour. As Marx put it,

> after different forms of concrete labour, such as agriculture, manufacture, navigation, trade etc, had each been declared the true source of wealth, Adam Smith proclaimed labour in general ... to be the only source of material wealth.
>
> 1904 [1859]: 67

Writing at the time of the rise of manufactures, Smith understood the significance of exchange value, and the specific importance of the commodity. The division of labour framed how various forms of labour were productive and connected this to his theory of value. Smith states that "labour, therefore ... is the only universal as well as the only accurate measure of value, or the only standard which we can compare the values of different commodities at different times and places" (1937 [1776]: 36). His emphasis on the idea that the division of labour increases productivity and output also allowed Smith to break with the restricted notions of agricultural production held by the Physiocrats. Smith was likewise able to broaden the conception of capital. As Rubin points out, this meant that Smith was able to pick up and develop some of the ideas of Petty in a way that eluded the Physiocrats (1989 [1929]: 215). With Smith, a more fully developed labour theory of value and a broadened conception of capital emerged.

Smith was able to connect the division of labour to a labour theory of value. However, in doing so, he often oscillated between emphasising different determinations of value, and he also stumbled in maintaining his theory of value in the face of capitalist production. Although Smith aims to elaborate a theory of exchange-value rather than use-value, he is unable to overcome a duality in his approach to the labour theory of value. In the first place, Smith develops a theory of value based on labour in connection with pursuing an explanation for changes in value. Secondly, Smith attempts to establish a consistent, or invariable standard and measure of value, that of labour time. This duality in Smith's approach leads him to a series of contradictions, including a conflation between objective and subjective approaches to value, and a certain confusion concerning the relationship between the labour expended in a commodity and the amount of labour that the commodity in turn commands. Further, Smith was unable to resolve the contradiction between materialised labour as exchanged in the commodity, and the process through which living-labour itself is traded as a commodity. Smith also confused the relationship between value and revenue – evident in the fact that Smith often derives value from revenue, rather than analysing revenue as the breaking up of value.

Unlike Smith, David Ricardo (1949 [1817]: 5–33) focused upon the expenditure of labour as the determining factor in the formation of value. This move allowed him to do away with the contradiction between labour expended on a commodity and labour purchased by a commodity, and to instead focus his attention upon the quantitative dimensions of value and measure (Rubin, 1989). As Marx points out, the primary focus of Ricardo is the magnitude of value, and its substance in labour time, but he does not engage the form of value (1975a: 164). Indeed, Ricardo sees the "capitalist form of labour as the eternal natural form of social labour" (Marx, 1904 [1859]: 69). It is in this generic sense that Ricardo marks a continuation of substantialist conceptions of labour and value. Nonetheless, Ricardo's consideration of the temporal aspects of value creation introduced a degree of complexity to the subject that is not found in previous theorists. For example, the categories of absolute and relative value articulated in Ricardo's late work demonstrate an attention to variations in value and in time, while restating the position of labour-time as substance of value.

The comments made above serve to highlight the various conceptualisations which inform analyses of value and labour throughout classical political economy. Of course, all theorists are bound to be influenced by the political and theoretical context in which they find themselves. As such, the above outline is not presented as a critique of the failure to reach the truth of the theory of value, but only to trace the recurrence of a particular theoretical premise, in order to further problematise this premise as it operates in contemporary theory. Finally, and as a brief aside, it is worth pointing out common themes that are concomitant with the labour theory of value in its substantialist guise: namely, the distinction between productive and unproductive labour, or material and immaterial commodities and forms of production. As we will see, while postworkerism moves beyond these related binaries, they nonetheless reinscribe a substantialist conception of value which undermines the critique of labour. The following section of the chapter will address these limitations.

As the sketch above shows, each of these conceptual distinctions is connected to a substantialist notion of value and labour. Already in Petty's formulation of the question of value, which accords primacy to non-perishable commodities over perishable ones, and productive over unproductive labour, we can discern the foundational premises of the substantialist approach to labour and value. The physiocratic perspective rearticulates this idea, most clearly in its conception of productive labour as agricultural labour. While both Petty and Quesnay recognise other forms of labour, they ultimately anchor value in tangible or non-perishable commodities and the labour that produces them. Smith and Ricardo go beyond the perspectives of Petty and also Quesnay, but each in their own way recreates the terms of a substantialist conception of labour and value. Smith, as the economist of the manufacturing period, and Ricardo as the economist of the industrial, both struggled to account for the creation and distribution of surplus value. Both Smith and Ricardo posed labour as magnitude and measure of value, yet neither managed to move beyond these formulations in their respective theoretical and analytical efforts. Neither posed the problem of the social form of production and value.

The above shortcomings become particularly apparent when one is confronted with a historical context in which service labour plays a key role. That is, the connection between productivity, value creation, and tangible objects produces a conceptual hurdle when one wishes to theorise the particularity of 'immaterial' commodities such as 'care' and the labour involved in their production. Though not alone in doing so, the postworkerists make a useful observation in drawing attention to the character of immaterial and affective labour. However, insofar as the postworkerists insist that the emergence of immaterial production fundamentally transforms the form and functionality of value, they adhere to the claim made by Dooley – they recapitulate the materialist fallacy. For postworkerism, the peculiar temporality and immateriality of services, for example, dislocates the operability of value as a property of tangible products, because the concrete manifestation of the commodity is no longer a physical object in which value is stored. However, the postworkerists then go on to identify immaterial labour and intangible commodities as the new foundation and source of all value. *In this respect they simultaneously break with and recuperate the classical tradition on the question of tangible value, while remaining entirely within the premises of a substantialist theory of labour.* It follows that contemporary attempts to recast a politics of value from below, such as we find in the postworkerist trinity of labour-value-affect, not only forget that the critique of value is also an articulation of the critique of labour as capital, but ends up reproducing the substantialist limit outlined above.

5   **Foundations of a New Substantialism: the Trinity of Labour-Value-Affect**

Postworkerism developed out of the Italian version of Marxism known as *operaismo*. According to Mario Tronti (2012), a key figure within *operaismo*, the *autonomia* movements of the 1970s in Italy mark the emergence of postworkerism as a theoretical field and perspective. This book, however, is primarily concerned with the variations of postworkerism that are clustered across the debates and projects of the journals *Futur Antérieur* founded in 1989, *Multitudes* founded in 2000, and the body of literature that has reached some prominence through the work of Michael Hardt and Antonio Negri, Christian Marazzi, Maurizio Lazzarato, Franco Bifo Berardi, Paolo Virno and Carlo Vercellone, amongst others. More specifically, this book focuses on the theories of immaterial, affective and biopolitical labour that define the perspective of postworkerism today. It is in these journals and books that the theses of immaterial production and cognitive capitalism were first formulated and developed into what can be called a coherent perspective.

Postworkerism begins from the premise of an epochal shift in the form of capitalism: from industrial capitalism to informationalised or cognitive capitalism (Negri and Vercellone, 2022). The emergence and hegemony of immaterial production is identified as one of the key characteristics of this alleged shift. Hardt and Negri (2000; 2004) insist that the hegemony of immaterial production is tendential and have gone to some lengths to argue that the tendency is realised in qualitative rather than quantitative terms. Nonetheless, they argue that since the 1970s, the "informatisation [of production] has been demonstrated by the migration from industry to service jobs" (Hardt and Negri, 2000: 285). For Hardt and Negri, "services cover a wide range of activities from health care, education, and finance to transportation, entertainment and advertising" (Hardt and Negri, 2000: 285). The shift to informatised production points to a further transformation in the character of labour.

For Hardt and Negri, with the "informatisation of production", communication, information and affect come to "play a foundational role in the production process" (2000: 289). In contrast to the characteristics and the output of industrial production, which privileged the production of tangible commodities that could be consumed as part of social life, immaterial labour allegedly produces the very substance of social life itself. With immaterial production, the entire social fabric of life is rendered productive. Thus, postworkerists argue that the temporality of immaterial production exceeds the clearly defined limits of industrial production: labour, value, and time become immeasurable. While industrial production was apparently demarcated by clear limits of clocking on and clocking off, within which time both necessary and surplus labour took place, today work time and the time of life are said to blur. From the perspective of postworkerism, with the informatisation of production there is no longer any clear delineation between working and non-working time, and thus between the moments in which one is or is not producing surplus value.

While the challenge to a limited focus on productive labour associated with industrial labour articulated by postworkerism is welcome, the construction of affective and immaterial production is the first step toward a valorisation of existing modes of labour. In particular, the critique of labour as a mode of expression of capital is lost.

The postworkerists have retained the analysis of labour and value, however unconventionally, as central components of their work. Noting that in many academic contexts the category of labour had "fallen into disuse" during the 1980s, Hardt and Negri emphasise the importance of labour to their own perspective (1994: 7). To quote this passage from Hardt and Negri at length, Hardt and Negri argue that "labour is too often defined narrowly in the realm of the capitalist work ethic that denies pleasures and desires". Against this definition, they claim the analysis of labour has "to open the concept ... across the spectrum of social production ... to grasp the contemporary processes of the production of social subjectivities, sociality and society itself". Continuing, for Hardt and Negri "the concept of labour refers primarily to the problematic of value". The expansion of labour to cover all social activity changes the understanding of value, whereby "labour functions as a social analytic that interprets the production of value across an entire social spectrum, equally in economic and cultural terms". While the formulation "by labour we understand a value creating practice" (Hardt and Negri, 1994: 7) appears consistent with Marx's argument that the only labour that 'counts' is labour that produces value, Hardt and Negri in fact re-determine the relationship between labour and value, specifically in terms of the labour process and the form of its measurability. However, as demonstrated above, Marx's understanding and critique of value centred upon the category of abstract labour, a social form that is not dependent upon the particularities of concrete labour processes. Hardt and Negri, by contrast, in pointing to the breakdown of value and defining affective production as immediately social, conflate the categories of concrete and abstract labour.

The alleged immeasurability of value is contingent upon a particular understanding of immaterial labour, specifically that it is 'immediately social' and productive of value. Their claim of immeasurability rests upon a conflation of the categories of concrete and abstract labour. Negri (1992: 78–79) has written that the theory of value as developed by Marx is necessarily bound to the conditions of manufacturing in the industrial revolution. That is, Negri tends to conceive of the relationship between concrete and abstract labour in a physicalist sense, whereby abstract labour is a certain quantity of direct hours of standardised industrial labour. Vercellone discusses this notion of value as a "labour-time theory of value" articulated through the aggregation of concrete hours of labour expended (2013: 423). Elsewhere, Vercellone argues that in the era of immaterial production "value-creating activity accords less and less with the criterion of the unity of time and space on which the regulation of collective time was based under Fordism" (2013: 433). The eventual outcome of this framing of value moves from a critique of value and labour into the valorisation of existing labour practices in the alleged inherently cooperative, immediately social dimensions to immaterial production.

The limits of the postworkerist perspective on the form and measurability of value arises primarily from an uncritical assumption that Marx had simply followed Ricardo in terms of understanding value. In *Multitude*, for example, Hardt and Negri argue that "Marx adopts from the classical political economists, such as Adam Smith and David Ricardo, the maxim that labour is the source of all value and wealth" (2004: 144). While Hardt and Negri acknowledge that taking the labour of the individual is not sufficient to understand value creation, that instead it is necessary to understand socially connected production, and abstract labour, Hardt and Negri conflate concrete and abstract labour, and thus misrepresent the problem of measure as Marx articulates it. Hardt and Negri state that:

> Marx poses the relation between labour and value in terms of corresponding quantities: a certain quantity of time of abstract labour equals a quantity of value. According to this law of value ... value is expressed in measurable, homogenous units of labour time ... this law cannot be maintained today in the form that Smith, Ricardo, and Marx himself conceived it.
>
> 2004: 145

The easy slippage from Ricardo into Marx that is demonstrated here points to the error of postworkerism on the question of value. Similarly, as Vercellone and Dughera have articulated the issue, "we must remember how, to Marx (but to Ricardo as well), the value of commodities depends on the difficulty of production and thus on labour time" (2019: 52). The reason for the breakdown, according to postworkerism, is the increased complexity and diffusion of labour beyond the factory walls, which in turn dissolves the homogenous, abstract character of simple labour (Hardt and Negri, 2004: 10). However, as Marx points out "labour ... measured by time, does not appear in reality as the labour of different individuals" (1904 [1859]: 24). As we saw above, and will continue to elaborate throughout the book, the construction of value by postworkerism misarticulates the relationship between concrete and abstract labour. The result of which leads to the valorisation of affective production as unmediated, that is, immediately social labour. In turn, the critique of labour is dispensed with.

I argue that the foundation of the postworkerist shift from a critique of labour as variable capital to an ontology of labour as immediately social, lies in the trinity of labour-value-affect. In a characteristically innovative construction, Negri (1999) outlines the coordinates of this trinity. Negri states that,

> The more the theory of value loses its reference to the subject (measure was this reference as a basis of mediation and command), the more the value of labour resides in affect, that is, in living labour that is made autonomous in the capital relation, and expresses – through all the pores of singular and collective bodies – its power of self-valorisation.
>
> 1999: 79–80

Negri's construction of a view of value from below is challenging, and to the extent it names a terrain of antagonism provides a provocative sounding board for thinking through the contestation of the reproduction of capitalist social relations. However, ultimately the critique of labour is supplanted with a valorisation of the construction labour-value-affect. The political implications of this reconstruction of labour and value will be critically unfolded throughout Chapters 3, 4 and 7 of this book.

The strength of the postworkerist approach to labour and work lies in its insistence on breaking down a hierarchy imposed in economistic terms between productive, unproductive and reproductive work, and seeking a terrain from which construct a communist politics upon this basis. However, it ultimately fails to pursue this insight in a way that maintains a critique of value as the historically specific form of mediation and domination intrinsic to capitalism. Instead, it relies upon an ontological argument in favour of recognising value-creating activity, and in so doing rearticulates a valorisation of labour and work as a basis for politics. Subsequent chapters unpack the limitation of the postworkerist perspective in detail. For now, engaging the perspectives found within the so-called value-form perspective, can help to illuminate some of the limitations of the postworkerist perspective to be explored later in the book.

In light of the value-form perspective outlined earlier in the chapter, we can turn attention directly to the questions raised by immaterial production with regards to the form of value. For Heinrich (2012) and Postone (2012), the alleged novelty of immaterial or biopolitical production presents no difficulty for the theory of value. Heinrich is quick to dismiss the argument made by Hardt and Negri that with immaterial production the labour theory of value is no longer operative. Heinrich notes the pivotal significance of exchange in understanding value and commodities:

> the difference between services and physical objects consists of a distinction of the *material* content; the question as to whether they are commodities pertains to their *social form*, and that depends on whether objects and services are exchanged.
>
> 2012: 44

For Heinrich, a consideration of the social form of commodities and exchange demonstrates that Marx's theory of value is maintained through the "transition from an industrial to a service economy ... or from material to immaterial production", even though theorists of such a transition often claim otherwise (2012: 44). If we follow Heinrich on this point, then we can engage some of the nuances of immaterial labour, while maintaining a critique of value as a historically specific social form.

In a similar fashion, Moishe Postone (2012) has criticised the idea that biopolitical and immaterial production obviate the task of understanding and critiquing value as part of a political project. Postone also emphasises the process of exchange and the social context within which an object of service exists. While theorists of biopolitical production argue that the 'immeasurability' of immaterial commodities by definition unhinges value theory, Postone points out that:

> the question of measurability is, basically, one of commensurability. That, however, is not an ontological attribute of the objects themselves. Rather, it is a function of the nature of the social context within which they exist.
>
> 2012: 247

Postone continues that the context in which measurability exists is a historically specific context in which the exchangeability of commodities dominates re-/production. Further,

> what renders them [ie. immaterial or material commodities] commensurable is value, a historically specific form of wealth that has nothing to do with their properties, whether material or immaterial, but is the crystallised expression of a historically specific form of social mediation that, in Marx's analysis, is constituted by a historically specific form of labor.
>
> POSTONE, 2012: 247

Each of these perspectives highlight a significant flaw in the postworkerist analysis, a flaw which was arguably inherited from earlier incarnations of *operaismo*, in which there is little consideration of exchange, exchange-value or the value-form.[5] Chapters 3 and 4 will return to this limitation within postworkerism in greater detail.

6   Notation: against a Productivist Foundation of Politics

The critique of the postworkerist ontology of labour-value-affect turns upon a consideration of how affective and immaterial labour are articulated within the composition of capital and class. Chapters 5 and 6 demonstrate how the affective sciences have been integrated into both managerial imperatives and the technological articulation of affective labour. The affective sciences are thus incorporated into the technical composition of capital and class, as immaterial forms of labour remain a "mode of existence of capital", insofar as the labour performed is rendered as variable capital (Marx, 1990 [1867]: 451). The critique of the commodification of labour and affect destabilises the productivist ontology of labour-value-affect. This ontology, as we will see through later chapters, renders all social activity as immediately social and therefore productive of value. However, from the perspective of the critique of capital, to be a productive worker is simply to occupy a certain position within the broader totality of capitalist production, circulation, and reproduction. To be 'productive' carries no ethical, political, or moral quality with it. This is especially so from a communist perspective. Marx's consideration of production and reproduction takes place at the level of social totality, which is to say, a circuitous whole, whereby every act of production is also one of reproduction, and vice versa (Marx, 1990 [1867]). The totality of capitalist reproduction draws into its orbit social activities that are productive and unproductive, waged and unwaged, directly market mediated and indirectly market mediated (Endnotes, 2013: 57–77). All these forms of social activity, even when not recognised as

---

5   It is true that Negri, and others such as Sergio Bologna, have engaged with exchange and exchange-value, yet it is my contention that for the tendency of postworkerism, this engagement remains very limited and bound up in physicalist conceptions of value. The rejection of value by Negri laid the foundations for later postworkerist perspectives. That said, taking 'Autonomist Marxism' in the broadest sense, it would be unfair to lay this charge against all theorists that fall under this title. For example, the work of the Midnight Notes Collective developed a contrary perspective to Negri and later postworkerists on precisely this question, among others.

such in the balance sheets of capital, become part of the reproduction of the totality, and the contestation of the totality may emerge at any of these points of activity.

7　Conclusion

Robert Kurz of *wertkritik* has argued that "no socialism of any kind is possible within the horizons of the ontology of labour, which is to say that the commodity form of social reproduction can only be overthrown together with 'labour'" (1991: 1). Although there are ambivalences in terms of how Marx himself engaged with this problem, there is sufficient evidence outlined throughout this chapter that Marx developed a rigorous critique of labour as a trans-historical and ontological category. In any case, it is this viewpoint that most illuminates the critique of labour and the reproduction of capitalist social relations. While postworkerism emerged through a critical consideration that sought to simultaneously negate the condition of labour as variable capital and valorise the subjective expressions of class struggle, the drift into an affirmationist ontology is realised with the construction of labour-value-affect.

In the perspectives of the postworkerists, particularly Hardt and Negri, we can detect a continuing tendency to reiterate a unique, but nonetheless substantialist account of labour and value. The recapitulation of labour as substance or foundation is expressed most clearly in the project of re-founding value from below, as labour-value-affect. The flattening of the contradictions of labour into a singular ontological substance of labour-value-affect, sidesteps the task of critiquing labour and thereby divests the political critique of labour of all negationist purchase. This problem is compounded when read against the value-form contributions. The difficulty lies in bridging the respective insights of value-form theorists and those that have developed labour process or compositionist critiques of capitalism. The slippage from *operaismo's* perspective on the refusal of work, to the postworkerist ontology of affective labour, highlights the political impasse postworkerism has reached. The theorisation of an ontology of immaterial being, which opened this chapter, rests upon an ontological conception of labour and the so-called immeasurability of value, labour, and time in the contemporary context of post-Fordism. In the following chapter, we trace out the historical and theoretical contexts in which this turn to ontology occurred, what its limitations are, and identify the enduring relevance of class composition analysis in the critique of class, capital, and labour.

Class Composition and the Prehistory of Immaterial Production

1 Introduction

At the turn of the millennium, the theoretical and political perspective now known as postworkerism gained international traction among academic and movement circles. The extra-parliamentary left in Italy had been a rich laboratory of political movement and theoretical production throughout the 1960s and 70s but was much less known elsewhere (Piccone, 1972). The publication of *Empire* in the context of the wave of global struggle known as the alter-globalisation movement, put postworkerist theories of labour, capital, and the state, among other themes, to an international audience. However, the relationship between the perspectives of postworkerism and its origins within *operaismo* were not clear at the time to many in the English-speaking world. Since that time significant translation work, along with wider studies of *operaismo*, have helped to clarify the continuities and ruptures between *operaismo* and postworkerism (Wright, 2002; Wright, 2021; Tronti, 2019; Balestrini and Morini; 2018). Nonetheless, tracing out the key steps that lead from *operaismo* to postworkerism is important to the aims of this book for two reasons. First, doing so helps to situate the postworkerist arguments in their historical context. Second, we can assess the extent to which the categories of *operaismo* remain valuable in the critique of the conditions of labour theorised by postworkerism. This chapter thus clarifies the arguments of postworkerism through revisiting the historical and political context of its emergence.

The analysis throughout the chapter turns around the concept of class composition. Encompassing the categories of the technical and political composition of class, the perspective of class composition analysis is in many ways the enduring legacy of *operaismo*. The framework allowed for both theoretical and practical innovations in Marxist and communist research and organisation. *Operaismo*, and indeed postworkerism, have always been oriented to the relationship between the technical and political composition of class, as a dynamic of class antagonism and capitalist development. However, the trajectory of postworkerism has in many ways flattened class composition analysis into a singular framework, if not outright dispensing with it. As we saw in the previous chapter, postworkerism ultimately arrives at a politics based on the valorisation of the ontological construction of labour-value-affect, in place of the critique of value, labour, and class composition. It is the contention of this book that the categories of class composition, particularly the technical composition of class, remain significant for the critique of affective production. Later chapters explore how affect has been integrated into the technical composition of class via managerial and technological articulations of the affective sciences. Those chapters analyse why postworkerism's dispensing with class composition analysis leaves it ill equipped to critique the affective compositions of labour and capital. This chapter provides a critical analysis of key theoretical steps that have informed the trajectory of postworkerism in arriving at the theory of immaterial and affective production, and the political implications that result from it.

Reflecting on the analysis of the previous chapter, the first section of the chapter illustrates why class composition analysis remains important for the critique of value and contemporary labour-capital relations. Specifically, class composition analysis consistently draws attention to the persistence of antagonism within the dynamics of the labour-capital relation, and as such offers a way out of the political limits of value-form theory. The second section of the chapter presents a critical analysis of the frameworks of class composition within *operaismo*. *Operaismo's* theories of class composition were developed in part to interrogate the immediate dynamics of work and class antagonism, but also informed an approach to historical periodisation. I argue that class composition analysis remains an important framework for interrogating the conditions of work, class movements, and capital. However, I also note limitations to this framework, which I return to in chapter 7. The third section of the chapter engages with the workerist-feminist critiques of *operaismo* and draws insights from them for the critique of postworkerism. The workerist-feminists developed one of the most important criticisms of *operaismo*, rupturing the narrow focus on the factory to expand the scope of investigation to new terrains of class movement and social reproduction, the implications of which we return to in Chapters 5 and 7. The final sections of the chapter analyse the prehistory of postworkerism and immaterial production in the early articulations of the socialised worker (*operaio sociale*) and the influence of the 'Fragment on Machines' and the 'General Intellect' on the tendency that became postworkerism. It is in these early departures from class composition analysis that the construction of labour-value-affect as the foundation of postworkerism begin to take shape.

2   Value and Antagonism

As we saw in the previous chapter, through its insistence upon the critique of value as a historically specific form of social mediation, the perspective of value-critique undercuts the substantialist concept of labour as a transhistorical category and foundational source of value. This aspect of value-theory is important in emphasising that the critique of capitalist social relations is necessarily also the critique of labour as a historically specific form of domination and mediation, of abstract labour as value. However, a significant shortcoming of this perspective lies in its inability to consider the lived temporalities and dimensions of work. The theoretical plane of value and equivalence is ill-equipped to deal with the temporal punctuations of work and the stratifications of class. In much the same way as exchange-value, for Marx (1990 [1867]: 128), contains not an atom of use-value, or inasmuch as abstract labour cares not for the concrete forms of labour, *value-form theory has little to say about the life or refusal of work*. In contrast, I turn to class composition analysis to address the immediate contours of class antagonism and address these limitations of value theory. A combination of value critique and class composition analysis provides a framework to navigate the relationship between what Samuel Fisher has dubbed the abstract models and concrete frictions characteristic of capital (2024). For now, it remains pertinent to ask if this limitation can be overcome in a way that both maintains a critique of value and avoids the problem of re-inscribing a substantialist account of labour.

The perspective and mode of analysis developed in value-form theory effectively removes the lived dimension of re-/production and any notion of an antagonistic subject from the critique of capital. For example, Werner Bonefeld, a key theorist within the Open Marxism perspective, has critiqued Postone's *Time, Labour and Social Domination* on the grounds of its attempts to "banish the class antagonism from the critique of political economy" (2004: 110). For Bonefeld, Postone "fails to conceptualise [the] essential relationship, that is the antagonism between capital and labour", and only "conceives of human social 'action' as something that is embedded within the framework of abstract social forms" (2004: 110). In this manoeuvre, the critique of capital is "replaced with a theory of capital and critique of labour", the effect of which is to remove and ignore the conflict between labour as a living subject and capital. Value-form theory, as a result, is defined by an absence of politics, if we define politics as the working class's confrontation with, and attempts to negate, its own labour as capital (Tronti, 2019 [1965]: 274). However, this implication of value-form theory has been received positively by some. Authors associated with the perspective of communisation[1] articulate this aspect of value-form theory as a kind of 'anti-politics', or at least an anti-programmatism, arguing that the "critical import of value-form theory is that it calls into question any political conception based on the affirmation of the proletariat as the producer of value" (Endnotes Collective, 2010: 93). The perspective of Endnotes here raises a wider debate on the determination and scope of programmatism, its historical context, and its relationship to affirmationist and negationist tendencies in class struggle. I am sympathetic to a perspective that questions the "affirmation of the proletariat as the producer of value" as a political horizon, given that it is this condition that must be overcome. Nonetheless, I argue that the limitation of value-form theory in articulating the dynamics of class conflict can be addressed through retaining the framework of class composition analysis.

The shortcomings of value-form theory might also be attributed to a certain imprecision concerning the shifting forms of work and the new labour processes that emerge as capital and class recompose themselves. In this sense, we might be able to speak of two materialities of value and class struggle which necessarily inform the materialist critique of capitalism: on the one hand, the materiality of the value-form expressed in the dual nature of labour at the level of social totality, and on the other, a materiality which consists of the dynamic antagonism that imbues the everyday organisation of work, waged and unwaged. The contradictions in the organisation of work are expressed in the categories of class composition analysis, which we turn to throughout this chapter. In a different register, Samuel Knafo (2007) and Massimo De Angelis (1995 and 2007), among others (e.g., Lebowitz, 2003) provide examples of analysing the relationship between the labour process and the creation of value. These theorists have attempted to analyse how antagonism in the labour process cannot be divorced from the question of value, but rather plays a determining role in its creation and magnitude. Nonetheless, these efforts have either, in the case of De Angelis, cut out some of the critical contributions of value-form theory, or otherwise neglected the implications of emergent forms of work and techniques of control (Knafo, 2007). The limits and the potential of the value-form perspective lie in the difficulty of bridging the abstract and the concrete. As Chris Arthur (1979) has pointed out, while value as abstract labour constantly seeks to rid itself of the bodily figure of the

---

1   Communisation emerged primarily in the French context of the 1970s, in the work of Gille Dauve and the group Troploin, as well as the group Theorie Comuniste. See the journals Endnotes 1 and 2, and Sic.

proletariat, of the concrete, this is never fully achievable. Put differently, the historical *contradiction* of capitalism is at least in part the *lived antagonism* of the body of labour with the forms of capital – and the problematic of value resides in this very tension.

Riccardo Bellofiore (2009), a theorist and economist whose work spans a critical engagement with *operaismo* and value theory, has used the metaphor of a ghost to explore the tension between the abstract and the concrete conditions, or the form and content of labour. As Bellofiore writes,

> the content which moves the exposition of *Capital* is the commodity – that is, it is neither the substance of value nor the form of value alone, but rather the contradictory polarities of value and use-value and the development of this contradiction.
>
> 2009: 182

The commodity, whether it be tangible or intangible, as a historical form which dominates production, draws together both substance and form, each presupposing the other. Continuing with Bellofiore, "in Marx, the movement goes from content to form, but the content is always, in a sense, form determined" while "(surplus) value production is *demand-driven*, while the *actual extraction* of living-labour depends on *class struggle in production*" (Bellofiore, 2009: 182). What is of significance in Bellofiore's formulation is the complex interrelation he draws between form and content, and the degree to which these factors determine each other. While this is perhaps most simply applied to the image of mass industrial production, we can use this same formulation to analyse the content and form of service, immaterial and affective labour. From this perspective we can connect the latter with the problem of value-form, and in so doing create an opportunity to break with the ontological turn of post-workerist theory. At the same time, it will be possible to retain an attention to the dynamics of contradiction articulated in the encounter between fixed and variable capital. Class composition analysis provides a key point of orientation in developing both the critique of labour and value as historical forms at the same time as identifying elements of class antagonism in the organisation of work.

3   Class Composition Analysis as Method and Perspective

Operaismo forms part of a lineage of Marxist and communist thinking that has often been considered heretical from the point of view of 'traditional Marxism'.

Examples of this class struggle or subjectivist Marxist perspective include the *Johnson-Forrest Tendency* and *Socialisme ou Barbarie* (Cleaver, 1979).[2] Among these 'heretical' tendencies, *operaismo* developed a unique contribution in its approach to communist theory and practice with the categories of class composition analysis. It was in the pages of the journals *Quaderni Rossi* (Red Notebooks) and *Classe Operaia* (Working Class) that the categories of class composition analysis were first developed.[3] With the express aim of understanding and articulating the relations between living-labour and capital as expressions of class antagonism, class composition explores these dynamics through the categories of the technical and political composition of class. According to *operaismo*, the dynamic interplay between the technical and political composition of class generates broader cycles of class decomposition and recomposition, which shape the contours of capitalist development, and the possibilities for communism.

In theorising the dynamics of class composition analysis, *operaismo* draws from, but ultimately reinvents, Marx's concept of the composition of capital. For Marx, "the composition of capital is to be understood in a twofold sense": the value composition and the material composition, or the value-composition and the technical composition of capital. The value composition of capital is "determined by the proportion in which it is divided into constant capital ... and variable capital" (1991: 762–763). The technical composition is "determined by the mass of the means of production employed ... and the mass of labour necessary for their employment" (1991: 762–763). Continuing, Marx states that the organic composition of capital is equal to the value composition of capital "in so far as it is determined by its technical composition and mirrors the changes in the latter" (1991: 762–763). On the basis of Marx's categories, it is

---

2   The Johnson Forest Tendency, the name referring to pseudonyms taken by C.L.R. James and Raya Dunayevskaya, emerged within and then split from the US Trotskyist movement in the 1940s. Socialisme ou Barbarie emerged in France in 1949 developing a critique of orthodox Marxism in the French context. For a discussion of how these two perspectives fit into a common lineage with operaismo see Harry Cleaver (1979: 45–51).

3   The early theorists in this tradition undertook a re-reading of Marx within the context of emerging leftist struggle in Italy in the early 1960s, and over time contributed to the development of a strong extra-parliamentary left movement. This project was undertaken as a break with the existing communist (PCI) and socialist (PSI) parties of the day and aimed to develop and explore a radical political practice. From its origin the 'perspective of autonomy' (Dyer-Witheford, 1999; Eden, 2012) was a heretical theory and practice. It is no surprise that a number of the theses that were developed by these theorists, while based in a reading of Marx, were and remain contrary to or beyond a good part of more so-called 'orthodox' Marxisms, and the various incarnations of the 'official' labour movement. The peculiarity of autonomist perspectives on class composition is no exception to this. See Steve Wright (2002).

possible to articulate the relationship between machinery, science, technology, production and living-labour. However, where for Marx the composition of capital expresses the relationship between constant and variable capital, and the shifting proportional relationship between these components, *operaismo* made an explicit attempt to draw out the subjective and political forces in motion within a given compositional relationship. In doing so, the analysis of the composition of capital, became that of the composition of class.

The inversion of perspective, from that of capital to class, is perhaps what *operaismo* is best known for. Tronti (2019 [1966]) provides the most famous articulation of *operaismo's* Copernican Inversion of class perspective, which grounds the orientation of the subjective perspective of class struggle characteristic of *operaismo*. Tronti states:

> We too saw capitalist development first and the workers second. This is a mistake. Now we have to turn the problem on its head, change orientation, and start again from first principles, which means focusing on the struggle of the working class. At the level of socially developed capital, capitalist development is subordinate to working-class struggles; not only does it come after them, but it must make the political mechanism of capitalist production respond to them.
>
> 2019 [1966]: 67

While Tronti's argument emphasises the activity of the working class as the dynamic force of change within capitalism, it was the investigations into the rapidly forming industrial zones of northern Italy that fed content into the perspective of *operaismo*. In the investigations into production dynamics and class behaviours of workers in the industrial centres, the tools of *operaismo* were first honed (Alquati, 2013 [1961]; Wright, 2002). These tools took their clearest shape in the categories of class composition analysis, workers inquiries and co-research.

3.1   *The Technical and Political Composition of Class*

In its original formulations by the *operaisti*, a class composition perspective involved the analysis of both the technical and the political expressions of class. The technical composition of class involves the arrangements of work and reproduction, the division of labour, tasks, skills, science and technology, and forms of cooperation at work. Political composition, by contrast, names the forms of organisation, collectivity, and cultures that workers develop against the stratifications imposed on them. While Tronti's Copernican Inversion gives primacy to working class struggle, that is the political composition of class, as the dynamic variable in capitalist development, the relationship between the categories of class composition was contested within *operaismo*. In general, the concept of political composition was not reducible to or determined absolutely by the technical composition of class and production. Instead, the two categories were seen to work upon each other through a dynamic interaction. Nonetheless, it was also the case at times that there was an over-emphasis on the technical as a determinate factor upon the political composition of class (Wright, 2002: 78). Despite this, the technical composition need not be understood as deterministic. As Wright puts it, as the organic composition of capital changes, so too does the technical composition of class (2002: 163). Indeed, it can be working class struggle that influences changes in the organic composition of capital. The significance of retaining an analysis of the technical composition of class lies in the fact that as a category it focuses upon the critique of labour as a component of capital, not that it determines absolutely the formation of political composition.

On first appearance the technical composition of class is an expression of the structural organisation of labour-power in the production process, and the conditions of the reproduction of labour-power. The technical composition of class expresses the technological conditions, or lack thereof, that determine the characteristics of the labour and valorisation process within a given production process. As Steve Wright has put it, the technical composition of class is the expression of "the workforce's material articulation within the organic composition of capital" (2002: 78). The analysis of the technical composition of class is thus an engagement with the myriad features of what is required to perform specific tasks 'on the job', the modes of managerial oversight and mediation, the scientific and technological basis of the labour, the character of organisation in terms of production, and the organisation of work spatially and temporally. The technical composition of class, as Gigi Roggero puts it, expresses "capital's articulation and hierarchisation of the workforce, and the relation between workers and machines" (2014: 517). However, what sets it apart as an analytical category from others that focus upon similar issues, such as labour process theory or Marx's discussion of the technical composition of capital, is that it is linked immediately with a subjective inflection, and as such is not a static category.

Class composition analysis situates class dynamics in the encounter between variable and fixed capital but emphasises the subjective and material variability of labour. While the technical composition of class expresses the material articulation of labour as a component of capital, it also maps coordinates for class struggle. Similarly, the technical composition of class can be understood as the crystallisation of previous relations of class contestation. As Rodrigo Nunes writes, with any given technical composition of class, "there correspond certain openings, behavioural patterns, a certain subjectivity among workers from which the forms of political organisation" will emerge (2007: 181). Further, Nunes argues that "a given technical composition implies a certain political composition which leads to a new cycle of struggles ... which in turn will lead to a new technical composition of the class" (2007: 181). In principle, the technical composition of class simultaneously expresses the material articulation of labour while also constituting some of the fundamental elements through which ongoing, recomposing developments of political struggle will emerge.

If the technical composition of class expresses the above dimensions of the labour-capital relation, then the political composition of class, as a theoretical and analytical category, names the forms and relations that proletarian struggle takes. As Sergio Bologna states:

> When we said political class composition we meant not only the technical composition, the structure of labour-power, but also the sum and interweaving of the forms of culture and of behaviours of the mass worker and all the strata subsumed to capital.
>
> 1977: np

Following Bologna, the political composition of class extends beyond technical determinations and takes into consideration, for example, the worker's

> link (or his [sic] break) with the family clan, his past as working-class emigrant, in contact with more advanced technologies, and with societies with more advanced command over labour-power, their past as political and or union activist, or his past as a member of a Catholic, patriarchal clan.
>
> 1977: np

The consideration of these elements operates as the texture for the development of political struggle, expressed in the following conclusion: these lived relations are

> all translated into acquisitions of struggle, into political wisdom, a sum of subcultures which catalyse each other, in contact with the massification of labour or with its inverse process, of fragmentation and dispersion over territory.
>
> BOLOGNA, 1977: np

The political composition of class, for Bologna, embraces this complex set of relations and indeed forms of attachment, detachment and intimacies.

Importantly, these relations of political composition emerge from, while also exceeding, the condition of the proletariat as variable capital and the specificities of any given labour process.

The political composition of class, then, extends beyond the determinations of the technical composition. However, it does not do so at a complete remove. Rather, the tension and antagonism expressed in the labour-capital relation and in the form of the political composition of class, takes place at least in part, across the grid of relations mobilised in the technical arrangements of work and reproduction. The consideration of the technical composition of class is important because it allows for the critique of labour as a component of capital, and thus the critique of work, to be materially grounded. Class, for *operaismo*, is not a pure consciousness waiting to be attained, nor an *a priori* reality preceding class antagonism. Rather, class is formed in struggle (Roggero, 2014: 517). The specificity of this struggle, for the *operaisti*, is expressed in the dynamic conflict between the technical and political composition of class. Roggero argues that:

> between technical and political composition, in fact, there is neither symmetry nor a dialectical reversal, because class does not pre-exist the material and contingent historical conditions of its subjective formation.
>
> 2011: 92

As Roggero suggests, the formation of class "is at once what is at stake and the condition of possibility of a conflict, rather than an a priori fact" (2011: 92). The subjective formation of class is thus not reducible to the specificities of technical composition, but neither does class struggle occur in a pure ideal space outside of technical composition.

Retaining a dynamic characterisation of the relationship between the technical and political composition of class challenges the perspectives that would seek to elevate either of the categories to a simple primacy. While I have drawn attention primarily to the technical composition, it is useful to note other examples, that follow Tronti's Copernican Inversion more closely, and begin with the political composition of class. For example, Nick Southall (2010: 283) has argued that the technical composition of class fails to understand the continuous struggle of the proletariat as an autonomous force. Rather, for Southall, the technical composition of class can only express the analysis of the proletariat at the level of variable capital. The editorial for the first issue of *Zerowork* articulates a similar position, arguing that rather than focusing on the technical constrictions on labour the journal will focus on "the forms by which workers ... affirm themselves as a class with political power". In this sense the "working class is defined by its struggle against capital", and the relations generated in this process, rather than by "its productive function" (Zerowork, 1975). I appreciate the perspectives of Southall and the Zerowork editorial in insisting on the dynamics of political composition. However, given the cyclical dynamic that characterises both the technical and political compositions of class and their variability, I insist a critique of the technical composition of class, that is labour as a mode of expression of capital, remains necessary.

The above outline of the categories of the technical and political composition of class explains the content of each category, and how these categories were understood to relate to each other. Beyond its function as a theoretical schema, the method and perspective of class composition analysis functioned as a mode of political interpretation and intervention. The following section provides a broad overview of the prominent expressions of class composition according to *operaismo*.

3.2   *History, Periodisation, Tendency*

Class composition analysis sought to locate the subjectivist perspective of class antagonism in its historically specific and contradictory forms. Although such an analysis paid significant attention to the minor-materiality of work and the hierarchies that existed within the working class, class composition also became a lens through which to generalise historical periods. It is possible to identify a tension between the levels of analysis. On the one hand, the attention to the particular enables a nuanced analysis of the arrangements of work and the struggle against it. On the other hand, class composition analysis operates as a framework to characterise broad and 'hegemonic' historical tendencies, expressed in a dominant formation of class composition, a qualitatively advanced sector of production, forms of the state, and the organisation of reproduction (see for example Negri, 1988 and Bologna, 1987). For the *operaisti*, the dynamic interplay between these layers of material reality remains in tension, but resolves into broad, identifiable periods corresponding to the advanced elements of capitalist production and class composition.

The process of historical periodisation, for *operaismo*, occurs across multiple contested levels, but the understanding of how they resolved and when, was subject to debate. Bologna argues that "with the category of class composition militant historiography is able to move to a terrain of social history and of political-institutional history" (1977: np). Tronti (1972), for his part, distinguishes between two approaches in understanding and analysing capitalist development and working-class struggle. The first approach is chronological, detailing events and facts in the cycles of labour struggles. The second approach, in Tronti's words, is to move through great historical events by pausing on macroscopic groups of facts yet untouched by the critical consciousness of labour thought (*pensiero operaio*) and therefore excluded from a class understanding that translates them into a political use of their consequences.

> 1972: 25

Going further, Tronti continues,

when relevant these events isolate a fundamental aspect of capitalist society. They cut a cross-section that goes from a series of struggles to a set of political-institutional, scientific, or organisational answers.

> 1972: 25

Framed as Tronti has above, the analysis of class composition encapsulates the minutiae of class antagonism at the level of class behaviours, as well as unfolding to broader historical periodisation. The tendency toward broader periodisation leads to theorisations of the composition of capital, the state form and forms of reproduction. Negri's theories of the state indicate how the analysis of historical tendency takes shape. Discussing the state, Negri has argued that "1848–71; 1871–1917. This periodisation seems to provide the only adequate framework for the theorisation of the contemporary state" (1988 [1968]: 9). Later, Negri would theorise the shift in state-forms through the configurations of the planner-state (1988 [1968]), the crisis-state (1988 [1980]), the nuclear-state (1989), and then with Hardt, as *Empire* (2000). As we will see below, one of the issues that emerges in the analysis of historical tendencies, particularly for Negri, is the erasure of class fragmentation in place of a valorisation of labour's socialisation.

The relationship between these two levels of periodisation is articulated through what the *operaisti* call cycles of struggle and class decomposition and recomposition (Dyer-Witheford, 1999; Cleaver, 1979). Following the relationship between the technical and political composition of class outlined above, the *operaisti* (and now postworkerists) theorise a series of antagonistic subjective practices (political composition) arising from the material structure of work (technical composition). It was by examining the tension between the technical and political composition of class that the workerists made sense of the rearrangements of capitalist reproduction and forms of work (Bologna, 1972). The *operaisti* trace the general movement of class figures from the professional worker of the late nineteenth century into the first decades of the twentieth; through decomposition and recomposition of the mass worker of Fordist production in the late 1960s, to the theorisation of the hybrid movements of *autonomia* (Bologna, 1972, 1977; Alquati, 2013 [1961]). However, in reality the proliferation of the *autonomia* movements challenged the precepts of *opera-ismo* (Wright, 2002; Wright, 2021; Bologna, 1972).

At its high point of activity, *operaismo* focused on the figure of the mass worker of the Fordist factory. Characterised by Keynesian state policies and Fordist arrangements of (re)production, the mass worker became the hegem-onic articulation of class composition for *operaismo*. The initial tracings of the contours of the mass worker came about through the worker inquiries at FIAT in the early 1960s (See Wright, 2002 and Wright, 2021 for extensive discussion of these inquiries and their implications for *operaismo*). It was here that the first indications of the new behaviours of the working class were identified. At a broader historical level, the mass worker emerged out the processes of decomposition and recomposition of class and capital preceding the domi-nance of Fordism (Bologna, 1972). As Bologna put it,

> Fordism not only profoundly altered the internal structure of the work-force by replacing the craftsman, or the 'labour aristocracy', with the modern line-worker, the mass worker; it also considerably altered both the structure of the wage and the labour (and capitalist) view of the wage ... For Ford ... the wage became a general quantity of income to be used as a means of controlling the dynamics of the system; it was an overall quantity of capital to be injected within an overall framework of planned development.
>
> 1972: 7

And in its consolidation, the mass worker reflected a broad apparatus of work and reproduction. For Negri's part, he outlined the characteristics of the mass worker in the following terms:

> 1) Within the organisation of the labour process, by *Taylorism*; 2) within the organisation of the working day and the organisation of wage relations, by *Fordism*; 3) within economic/political relations, by Keynesianism; 4) within general social and state relations, by the model and the practice of the *Planner-state*.
>
> 1988 [1982]: 205

The mass worker represented the key figure and prime source of antagonism arising from the technical composition of Fordism. There was, of course, ver-ification of the analyses of the *operaisti*, throughout the Hot Autumn of the late 1960s, and the struggles of the early 1970s. However, it was not long before the proliferation of social struggles beyond the factory superseded the framework of the mass worker, as the myriad struggles of *autonomia* took shape (Bologna, 2007; Wright, 2002; Wright, 2021). Some *operaisti* understood the composition of the *autonomia* movements to be animated by the socialised worker of tertiarised capitalism – an intuition that represents a precursor to contemporary postworkerism (Negri, 1988). However, before turning to the articulation of the socialised worker, one of the most powerful critiques of the limitations of the mass worker came from within *operaismo*, in the form of the workerist-feminist analysis of reproductive labour.

4   Workerist-Feminist Critiques, Wages for and against Housework

Limitations to class composition analyses which insist on a determinate relationship between the technical and political composition of class are myriad. Throughout the debates of *operaismo*, workerist-feminism, *autonomia*, postworkerism, and elsewhere, key points of contention arising from a technical determination of class have been identified (Dalla Costa and James, 1972; Federici, 2012 [1975]). These include a reductive conception of work arising from a narrow consideration of productive labour, which in turn gives primacy of political significance to certain layers of workers over others. Other limitations include an inability to articulate modes of organisation, struggle, and social antagonism that exceed the workplace or are outside of the technical-political relationship as expressed in production. One of the first, and most important challenges to classical *operaismo* emerged, in part at least, from within it in the form of the workerist-feminist critique of the mass worker.

Tronti's Copernican inversion of the class perspective allowed *operaismo* to relocate the point of departure for communist politics and capitalist restructuring in the struggle of the working class. However, it took further inversions of perspective within the theoretical development and political struggles of *operaismo* and *autonomia* to displace the narrow focus on the industrial or mass worker. The rise of the student movement and unemployed workers' struggles contributed to this displacement (Wright, 2002), as did migration from periphery to centre (Mitropoulos, 2006). Yet within the internal debates of the *operaisti*, perhaps the greatest contribution came from the women's movement. The workerist-feminists took Tronti's inversion further than the factory, focussing their analysis on the unwaged labour of the housewife, thus forging a far more nuanced approach to the critique of capitalist reproduction than previously expressed in the theory of the mass worker. In this new inversion, the worker-feminists both radicalised and ruptured the frameworks of *operaismo*.

Rather than representing a simple addition to the general perspective of *operaismo*, the interventions of workerist-feminist theorists such as Mariarosa Dalla Costa, Silvia Federici, and Leopoldina Fortunati represent a concerted effort to displace the workerists' myopic obsession with factory labour as the key site of class struggle, among a powerful constellation of movement groups (Wright, 2021: 478–506; Balestrini and Moroni, 2021 [1997]: 4481–512). Alongside the theoretical work carried out by these authors, the political work of groups such as Lotta Feminista in Italy, the Power of Women collective and debates within the collective Big Flame in the UK, the International Feminist Collective, and the Wages for Housework campaign, constitute a rupture and radicalisation of some of the core assumptions that inform the political perspective of *operaismo*. Finally, the theoretical foundations for these developments, to be analysed below, derived from a radical critique of the process of reproduction and unwaged domestic labour, in a project that sought to demonstrate how unwaged and domestic work produces value. Moreover, the workerist-feminists began from the premise that the totality of capitalist reproduction and exploitation relied on the unwaged work of the household. As Premilla Nadasen points out, within the wider, international Wages for Housework campaign there was a critique of the exploitation of colonial labour and slavery which was pivotal to displacing the attention limited to the waged sphere (2023: 120, see also Best, 2021 for a discussion of the significance of the workerist-feminist critique today). Within the immediate critique of *operaismo* and the mass worker, the subjective figure of the mass worker was replaced by that of the housewife. The strengths and weaknesses of the workerist-feminist perspective arise from this manoeuvre.

In 1971 Dalla Costa penned the essay "Women and the Subversion of the Community", and one year later it was read to a founding meeting of the International Feminist Collective (IFC) and launch of the Wages for Housework (WfH) campaign (Dalla Costa and James, 1975 [1972]). Dalla Costa's essay played an important role in opening what came to be an international debate on WfH, and in outlining the terms of a new Marxist Feminist critique of reproduction. WfH as a demand within, or component of, feminist history was not entirely novel, drawing on various historical precursors (Dalla Costa, 2012). However, the workerist categories that the Italian feminists brought to the question expanded the horizon of analysis, and indeed connected the issue to broader capitalist social relations.

Dalla Costa begins "Women and Subversion" by identifying the exclusion of children and women from the place of productive activity, namely the factory, and the organisation of this exclusion through the division of labour and the form of the family. Exclusion does not, for Dalla Costa, mean a removal from a relationship of exploitation. Rather, exclusion points to a more complex articulation of the relationship of exploitation. Dalla Costa argues that while it appeared as though the key moments in the exploitation of labour and the prominent organising force of capitalist society are found in the immediate point of production and the factory, relationships of exploitation are in fact not reducible to these. Marx may have been right to take us into the hidden abode of production in *Capital volume 1*, but this was not far enough to see just how far the relationship of exploitation went, or indeed to see exactly how it was organised. Dalla Costa in "Women and Subversion" begins to take a step further.

For both Marx and for the workerist-feminists the wage was an important focus of critique, although they approached this problem from different perspectives. Regarding labour-power, Marx's discussion of necessary labour, as distinct from socially necessary labour time, in *Capital* is essentially a discussion of the wage, or the value of labour-power represented as the bundle of commodities necessary to reproduce labour-power (Marx, 1990 [1867]: 325). This level is determined historically, socially, culturally and so on. As Marx puts it,

> the total sum of the necessary means of subsistence ... consists of various commodities, each the product of a distinct industry; and the value of each of those commodities enters as a component part into the value of labour-power.
>
> 1990 [1867]: 433

The reduction of the value of labour-power is achieved through the increased productivity in those branches of industry that produce commodities purchased in the reproduction of labour-power (Marx, 1990 [1867]: 432). Marx recognised that in actual life wages are often lower than this and had made clear the inherent contradictory relationship between labour and capital, subjectively at the level of need and desire, formally in the analysis of the value-form. The wage, for waged workers, expresses this contradiction at both the subjective and formal level. So, while the wage is formally a relationship between equivalents, it in fact obscures an inherent imbalance. Marx's critique of the wage as an index of reproduction remains primarily at this level – formal and at the point of production.

The unwaged labour of reproduction is what is missing from Marx's analysis. Marx did not define necessary labour as inclusive of the actual work performed in the household that was necessary for the reproduction of labour-power to occur.[4] It is here that the workerist-feminists departed from the classical rendering of Marx's theory of value. Beginning from the perspective of working-class housewives, the workerist-feminists criticised the restriction of the analysis of the wage to the level of "direct exploitation" of waged labour (Dalla Costa and James, 1975: 28). Dalla Costa also criticised the organisations of the formal labour movement and other working-class groups for failing to analyse how it "is precisely through the wage that the exploitation of non-waged labour has been organised" (1975: 28). Beyond the formal imbalance in the direct exploitation of waged labour was a deeper level of exploitation. For Dalla Costa, the wage "commanded a larger amount of labour than appeared in factory bargaining", and that in particular *where women are concerned their labour appears to be a personal service outside of capital*" (1975: 28 emphases in original). While women were excluded formally from the wage relationship and thus appeared to be performing a personal and natural service, Dalla Costa argued that working class housewives were involved in the production and reproduction of the commodity labour-power. Herein lies the key insight and point of departure for the workerist-feminists.

Dalla Costa identified the relationship between domestic labour and the overall process of the valorisation of value as the key problem, and this point continued to be taken up by later theorists. She argued that "within the wage, domestic labour produces not only use-values", that is not only use-values in terms of the sustenance of the members of the home, such as dinner and hygiene, but also the use-value of labour power. As a result of this, domestic labour for Dalla Costa was "essential to the production of surplus-value" (1975: 33). Dalla Costa's was a controversial argument, in that it amounted to a re-positing of domestic and reproductive labour as properly productive in a Marxian sense (1975: 53, footnote 12). She thus argued that the (re)production of labour-power in the home was productive of value in itself, and that domestic labour had a "precise and vital place in the capitalist division of labour, *in the pursuit of productivity at the social level*" (1975: 33, emphasis in original).

---

4   In both the 'Results on the immediate process of production' (or what is now the Appendix to *Capital volume I*) and in *Theories of Surplus Value*, Marx does carry out a more sustained analysis of labour in terms of the question of productive and unproductive forms of labour. While Marx's comments in these books are of relevance to my analysis of affect, and I will return to them, Dalla Costa and other workerist-feminists were making a different point to Marx that in effect challenged and modified the letter of Marx's theory of value in terms of the production of value. I will return later in this chapter to my own perspective on the workerist-feminist challenge and modification.

Viewed from this perspective, domestic labour was pivotal not only to understanding the condition of women, but also the accumulation of capital and the composition of class and struggle.

Fortunati (1981) sought to demonstrate just how this was so at a formal level nearly a decade later. Fortunati begins with the critique of reproduction, and the limitation of the concept of the reproduction of labour-power in Marx. Fortunati argues that Marx's perspective on the consumption process that is involved in the reproduction of labour-power renders invisible the work involved in such a process. For Fortunati, Marx sees the worker's reproduction as a simple act of productive consumption, assuming that the act of consuming the wage was simultaneous with the reproduction of the worker. Or, to the degree that the wage can be used to purchase labour, it does so in purchasing unproductive service labour. However, Fortunati rejects this perspective, insisting that reproductive labour does in fact produce value. Fortunati links the time spent in housework and sex work to the production of labour-power. She then argues that as a result of this time spent, housework and sex work produce a value expressed in labour-power. For Fortunati, then,

> the real difference between production and reproduction is not that between value/non-value, but that while production both *is* and *appears as* the creation of value, reproduction *is* the creation of value but *appears otherwise*.
>
> 1981: 8

Housework is said to produce value as "it raises the use-value of his [the workers'] labour-power, use-value being the element which creates value, and which is the substance that multiplies value" (Fortunati, 1981: 8). Fortunati's work is an attempt to represent formally how domestic or reproductive labour is directly productive of value.

The approach taken by the workerist-feminists was innovative, and yet also shared some of *operaismo's* inherent ambivalences. Silvia Federici (2012 [1975]) demonstrates the radical political potential of the workerist-feminist perspective when she argues that rather than seeking to embed women in the role of housewife, the demand for wages is in fact the refusal of this condition. Noting how any worker's relationship to capital is obscured, including through the wage, Federici argued that not only had housework been imposed on women, but that it had "been transformed into a natural attribute, rather than being recognised as work, because it was destined to be unwaged" (2012 [1975]: 16). That is, unwaged housework constitutes an even deeper level of mystification. Thus, for Federici, it was necessary to remember that "money is capital, i.e., it is the power to command labour" (2012: 19). Thus, the struggle for a wage meant to "undermine capital's power to extract more labour from" unwaged domestic labour and to refuse housework as a natural attribute of women. Although workerist feminism extended the framework of workerist critique then, it is nonetheless evident that several similarities connect the two perspectives. In particular the emphasis on the wage as a lever of struggle constitutes a key point of commonality (Wright, 2014: 373). While Federici insists on the political dimension of perspective of the wage and its capacity to demystify and dislocate the condition of women's unwaged work, it is possible to discern a productivist inflection within workerist-feminism. The trajectory of the workerist-feminists has remained staunchly critical of the theories of postworkerism, particularly of the theory of immaterial and affective production (Federici, 2013). And yet, there is a parallel with postworkerism's effort to demonstrate that all of labour is productive, increasingly expressed as a reproductive commons.

Despite the critical contribution of the workerist-feminists, the novelty and significance of their argument is sometimes left out of, or simply subsumed to the trajectory of *operaismo*. In other words, the contemporary presentation of the history of *operaismo* and postworkerism in the Anglophone world, tend assume an automatic theoretical and political affinity between the workerist-feminist perspective and that of classical *operaismo*. Viewed in this way, debates that remain contentious today within the perspective of autonomy, for example debates pertaining to affective, immaterial and precarious labour, are read backwards and erased from the political development of *operaismo* and postworkerism, in each instance with little acknowledgement. Thus, a presentation which subsumes the workerist-feminist contribution to the premises of *operaismo* obscures the reality of the theoretical and practical, political development of the workerist-feminist perspective and the active role it played in radicalising the premises of *operaismo*.

Writing about the various inspirations that the workerist-feminist perspective drew from in organising on the basis they did, James states,

> for them [official organs of the labour movement] the 'real' working class is white, male and over thirty. Here racism, male supremacy and age supremacy have a common lineage. They effectively want to make us auxiliary to the 'general'-struggle – as if they represented the generalisation of the struggle; as if there could be a generalised struggle without women, without men joining with women for women's demands.
>
> 2012 [1972]: 62

The workerist-feminist critique of the labour movement resonated with other marginalised sections of the working class. Thus, James argues that "what gave us the boldness to break, fearless of the consequences, was the power of the Black movement. We found that redefining class went hand-in-hand with rediscovering a Marx the Left would never understand" (2012 [1972]: 62). And importantly, the workerist-feminist perspective identified the specific sites of capitalist production and reproduction as terrains of work from which the labour-capital relation could be struggled against, and with an attention to the stratifications of class along lines of gender and race.

Within the context of *operaismo*, the workerist-feminist perspective, in its international expression of wages-for-housework and wages-against-housework, should be seen as a radicalisation and a rupturing of the foundational tenets. The analysis of the relationship between unwaged work and the production of value, the emphasis upon the unwaged housewife, provided an analysis that not only spoke directly to the various stratifications of the working class, but also to the ways in which political organisation across such stratification might be possible. Part of this involved a rejection of the masculinist conceptions of the factory worker as the hegemonic class figure. Workerist-feminism transformed Tronti's Copernican inversion into a more radical proposition. It also constituted a key rupture from within *operaismo* while signifying the arrival of new subjects of struggle that would eclipse the figure of the mass worker.

5   The Emergence of Postworkerism and the Composition of Class

It was the publication of Hardt and Negri's *Empire* that brought postworkerism to a larger audience, particularly in the English-speaking world, and in so doing situated the controversial thesis of immaterial production at the centre of much debate (Dean and Passavant, 2004). However, the lineage of thought that feeds into the postworkerist perspective on immaterial production can be traced back to the 1970s and the struggles of the *autonomia* movements. Negri locates the decade of the mass worker, its high point of struggle but also decline, between 1960 and 1970. While workers' struggles inside and against the factory were important throughout this period, the factory was by no means the sole site of struggle, and throughout the 1970s became less and less so. The 'area of autonomy' was characterised by a series of movements and tactics embracing rent strikes, self-reductions, feminist struggle, unemployed workers organising and work refusal. Many political observers, not least the *operaisti* and postworkerists, identified the shifting technological arrangements of work, the refusal of factory labour, the growth of non-standard, precarious work, the restructuring of the state, and the shifting global order, as the key features of an emerging form of class composition (Bologna, 2007). The genesis of the postworkerist thesis of immaterial production is identifiable in the analyses of the shifting terms of class composition developed during this period.

5.1   *The Socialised Worker*

The theorisation of the socialised worker (*operaio sociale*) is fundamentally bound to the experience of *Autonomia Operaia*, the tumult of the struggle in Italy of the early 1970s, and the processes of capitalist restructuring in that period (Wright, 2002: 152–175). The category of the socialised worker, associated primarily with the work of Negri, was proposed in the 1970s as the expression of an emergent class composition, one that coincided with the decline of the mass worker and the rise of the *autonomia* struggles. As a figure of class composition, it allegedly represented a higher level of socialisation and abstraction of labour beyond a given sector of production. In other words, unlike the mass worker, which was the reflection of class composition within Fordist factory production, or indeed the housewife located specifically at the acute node of reproduction, the socialised worker reflects abstract labour in total. In the next chapter the problems with the postworkerist theory of concrete and abstract labour are revisited. For now, the socialised worker was devoid of class stratifications, fully integrated with the time of capital, and defined not by its internalisation as a component of capital or the time of work within the factory, but throughout the entire social terrain.

For Negri, the identification of the subjective figure and hegemony of the mass worker had turned out to be an act of historical recognition, insofar as "the mass worker had been conceptualised and had become a reality just when its period of existence was in fact about to end" (1989: 75).[5] According to Negri, the socialised worker is the somewhat paradoxical product of the final conflicts of the mass worker. Negri argues that the 1970s saw a "ferocious conflict

---

5   For *operaismo*, class composition analysis constituted a perspective in which class analysis was not reducible to a project of historical interpretation or political economy but is rather an immediately political method in its orientation (Tronti, 1972; Bologna, 1977). However, a tension between the possibility of formulating a method of political analysis and intervention, and a tendency to become a form of historical interpretation remained at the heart of *operaismo* (Bologna, 1977). Bologna (1977) gave one summation of this tension when he noted that militant historiography is necessarily behind the times, and so while the analysis of class composition can be refined, and thus describe with better precision material reality, it nonetheless lags and is incapable of anticipating forms of political practice that have not yet formed.

that took place over the destruction (by the bosses) and the defence (by the workers) of the institutions of the mass worker" (1989: 76). However, within this conflict "neither side was victorious" (1989: 76). That is, for Negri, although employers managed to reimpose authority within production and force redundancies, by the time this occurred many workers were no longer interested in these terms of conflict and their results, and the "trade unions were left to fight alone". Indeed, as far as Negri was concerned, what followed was an arrangement of work and conflict that was not focused upon the usual questions that confronted the mass worker such as wages and conditions, but rather a new set of problems. According to Negri, it was the socialised worker that anticipated, expressed, and advanced this new political horizon.

Informing the discussion of the socialised worker and its emergence as a subjective figure of class composition were new forms of struggle taking place around the question and conditions of the welfare state. As Carlo Vercellone has pointed out, from the mid-1950s to 1970, Italy saw a significant growth in spending on social services (1996: 82). The proliferation of new forms of struggle in the 1970s points to the emergence of new sources of conflict at the intersection of the state, welfare and social reproduction. Indeed, the questions that were raised by the feminist movement and the workerist-feminists are crucial undercurrents to the thesis of the socialised worker, even if the importance of this undercurrent is not always acknowledged. Negri takes up the question of the welfare state in relation to the social worker.[6] For example, he states that "the high point of capitalist reformism, illustrated the connection between the expansion ... of the welfare state on the one hand, and the rejection of work ... on the other" (1989: 71). Negri articulates this process arguing that,

> in fleeing the factory, the worker sought socialised forms of production, and as a consequence, *the welfare state was transformed from an instrument designed to support the capitalist firm, into an instrument of socialised productivity. From the welfare state to the state as producer; from the mass worker to the socialised worker.*
>
> 1989: 71, emphasis in original

---

6   It is worth noting, that while there is a direct line of development between the theorisation of the socialised worker and the contemporary analyses of postworkerism, the question of welfare illustrates a key distinction in the particularity of each historical moment. The spaces and forms of struggle that correspond to the explicit theorisation of the social worker are characterised by the last years of the welfare state. The post-Fordist precarious worker is theorised in the context of the absence of the previous form of welfare and class deal. The theorisation of the socialised worker occurred in the last hours of the Fordist crisis, and thus despite theoretical continuity with immaterial production, remains out of step with the contemporary context.

The struggles that gave rise to the socialised worker were thus seen to elevate the antagonism between labour and capital to a higher level, a shift that immediately put into question the tenability of the social relation of capital.

Although the category of the social factory had long been a part of the workerists' vocabulary and conceptual arsenal, it had remained linked to a specific conception of the factory proper, as a kind of metronome of the city. In this formulation, capital facilitated the cooperative activity of labour within the factory and pulled the activity of the city into its orbit. The workerist-feminists, as discussed in the previous section, also began from the premise of the social factory to radicalise the critique of reproduction and displace the centrality of the male factory worker in their consideration of anti-capitalist struggle. However, for those who began to theorise through the lens of the socialised worker, a new unity of production, reproduction, and circulation was proposed. Now, it was no longer the factory that put society into motion, but socialised labour itself. In the articulation of the socialised worker, the transformation of the articulation between labour and capital was of primary importance in the shifting determinants of class composition.

The socialisation of labour decentred the factory, seeking instead to identify an undifferentiated social terrain in total as the basis of productive activity. With the emergence of the socialised worker, "work has even less to do with the factory. The latter is no longer recognised or even considered to be the specific site of the consolidation of labouring activity and its transformation into value" (Negri, 1989: 89). Negri continues that "work abandons the factory in order to find, precisely in the social, a place adequate to the functions of concentrating productive activity and transforming it into value" (1989: 89). One can already get a glimpse of how, for the *operaisti* and postworkerists, the specific spatial and temporal arrangement of factory production informs the theorisation of value, and in turn how the disruption of this arrangement destabilises value. Moreover, we can see how labour begins to move towards an articulation of being immediately social.

Already, writing in 1971, Negri was indicating the future directions he would take in theorising the autonomy, and immediately social character of labour. He argued at that point that,

> The exchange of labour-power is no longer something that occurs, in determinate quantity and specific quality, within the process of capital; rather, an interchange of activities determined by social needs and goals is now the precondition, the premise of social production as such; and sociality is the basis of production ... Work is now an immediate participation in the world of social wealth.
>
> NEGRI, 1971: 20

The final sentence of this quote is of particular interest, in that it immediately equates work with a direct participation in a world of social wealth. Moreover, such a world is understood to exist outside of capital. The category of the social worker represents a first attempt to develop this notion of unmediated productivity and the dislocation of labour and capital.

In the transition toward post-Fordism and the socialised worker Negri, and later postworkerism, identify the completion of the process of real subsumption. Negri argues that "[o]*nce subsumption is completely realised, the only possible development is a transition from socialised labour-power to the social worker to the new class subject*" (Negri, 1988: 222, emphasis in original). With the coincidence between the decline of the mass worker and the alleged emergence of the socialised worker, "work has become diffused throughout the entire society" (Negri, 1989: 77). What is of interest here is the idea that the subsumption of all existing social relations within the reproduction of capital allegedly dislocates the form of the antagonism between labour and capital as a component in the organisation of work. Negri states as much when he notes that

> while the ambiguous theory and methodology of the mass worker implied a dialectic of value which today the social worker rejects, there was articulated therein an inherent practical activity of subversion, a self-valorising independence (autonomy), which now the social worker lives as his own dignity and essence.
>
> 1988: 222

The struggle of the mass worker to move from work refusal to self-valorisation is now automatically expressed in the figure of the social worker. For Negri, the socialised worker is thus no longer locked into the condition of variable capital, but exists purely as living-labour, ontologically grounded in a use-value autonomous from capital. This condition finds its complete realisation in the postworkerist construct of labour-value-affect. Indeed, now the "socialised worker produces value naturally" (Negri, 1989: 79) and is the "producer of cooperation necessary for work" (Negri, 1989: 80). Negri retains a conception of antagonism to capital even in the context of the immediately social character of post-Fordist production. However, the dislocation of labour and capital in the organisation of work undermines the capacity to critique the persistent articulation of labour as a component of capital.

For the postworkerists, the condition that enables this alleged immediate autonomy, thus closing the character of antagonism that characterises Marx's discussion of the dual nature of labour, is the growing significance of communicative and intellectual labour. The tertiarisation of labour in this period is assumed to have transformed the mass worker into the subjective figure of the communicative worker – the socialised worker. Now, the socialised worker, combines "the conception and execution of labour across a universal horizon" (Negri, 1989: 78). The immediately social labour of the socialised worker emerges through a direct inversion of Marx's analysis of fixed and variable capital and a re-reading of the concept of general intellect, in a condition where "variable capital represents itself as fixed capital" (Negri, 2008: 160). The inversion of the categories of fixed and variable capital place the body of the worker, the intellectual, linguistic and affective capacities of labour, at the centre of analysis.

5.2 *General Intellect and the* Grundrisse

The postworkerist conception of the contemporary relationship between labour and capital draws heavily from the *Grundrisse*.[7] Negri's (1991) *Marx beyond Marx* is the pivotal reference point for the autonomist analysis of the *Grundrisse*, but as early as 1964, the section that came to be known as the 'Fragment on machines' was heavily influential on the *operaisti* (Tronti, 2008; Bologna, 1987). The fragment on machines is a short section of about twenty pages, which is found across the last pages of notebook VI and the first pages of notebook VII in the *Grundrisse*. In the 'Fragment', Marx takes some of his key arguments to their extreme and draws the contradiction between living-labour and capital as dead labour to a head. Marx outlines the process by which industrial capitalism leads to a massive accumulation of fixed capital, encompassing the general social knowledge of society, embodied in and organised through a vast automatic system of machinery. As a result of this process, variable capital is marginalised and reduced to a simple automaton that administers the vast productive power of machinery. Marx speculates that in such a situation, self-valorising value as the organising principle of capitalist society goes into crisis, as do the indexing mechanisms of the economy – labour-time as a form

---

7   The first unabridged Italian translation of the *Grundrisse* was published in 2 volumes, the first in 1968, and the second volume in 1970. The decision to publish it in two volumes ended the first volume where Marx turns to the discussion of circulation, after the analysis of production (page 401 of Marx, 1993 [1939]). However, this was not the first time a section of the text had been translated and circulated. Various sections of the book had been published since at least 1964 by the operaisti. The original journal of operaismo, *Quaderni Rossi*, in its fourth edition, published the 'fragment on machines' (Marx, 1973: 692–712), while the journal *Classe Operaio* published three other extracts from the *Grundrisse* over the course of 1964 (Tronti, 2008: 229). Not everyone was as enthusiastic as the operaisti about the 'new' work of Marx. Indeed, the operaisti were accused on making up these passages and denounced.

of measure is undermined by the relationship between science, machinery and labour. That is, capital assumes a life of its own, and living-labour is reduced to a diminishing life-blood among the grease and cogs of industry.

The 'Fragment' is characterised by a certain ambivalence: a tension between the development of productive forces as a condition for the freeing of labour, and the ongoing domination of labour by general social knowledge as capital. The first tendency leads Marx to speculate that the crisis of value may be immanent within the very logic of capitalist development. The massive proportional increase in the ratio between fixed capital in the form of machinery over variable capital (Marx, 1993 [1939]: 702–703) would seem to lead inexorably to such a crisis. The worker steps to the side of production, rather than being its chief actor (1993 [1939]: 705). It is "neither the direct human labour" a worker performs, "nor the time during which he [sic] works" which is critical to production (1993 [1939]: 705). Rather it is the worker as an element of a social body, the great productive power of society, mobilised as a whole: "the development of the social individual ... appears as the great foundation stone of production and of wealth" (1993 [1939]: 705). As a result, Marx continues, labour time no longer functions as a basis of measure, and thus production based on exchange value breaks down. However, Marx's discussion of the crisis of value is at best ambivalent on the question of whether or not such a crisis would lead to the emancipation of labour or the definitive overcoming of value. Here in the 'Fragment' as elsewhere in his oeuvre, Marx reiterates the idea that the reduction of human labour is a condition of the emancipation of/from labour. Yet Marx does not go so far as to proclaim that the overcoming of capitalist social relations is already given within the historical unfolding of capitalism. The 'Fragment' is characterised as much by speculations and meditations on the ongoing domination of labour by science, machinery and knowledge in the form of capital, as it is by the idea of an inevitable crisis.

Throughout the commentary that makes up the 'Fragment', Marx makes some telling comments on the relationship between the categories of capital and the dynamic contradiction that is set in motion. Here Marx (1993 [1939]: 694) argues that 'the accumulation of knowledge and of skill, of the general productive forces of the social brain, is thus absorbed into capital, as opposed to labour, and more specifically of fixed capital'. Later Marx argues:

> The development of fixed capital indicates to what degree general social knowledge has become a direct force of production, and to what degree, hence, the conditions of the process of social life itself have come under

the control of the general intellect and been transformed in accordance with it. To what degree the powers of social production have been produced, not only in the form of knowledge, but also as immediate organs of social practice, of the real life process.

1993 [1939]: 706

For Marx this is a question that arises from the contradiction between the relative productive powers of fixed capital over living-labour. This is really a discussion on the production of relative surplus-value taken to an extreme (see Marx, 1990 [1867]: 643–654). Marx is thus grappling with the relationship between the accumulation of dead labour in the form of fixed capital and the extent to which this expresses the immanent command of general social knowledge within the relations of production – the objectification of social knowledge, which comes to mobilise the activity of living-labour and reduce its creative activity to that of a scattered intellectual organ across the machine.

The 'Fragment' has been read several times by those associated with post-workerism, but perhaps two key periods stand out. First, the Italian translation of the 'Fragment' and the *Grundrisse* first circulated between 1964 and 1968, that is, in a condition of increasing massification of industrial production. Thus, the image presented in the 'Fragment' was in several respects a very real depiction of the realities of factory labour and class struggle at the time: a time when labour was confronting the image of itself in the massified dead labour of machinery. Indeed, Panzieri's enthusiasm for the fragment was precisely to antagonise the alleged neutrality of science and capitalist rationality and the dispossession of labour realised in machinery (Panzieri, 1980; Bologna, 1987). Against such a backdrop it is not surprising why this passage was so significant for the *operaisti*. However, another, more recent reading, brings us to the current conjuncture and the engagement with post-Fordism and postworkerism.

The *Grundrisse* and the 'Fragment' is a touchstone document in the shift from *operaismo* to postworkerism and the analysis of post-Fordism. Paolo Virno states that "post-Fordism is the empirical realisation of the fragment on machines" (2004:100). Similarly, Hardt and Negri, in reference to the 'Fragment', proclaim that "what Marx saw as the future is our era": the era of cognitive, linguistic, cultural, and affective production materially manifest in the condition of post-Fordism and the hegemony of immaterial production (2000: 364). Given both the emphasis upon the immediately social character of production associated with the socialised worker and immaterial production on the one hand, and the daunting image of machinery depicted in the 'Fragment', it is not immediately apparent why it remains so significant for the postworkerists. Nonetheless, the concept of the general intellect, outlined in the 'Fragment on machines', has been of key importance for the postworkerists.

Through a reconsideration of Marx's thesis on the general intellect, the postworkerists have reconstructed the relationship between living-labour and fixed capital. Whereas for Marx, the general intellect was expressed as a characteristic of fixed capital in the form of machinery and scientific rationality, the postworkerists invert this relationship. Virno argues that "in post-Fordism, the *general intellect* does not coincide with fixed capital, but manifests itself principally as a linguistic reiteration of living-labour" (2004: 106). Elsewhere, Virno argues that "mass intellectuality – as an ensemble, as a social body – is the repository of the indivisible knowledges of living subjects and of their linguistic cooperation" (1996: 270). Hardt and Negri similarly argue that "living beings as fixed capital are at the centre of this transformation" from Fordism to post-Fordism (2009: 132). And in *Empire* they identify the "principal powers" of the general intellect as those of "science, knowledge, affect and communication" (2000: 365). The general intellect having thus been inverted becomes the instrument through which to analyse the intellectual and affective dimensions of contemporary forms of labour, as well as the political foundation upon which to construct the common. For postworkerism, Marx's observation that "in machinery, knowledge appears as alien, external to him (sic)" (1993 [1939]: 695), is inverted in the transition to post-Fordism. General intellect no longer resides in fixed capital, but rather flows through and beyond variable capital. Moreover, it is expressed as an innate characteristic of the individual, of the bios, and gives expression to the alleged immediately social character of production.

5.3 *From the Socialised Worker to the Common of Immaterial Production*

Postworkerist theorists such as Hardt (1999), Negri (1999), Virno (2004), and Bifo (2009a), offer a unique rethinking of labour and the organisation of capitalism in a contemporary and post-Fordist context, one that relies heavily on the concept of immaterial production. Negri's theorisation of the socialised worker throughout the 1970s and 80s contains elements of the contemporary postworkerist perspective of immaterial production. However, the thesis of the hegemony of immaterial production and the analysis of the forms of labour that allegedly demonstrate its existence, have moved beyond the initial terms set out with the socialised worker. As postworkerism developed throughout the 1990s, it brought to the critique of post-Fordism its critical Marxist perspective, now entwined with the work of Deleuze, Guattari and Foucault. Pivotal to the development of this perspective was the theorisation of immaterial labour developed in the journal *Futur Anterieur*. While approaches to post-Fordism had often been inflected by the triumphalist note associated with information revolutions and theorists of the knowledge economy (Dyer-Witheford, 1999), or otherwise with the more structural accounts of the Regulation School, the postworkerists attempted to introduce the thematic of class struggle, and arguably their very own triumphalist inflection, into the account. This section outlines some of the pivotal steps that informed the development in post-workerism from the thematic of the socialised worker to that of immaterial production, drawing attention in particular to the work of Maurizio Lazzarato and Paolo Virno.

Maurizio Lazzarato's (1996) work on immaterial labour remains important for the analysis of postworkerism.[8] Lazzarato condenses previous research into the restructuring of various forms of work and class composition into a set of working hypotheses and speculations. Lazzarato pays a closer attention to what one might continue to call the technical composition of class in the transition to post-Fordism, while also introducing in explicit terms the problematic of subjectivity and its production in relation to immaterial labour. In doing so, Lazzarato's (1996; 2014) analysis of immaterial labour is considerably more cautious and restrictive than that of other contemporary postworkerists. Despite his recent criticisms of some of the central tenets of theories of cognitive capitalism and immaterial production, it also remains the case that his work foreshadows the ontological turn characteristic of postworkerism.

For Lazzarato the "various different post-Fordist models have been constructed both on the defeat of the Fordist worker and on the recognition of the centrality of (an ever increasingly intellectualised) living labour within production" (1996: 134). The "increasingly intellectualised" character of labour shifts the position of the worker from the role of automaton, as Marx had it in the *Grundrisse* to that of an "interface". The notion of the interface denotes the shift in the position and role of the worker such that the worker comes to be directly involved in the organisation of labour and the labour-process, in decision-making and in moving between different work functions. Immaterial

---

8 Maurizio Lazzarato is credited with coining the term immaterial labour, particularly in the English-speaking world. Lazzarato's work on immaterial labour remains of significance for my presentation of the concept. However, it is necessary to note that Lazzarato has, in a number of significant respects, moved away from key categories associated with postworkerism. In particular, he has moved away from notions of immaterial labour, cognitive capitalism, and the knowledge economy. See Lazzarato (2024).

labour, understood as increasingly intellectualised, thus allegedly breaks down the distinction between manual and mental labour.

The indistinction between mental and manual labour that Lazzarato and other postworkerists have sought to emphasise remains a pivotal point of tension in their conception of the political and technical composition of immaterial labour. Lazzarato states that,

> the split between conception and execution, between labour and creativity, between author and audience, is simultaneously transcended within the 'labour process' and reimposed as political command within the 'valorisation process'.
>
> 1996: 134

For Lazzarato the intellectualisation of labour necessitates a reconsideration of how labour, the labour-process and valorisation are related and organised. Ultimately, the implications found in Lazzarato's argument here are followed to their conclusion in the separation of labour and capital in the cooperative practices of immaterial production.

Christian Marazzi (2008: 41) brings this complexity to the fore, emphasising the centrality of language and communicative-relational action in post-Fordist production. Marazzi argues that "the chain of production has ... become a *linguistic chain*, a *semantic connection*, in which communication, the transmission of information has become both a raw material and instrument of work" (50, emphasis in original). That is, language and communication become the very stuff of production; production sees the linking of material and execution of labour in language and communication. Further, while the division of labour that characterised the mass worker saw a split between the work of innovation, carried out by higher layers of workers and management, and the implementation of such decisions by the de-skilled mass worker, immaterial production allegedly collapses this division.

Paolo Virno argues that the contemporary form of work can be described as the loquacious factory. Virno too focuses upon the linguistic nature of post-Fordist production puts it as follows: the "communication industry ... plays the role of *industry of the means of production*", in so far as techniques of communication and relation become means of production in post-Fordism (2004: 61, emphasis in original). The passage to post-Fordism, which brings us to the present conjuncture, complicates the relationship between time and labour, and the techniques that articulate this relationship. The theoretical prism that postworkerists use to explain these changes is the inversion of the general intellect. Christian Marazzi argues that "in post-Fordism, the *general intellect* is not fixed in machines but in the bodies of workers. The body has become … the toolbox of mental work" (2008 [2002]: 44). A vitalisation of work is evident here, in that "the new form of fixed capital is constituted by a network of social and vital relations" (Marazzi, 2011 [1994]: 94). Berardi's thesis of semiocapitalism maintains that "productive life is overloaded with symbols that not only have an operational value, but also an affective, emotional, imperative and dissuasive one" (2009a: 107). In the passage to post-Fordism, the labour of producing affects, communication, knowledge, the creation and maintenance of relationships and the cultivation of attention emerge as key economic terrains.

Hardt and Negri's collaborative work (1994; 2000; 2004; 2009; 2017) expands on the concept of immaterial production as developed in *Futur Anterieur* and Lazzarato's work. In particular, they add the concept of affective labour to the more explicitly intellectual and cognitive inflection that had hitherto characterised the theorisation of immaterial production. For Hardt and Negri, immaterial production sees 'images, information, knowledge, affects, codes, and social relationships … coming to outweigh material commodities in the capitalist valorisation process' (2009: 132). The concept of immaterial production responds to the increasing amount of labour carried out in service industries generally. Perhaps more importantly, with immaterial production the work of communication, cultivating relationships and producing affect comes to constitute primary points in the organisation of accumulation in contemporary capitalism. In other words, the resources, raw materials and labour used in immaterial production are directly affect, language and knowledge. This is what is meant when it is said that today, fixed capital and the general intellect are increasingly located not in machinery but in the bodies and brains of workers.

6 Conclusion

This chapter has traced the fundamental steps that mark the specific trajectory of postworkerism as it emerged from its origins in *operaismo*. The analysis of *operaismo* and particularly of the categories associated with class composition analysis will be returned to in Chapters 5, 6 and 7, where I analyse the incorporation of the affective sciences into the technical composition of class. The outline of class composition analysis in this chapter also helps to demonstrate the specific ways in which postworkerism has broken with its earlier frameworks of analysis. This chapter also engaged with the workerist-feminist critiques of *operaismo* and the mass worker, which expanded and radicalised the scope of analysis of labour. The insights of the workerist-feminists are significant in problematising productivist notions of labour and expanding the frameworks of class composition analysis. I return to these insights in Chapters 5 and 7. Finally, this chapter outlined how the initial theorisation of the socialised worker and the higher abstraction of labour, laid the foundations for what has matured into the postworkerist theses of immaterial labour, autonomous production, via the reading of the *Grundrisse*.

The inversion of the categories of fixed capital and living labour introduces a series of theoretical difficulties for postworkerism. In the first place it tends to collapse the dynamic relationship between the technical and political composition of class, into the singular substance and potential of living labour. This occurs, as analysed above, through the identification of language, intellect and affect as simultaneously constituting fixed capital and an inherent autonomy due to their characteristic as innate human capacities. The postworkerist analysis of the general intellect, significantly limits in the postworkerist capacity to develop a critique of labour. While for *operaismo* the analysis of the technical composition of class had allowed for an acute sensitivity to the relations within which the labour-capital relation is organised, postworkerism largely dispenses with this. The analysis of the technical composition of class not only provided a framework to locate the changing material structures of work historically, but also identified how labour was incorporated into the reproduction of capital. In the absence of this perspective, which provides a basis upon which to develop a critique of labour as an expression of capital, of exploitation, the wage, and surplus-value, instead labour becomes an unmediated, immediately social concept. One of the crucial points of continuity between the socialised worker and the constitution of labour-value-affect as the foundation of postworkerism is thus found in the dislocation of labour and capital through the analysis of cooperation. With the socialised worker, labour no longer finds itself as a mode of expression of capital, as variable capital, but confronts capital as an external force. This marks a fundamental difference with the consideration of the mass worker and sets in motion the trajectory of analysis that arrives at the autonomy of labour in immaterial production. The following chapter explores the limits of the critique of political economy that emerge from the postworkerist productivist ontology of labour-value-affect. Chapters 5, 6 and 7 revisit the categories of class composition analysis, identifying the incorporation of the affective sciences into the technical composition of class. On this basis it is possible to develop a critique of affective production without recapitulating the productivist ontology of postworkerism.

CHAPTER 4

Affective Ontology, Cooperation, and the Crisis of Value

1 Introduction

Writing in *Volume III* of *Capital,* Marx comments on the antagonism within the labour-capital relation expressed in the division between surplus-value and wages. Marx states that it is the "function of these two independent variables that set limits on one another" (1992 [1894]: 486). For *operaismo,* this articulation of the conflict between labour and capital saw its clearest expression in the struggles of the mass worker (Wright, 2002: 155; Negri, 2018: 4). In this formulation, the wage is understood as the expression of labour's incorporation into capital and thus a condition to be negated, as well as a terrain upon which to directly assault capital and extend the struggle for working-class needs. For *operaismo,* this was also the foundation upon which the 'law of value' would be sent into crisis. Or rather, the fracturing of this foundation through the pressures of the global wave of struggle in the 1960s and 70s, and the counter-revolution orchestrated against it, would provoke the crisis of value. (Wright, 2013; Cooper, 2024). As we saw in the previous chapter, for the postworkerists, rather than leading to a process of class fragmentation and decomposition, the outcome of the crisis was a higher socialisation of labour, beyond its articulation as a component of capital. The conclusion of the postworkerist argument, expressed in the theses of immaterial production, is the dislocation of labour and capital and their rearticulation in new forms.

In the postworkerist telling, while labour still confronts capital in an antagonistic dynamic, the shape of the conflict has been transformed. Now, in the conditions of immaterial and affective production that emerged from those of the socialised worker, labour expresses itself autonomously from capital, through the self-organisational capacities of immaterial labour. Capital, on the other hand, steps outside of the production process, and no longer exploits labour but rather extracts profit as a form of rent, in a dynamic that has been called the becoming-rent of profit (Vercellone, 2013). Underpinning the postworkerist argument of autonomous production is the foundation of labour-value-affect as the materialisation of 'the common' – a form of communicative and affective production beyond the mediation of capital. The reconstruction of the labour-capital relation outlined in postworkerism sees the maturation of their ontological turn in theorising labour and politics. Without doubt, the theses of immaterial production and rent developed by the postworkerists offer innovative readings of both Marx and the dynamics of contemporary social conflicts. However, the alleged dislocation of labour and capital risks misarticulating the dynamics of exploitation still contained within the labour-capital relation and the wage, even in conditions of immaterial and affective production. This chapter develops a critique of the ontological articulation of labour characteristic of postworkerism, and the implications it holds for the critique of political economy and class composition.

2   The Crisis of Value

2.1   *Value and Composition*

Postworkerist reflections on the crisis of the 'law of value' emerged through the analysis of class composition, workers' and social struggles in the late 1960s and throughout the 1970s, and the responses of the state and institutions of capital. In a detailed essay exploring the analysis of value and money within *operaismo*, Steve Wright argues that:

> by early 1974, and for all their many other differences, the *operaisti* were largely agreed that if the so-called 'law of value' had not collapsed altogether, it was in the very least in serious crisis, due above all to capital's uncertainties at that point concerning its capacity to harness labourpower to its own ends.
>
> 2013: 377

As Wright points out, the *operaisti* understood the crisis of value to have emerged as a result of the struggles of workers from below, and the 'revolution from above' carried out by capital. Their theorisation of value is thus directly related to the consideration of class de- and recomposition. Locating the 'revolution from above' as a direct response to the revolts of the working class, the unemployed, and the refusal of the reproductive order of capital is an important insight. Melinda Cooper (2024) also locates the origin of the long counterrevolution in the 1970s, which was unleashed upon the forms of social contestation that had pushed the limits on the structures of Fordism and Keynesian reproduction to a breaking point. For Cooper, the long counterrevolution is orchestrated through a combination of fiscal and monetary policies of austerity in social provisioning and extravagance in private wealth transfer. These historical processes have seen massive reconcentration of wealth through capital gains and asset appreciation, the recomposition of state and capital, alongside the decomposition of labour. While writing from a different vantage point and political perspective than that of *operaismo* or postworkerism, Cooper's analysis helps to illuminate the insights of the *operaisti* into the origins of this process, which they gained through the experience of the movements they were part of. Nonetheless, the limitation in the postworkerist argument that I want to draw attention to lies in their theorisation of labour, value, and measure as articulated through the crisis of the mass worker and the emergence of immaterial production.

As illustrated in the previous chapter, the *operaisti* were well attuned to the connections between the technical and political composition of class from the subjective viewpoint. The analyses of class composition have a direct bearing upon *operaismo's* theorisation of value, such that their theory of the alleged crisis of the law of value, for example, is understood as a response to the *autonomia* struggles of factory workers and other social movements of the 1970s. Negri posits this connection explicitly in his lectures on the *Grundrisse*, where he argues that in the context of *autonomia* "the theory of value is worn to threads, as far as our struggles are concerned" (1991: 17). Earlier, the *operaisti* contended that the unruliness of the factory struggles had placed the control of labour-power beyond the reach of capital. It was, then, the struggle of workers from below which dislocated the operability of the law of value through a rupture of the rhythms and balance of the factory. Struggles over the commodity labour-power put the law of value into crisis and saw labour breach the factory walls. Some *operaisti* understood this as a move towards the deeper socialisation of labour (Negri, 1988), while others saw a growing fragmentation of class experience (Bologna, 2023). In any case, as Wright argues, from the perspective of *operaismo*, what is clear is that workers' struggles precipitated a process of class decomposition and recomposition which also impacted the form of money.

A key moment in the *operaista* perspective on the crisis of value was the collapse of Bretton Woods and the abandonment of the dollar-gold standard by Nixon in 1971 (see Bologna, 1993a [1973]; Bologna, 1993b [1973]; Negri, 1991 [1978]; Negri, 2005 [1971]; Marazzi, 2014: 27–33). Following Wright (2013) once again, it is apparent that for the *operaisti* this event represented the capitalist attempt to orchestrate the decomposition of working-class struggle. Marazzi has argued that the "declaration of dollar inconvertibility" must be understood in the context of global class struggle; more specifically, that it "set the strategic framework for the reorganisation of capital by means of the crisis – *a planned crisis against the global working class through the manipulation of money*" (1977: 96). The manipulation of money was facilitated by the fact that it was no longer being anchored in a specific commodity – gold. In this way the delinking of the standard was, for the *operaisti*, a pivotal moment in the so-called crisis of value. As Bifo argues, "after Nixon's decision, measurement ended. Standardisation ended. The possibility of determining the average amount of time necessary to produce a good ended" (Berardi, 2012: 88). Money without anchor was no longer able to provide a stable index of measure. Such is the crisis of the law of value set in motion from above as a mechanism of class decomposition.

The theoretical and political creativity of the workerist response to the shifting conditions of capitalist crisis does not need to be rehearsed here. The issue I would like to press on, however, is the degree to which postworkerism confines the problematic of value to a particular technical form of production, in turn embedded in a specific labour process and standard form of measure. That is, the postworkerists assume a periodisation of value in which *commodity-money anchored in gold, Fordist labour processes, and Keynesian policy effectively come to represent the historical fulfilment of Marx's law of value*. As far as *operaismo* and postworkerism are concerned, the breakdown of this triangulation must also lead to the breakdown of the law of value. For *operaismo* and postworkerism, a series of conceptual splits characterise the functionality of the law of value. These include the spatial and temporal organisation of the working day; the contractual forms of mediation between labour and capital during this period; a sense of clear demarcation in the categories of fixed/constant and variable capital; and finally, the distinction between the spheres of production, circulation and reproduction (De Angelis, 1994). This conceptualisation leads the *operaisti* and the postworkerists to posit Fordism as the clearest historical, and ultimately final, expression to the law of value as constructed by Marx. The creativity of the *operaisti* in forging concepts in the heat of the class battles in which they found themselves notwithstanding, then, their tendency to reduce value to a specific technical organisation of production represents a considerable limitation in the critique of labour. For the theorists of postworkerism, this initial limitation found in *operaismo* has developed into a fundamental political impasse.

2.2   *The Technical Determination of Value*

Considered in broad strokes, 'the long '68' and the collapse of the gold standard marks a decisive historical threshold for the postworkerist understanding of the crisis of value. However, the other side of the crisis of the law of value is the consideration of labour that dominates postworkerist thought. On one hand, the postworkerists argued that the abandonment of the dollar-gold standard had unhinged the capacity of money to function as a form of measure. On the other hand, they thought that workers' struggles and the subsequent emergence of 'new' forms of affective and immaterial labour beyond the factory walls had set labour apart from capital, thus rendering labour immeasurable and generating a crisis of value. However, there are limits to constructing such a close relationship between the labour process, concrete labour, a standard of measure, and the crisis of value. I have already pointed out in Chapter 2 that the postworkerist reading of value is ultimately a Ricardian one, but it is worth deepening the critique of how the postworkerists come to understand value as a simple aggregation of concrete hours of labour. If the 'new' forms of labour resist measurability, and consistently elude the problem of value, the implication is that a previous form of labour was not so elusive. The logic that informs this reasoning illustrates the limits of postworkerist analyses of labour and value.

The pivotal factor in the postworkerist analysis of value is the question of value's measurability. Marx's consideration of the measure/magnitude, substance and, most significantly, the form of value was covered in Chapter 2. For Marx, and other theorists, the key to understanding value comes through an analysis of value-form. Postworkerism, by contrast, has built its consideration of value solely around the question of measure. In particular, the object of measure is concrete labour. Negri argues that the key limitation of "Marx's consideration consists in the fact of reducing the form of value to an objective measure" (1992: 71). Elsewhere Negri argues that what has fundamentally changed since the "time of the classical theory of value" is "the possibility of considering value as a measure of concrete labour" (1999: 78). Thus, Negri concludes that labour can no longer be expressed as units of homogenous time. The implication of this perspective, however, is that there was a time when value was a measure of concrete labour based upon homogenous units of labour time. It is in this construction of value that the substantialist conception of value is recapitulated even as it is criticised.

The exemplary model of labour in which the law of value could operate was, according to postworkerism, Fordist factory labour. The postworkerist narrative posits clear demarcations between the functionality of time and activity: of productive working life. In other words, there were clear sites and times in which living-labour or variable capital confronted fixed capital, and in this interaction undertook value-creating activity. This is the unity of time and space that underpins the construction of value for postworkerism. Fordism was thus characterised by "regular rhythms of factory production and its clear divisions of work time and non-work time", in which there was a "temporal unity of labour as the basic measure of value" (Hardt and Negri, 2004: 145). Within this formulation labour is an external standard of measure, and value is measurable by labour as the difference between input costs, particularly that of variable capital (wages), and the value of the commodity output (Eden,

2012).[1] As Vercellone and Giuliani understand it, "the law of value founded on abstract labour time where value is expressed as a definite quantity of simple and homogeneous unskilled labour enters into crisis" (2019: 16). Continuing, they state that "Knowledge and the immaterial become the principal source of value, replacing the criteria of output productivity and of direct labour time proper to industrial capitalism" (2019: 30). Even Marazzi will argue that with post-Fordism "we have witnessed the crisis of industrial time as homogenous, abstract, chronometric, computable objectifiable time, external to human beings and to things" (2002: 51). The postworkerists thus posit a direct relationship between the amount of 'concrete' hours worked by an individual worker and the measurability of value.

Rather than a critique of the value-form, postworkerism instead focuses on the particularity of the labour process. Dave Eden (2012: 95–108) argues that in the work of Virno and Negri, the theory of value is reducible to a fixation upon the labour process and concrete labour. As a result, value is constructed as "a technical determination rather than a product of social relations predicated on production for exchange" (Eden, 2012: 96). Eden's critique focuses upon the absence of exchange and the failure of Negri and Virno to develop a critique of the commodity, and notes that this arises from the primacy of production within the framework of *operaismo*. Eden is correct to note this absence, and indeed Negri (2005 [1971]: 20) was proclaiming the obsolescence of exchange as early as 1971. For Negri, the paradox of exchange lies in the fact that the real subsumption of labour to capital, while subjecting all relations to exchange, also undermines the meaning of exchange-value in Marx. If, for Marx, exchange is what transforms private labour into social labour (Marx, 1991; Rubin, 1990 [1928]), postworkerists posit an entirely different reading of exchange. Negri is again exemplary here, arguing that within the condition of real subsumption, "the labour of the single producer is posited from the outset as social labour" (2005 [1971]: 20). Herein lies a significant clue to understanding

---

1   Angela Mitropoulos (2012) analysis of oikonomia and neocontractualism presents a convincing argument that what is missing from the theory of the wage from Marx onwards, is that it is an expropriation of surplus labour not only from that formally exploited in the workplace/workday, but through the racial and gendered ordering of the household. Mitropoulos reworks the theory of value into the law of the household and oikonomia. Her work constitutes, amongst other things, an important contribution to value theory. The exploitation of labour has always drawn from an 'immeasurable' pool of free labour. However, this does not render the theory of value untenable, or transform all social activity into a smooth productive substance. Indeed, the extraction of free labour has been arranged in numerous and shifting arrangements over time, including the unpaid portion of the working day, but also from a pool of labour never even formally recognised as such.

the trajectory of Negri and postworkerism more generally. Later Negri would claim that "exchange is inadequate to the possibility for capital to set in motion the collective power of socially cooperative labour: hence the obsolescence of exchange is total and radical" (2005 [1977]: 182). Removing the consideration of exchange from the critique of work makes it that much easier to posit labour as a smooth, singular substance. The absence of exchange is thus one indication of how the postworkerist account of value undermines its capacities for the critique of labour.

The absence of exchange is informed by a problematic conceptualisation of the relationship between concrete and abstract labour. Specifically, the concept of abstract labour is read back into, or through, the labour process by postworkerism. Here again, the Fordist factory plays a pivotal role. Industrial factory labour is posited as a clear illustration of a simplified, and thus measurable labour. Bifo argues that "industrial labour was generally abstract since its specific quality and concrete utility was irrelevant compared to its economic function of valorisation" (Berardi, 2009: 75–76). More specifically, that "the more industrial labour is simplified the more it is interchangeable". For Bifo, abstract labour is constituted through a particular form of concrete labour performed within the workplace or labour process of mass industrial production. Thus, part of the explanation for the immeasurability of value lies in the fact that the labour of post-Fordist workers is not "interchangeable" in the same way industrial labour was. However, the real difficulty that Bifo has identified here is the relationship between simple and complex labour, which is a different problem to that of the measurability of value.[2]

The abstraction of labour, and the character of labour as homogenous as rendered in exchange-value and the process of exchange, does not arise from the conditions of any given labour process. Indeed, it is unrelated to the labour process or the labour of the individual. Beverley Best has put it as follows, "every bearer of the collective worker performs necessary labour and surplus labour regardless of the concrete labour they perform" and "no individual producer or enterprise actually generates value at all" as value is fundamentally social, a mediated mode of sociality (2024: 196). As Marx argues, "the homogenous simplicity of labour means ... the equality of the labours of various

---

2   Jacques Bidet (2005: 16–30 and 94–99) has argued that the attempts by Marx to grapple with simple and complex, or skilled and unskilled, labour in relation to value are undermined by the trajectory of his own argument. Marx's own argument concerning the determination of the value of labour-power circumvent the difficulties that Marx continued to pursue in trying to understand distinct categories of simple and complex labour. Bidet argues that in reality, complex labour is an unnecessary category. For a rejoinder to Bidet's reading of Marx and market socialism see Helmut Richelt (1993).

individuals … the actual reduction of all kinds of labour to uniform labour"
(Marx, 1904 [1859]: 26). Exchange plays a fundamental role in rendering the
equality of labours, in the articulation of their social character. But the functionality of this process does not arise from the specific character of labour or
types of labour processes that characterise production. To locate value in the
concrete specificity of a given labour process misarticulates the persistence
of mediation, and as a result undermines the critique of labour as a mode of
expression of capital. The misarticulation of mediation also underplays the
persistence of the wage in the organisation of labour, the organisation of
exploitation, and a variable of contestation within the labour capital relation.
Below, I return to the significance of the wage in the articulation of labour, but
first it is useful to unpack the conditions of autonomous production further.

3   Cooperation, Autonomous Production, and Measure

For postworkerists the crisis of the law of value emerges as the result of transformations in labour that constitute contemporary capitalism and the spatial
and temporal rhythms of work. These are summed up as the movement from
Fordist to post-Fordist capitalism, or from industrial to cognitive capitalism
(Moulier-Boutang, 2011; Vercellone, 2010; Virno, 2004). Vercellone argues that
if we are to understand the crisis of value, then it must be seen as "a crisis
of measurement that destabilises the very sense of the fundamental categories of the political economy; labour, capital, and obviously value" (Vercellone,
2010: 90). Vercellone continues, "the crisis of the *law of labour time-value* is
not limited to a measurement crisis but corresponds to two elements … the
exhaustion of the progressive force of capital and its increasingly parasitical
character" (2010: 90). To continue with Vercellone, the crisis of the law of value
can be seen insofar as, pertaining to industrial capitalism, "abstract labour,
measured in a unit of simple, non-qualified labour", which is the "tool allowing
for the control over … labour" no longer holds (2010: 90). In order to explain
why this is the case, Vercellone argues, it is necessary to look to the reconfig-
uration of the categories of capital that occurs with the "power and growth of
the power of labour's cognitive dimension" (2010: 90–91).

As noted in previous chapters, throughout the 1980s and 1990s postworkerism begins to posit the self-organised cooperative practices of the living,
general intellect as the pivotal terrain of production. As Pasquinelli puts it,
"only at that time [1990s] would *operaismo's* idea of the autonomy and primacy
of living labour be extended to living knowledge, rediscovering that so-called

'Fragment on machines'" (2014: 186). Thus, the general intellect was extracted from "the greasy gears of the industrial machines" to circulate through the body of labour. Whereas the Fordist factory established a clear demarcation between labour and machinery, or variable and constant capital, today the expansion of cognitive and affective labour means that variable capital directly incorporates aspects of fixed capital or 'machinery', for example, the capacity to communicate or care. Therefore, "when speaking of cognitive work, we are speaking of this new faculty of the workforce: *the means of production has become internal to the singularities engaged in the organisation of labour*" (Negri, 2008: 66). Elsewhere, Lazzarato has argued that the "cycle of immaterial labour takes as its starting point a social labour power that is independent and able to organise both its own work and its relations with business entities" (1996: 138). Indeed, "industry does not form or create this new labour power, but simply takes it on board and adapts it" (1996: 138). What opens here, even if one were to accept the renewal of Marxian categories, is the possibility of sliding from the critique of political economy towards an ontological conception of labour, where labour is understood as not only capable of, but engaged in sustaining its own autonomous social organisation of production. If we accept this premise, it follows that exploitation takes on the form of "value expropriation that proceed[s] in a position of exteriority in respect of the organisation of production" (Vercellone, 2010: 91). Labour, now incorporating elements of fixed capital, can organise itself, and so exploitation is expressed as a parasitic drain on the common.

Postworkerism's argument concerning immaterial production, the general intellect and autonomous labour, has implications for how work is understood. That is, the hypothesis of autonomous labour illustrates how postworkerism has moved from a critique of labour to its valorisation. For example, Hardt and Negri argue that:

> when the multitude works, it produces autonomously and reproduces the entire world of life. Producing and reproducing autonomously means constructing a new ontological reality. In effect, by working, the multitude produces itself as singularity.
>
> 2000: 395

Based upon the premises of postworkerism, work is already a construction of a new world. Postworkerism moves from a world beyond exchange in which, "work is an immediate participation in the world of social wealth" (Negri, 1971: 20), to a condition of properly autonomous production.

As far as postworkerism is concerned, the pin that holds together this new class composition of autonomous production is the character of cooperation within the organisation of immaterial labour. In this formulation, because the technical composition of class approximates an immediately social character through affective and immaterial production, capital no longer functionally organises cooperation between labour. Thus, for Negri, "stripping capital of this function means recuperating for labour-power autonomous capacities of cooperation" in the common (2013b: np). Negri's comments highlight the significance of the role of affect in the ontological turn of postworkerism, and the particular conception of cooperation arising therefrom.

The question of cooperation is significant to both the analysis of class composition in general, as well as specifically to the postworkerist conception of affective labour and autonomous production. Marx's characterisation of cooperation in *Capital volume I* is the image against which postworkerism assesses the present arrangements of labour. Marx wrote of cooperation that "as a general rule, workers cannot cooperate without being brought together: their assembly in one place is a necessary condition for their cooperation" (1990 [1867]: 447). Marx continues, "hence workers cannot cooperate unless they are employed simultaneously by the same capital, the same capitalist, and therefore unless their labour-powers are bought simultaneous by him" (1990 [1867]: 447). Finally, Marx argues that,

> their cooperation only begins with the labour process, but by then they have ceased to belong to themselves. On entering the labour process they are incorporated into capital. As co-operators, as members of a working organism, they merely form a particular mode of existence of capital.
>
> 1990 [1867]: 451

It is not difficult to see why postworkerists have taken the opportunity to update this image of cooperation. The image cast in Marx's description does not immediately resonate with various contemporary arrangements of work or the widespread integration of technologies into everyday life (Smith, 2020). The dispersed character of so much labour, coordinated via platforms with workers scattered across urban space, presents a different image of coordination and cooperation than the massification of labour in industrial factory zones indicated by Marx. Of course, we should not forget that the contemporary geography of production includes the hinterland as "a heavily industrialised space" of farms and large-scale logistics complexes (Neel, 2018: 16). Nonetheless, some forms and means of cooperation are distinct from that of the factory, in a range of contexts like care, or logistics, among others. However, even in these contexts, Marx's final phrase above should not be forgotten. Namely, that one's condition as variable capital still marks working time and activity as a "particular mode of existence of capital". It is this condition that stamps the technical composition of class, and which remains the object of critique.

The postworkerist perspective on affective labour inaugurating a regime of autonomous production has theoretical and political implications beyond the conception of cooperation. Dispensing with the categories of class composition analysis, specifically that of the technical composition of class, forms one plank of the argument concerning the immeasurability of labour and value. While the premises of the immeasurability of labour and value are presented in philosophical and political-economic terms, they also emerge from the postworkerist consideration of contemporary class composition. Negri's (2003) work constitutes the most philosophical articulation of the immeasurability thesis, while the work of Marazzi (2008 [2002]) presents a more rigorous engagement with questions of finance, circulation, and labour. Despite the distinct perspectives on the concept of immeasurability presented by Marazzi and Negri, they nonetheless parallel and inform one another. Once again, the thesis of immeasurability rests largely upon the idea that class composition and the organisation of labour have undergone profound qualitative changes.

The immeasurability of labour and value allegedly rests upon the shifting work arrangements of post-Fordism, the collapse of the gold standard, and the proliferation of financial logics to ever-widening aspects of socio-economic life (Wright, 2013). Marazzi argues that the emergence of post-Fordism ushered in an expansion of work time and a reduction in wages, while also putting to work "the most common, most public ('informal') qualities of the workforce – or better, language, communicative relational language" (2008 [2002]: 41). Marazzi goes on to state that "the centrality of language in post-Fordist production and the putting to work of the cognitive properties of the workforce leads to the *crisis of measurability* of single work operations" (2008 [2002]: 43, emphasis in original). In this formulation, the rise of communicative and relational labour expressed through the general intellect is understood to have provoked a general crisis of measurability. But the implication of single work operations is also telling. Ultimately, the position outlined by Marazzi recapitulates the technical determination of value that was presented earlier in the chapter.

Negri's, entwining of Spinozist affect and labour positions labour beyond measure:

> in this paradoxical way, labor becomes affect, or better, labor finds its value in affect, if affect is defined as the 'power to act' (Spinoza). The

paradox can thus be reformulated in these terms: The more the theory of value loses its reference to the subject (measure was this reference as a basis of mediation and command), the more the value of labor resides in affect, that is, in living labor that is made autonomous in the capital relation, and expresses ... its power of self-valorisation.

1999: 79–80

Labour and value are thus reconceptualised through the category of immeasurable affect or value-affect.[3] As production subsumes the totality of social life, so the basis of value as measure collapses. As labour becomes life in biopolitical production, the labour theory of value implodes, and the task of theory becomes that of decoupling value from measurable labour. Having made this move, Negri then attempts to reconstruct the theory of value in terms of value-affect, where affect is posited as an immediately cooperative and immeasurable political force.

Reflections on the relationship between time, value, and class composition, are woven throughout postworkerism. Negri's (2003 [1981]) essay *The Constitution of Time*, written from prison during his first incarceration, presents a dense articulation of his analysis of the immeasurability of labour and value, the implications of which inform much of postworkerism. Negri locates the immeasurability of value and labour in the real subsumption of labour to capital. In the most basic of terms, Negri argues that in a condition of real subsumption, which he takes to mean the subjection of all social and creative time to the time of capital, labour time ceases to be the measure of value:

---

3   Despite the postworkerist insistence that the conditions of immaterial production render labour and value immeasurable, the issue of measure remains heavily contested within the broader field of autonomist marxism. Contra postworkerism, theorists such as Caffentzis (2011a) and De Angelis (1995; 2007) continue to insist on the problem, and indeed the practice of measure. Both Caffentzis and De Angelis consider the question of measure in relation to the ongoing viability of the theory of value. De Angelis and Caffentzis exemplify a tendency in autonomist Marxism to retain an engagement with the theory of value that both challenges its marginalisation within postworkerism while also retaining an emphasis on working class self-activity within the value relation. For example, De Angelis (1995) develops a political reading of abstract labour. He argues that abstract labour is "work in the capitalist form" and that as a result abstract labour is ultimately a "relation of struggle" (1995: 108). More recently, De Angelis (2007) has reframed his analysis of abstract labour in terms of 'value struggles'. For De Angelis a pivotal feature of value struggles, struggles over the determination of what is considered valuable, are conflicts over forms of measure. De Angelis' perspective fits into a broader debate about the relationship between class struggle, particularly at the point of production and the determination of value (see for example, Knafo, 2007; Kicillof and Starosta, 2007).

"time as measure of value is smashed" (2003: 42). Or as Alexander Brown has put it in his commentary on this essay, "for Negri, there is no outside to time, because time is constitutive of being in its entirety" (2012: 179). For Negri, this situation engenders two counter-posed forms of time: on the one hand, the time of productive cooperation of the socialised worker (now multitude), and on the other, the time of capital as exterior command. It is for Negri, perhaps counterintuitively, the real subsumption of labour to capital that facilitates the dislocation and separation of labour and capital in the production process, in terms of composition, cooperation, and exploitation.

Further, Negri argues there is a "radical difference of ... two practices of time: analytic on the capitalist side, productive on the proletarian" (2003: 75). The time of productive cooperation elevates the condition of labour to an ontological and ethical status that is temporally opposed to capital. Indeed, for Negri the opposition of time is marked by a radical separation between the productive cooperation of the proletariat and capital's time of domination. Thus, this is a "separation that does not divide the working day by internal lines, but that co-extensively counterposes capital and labour" (Negri, 2003: 80). Negri's (2003) argument concerning the separation of time retains an engagement with a politics of negation and refusal. However, the productivist conception and ontology of labour emerges as the dominant tendency, even in this essay. For example, Negri argues that "time is ... defined as transformation of refusal into cooperation, cooperation into production, production into liberation" (2003: 80). While highly philosophical in register, the affirmationist tendency that determines the immeasurability of labour and value articulated by Negri above arises in the consideration of the composition of class in the wake of the mass worker.

The tendency that Negri articulates above is traceable throughout his co-authored work with Hardt and reflected in wider postworkerist perspectives (see for example Vercellone, 2013 and Vercellone and Dughera, 2019). Hardt and Negri argue that "value will be determined only by humanity's own continuous innovation and creation" (2000: 356). In Chapter 2, I suggested that this perspective on value is simultaneously an argument for a conception of value from below and a moralist argument for the recognition of productive activity. Hardt and Negri continue: "the temporal regimentation of labour and all the other economic and/or political measures that have been imposed on it are blown apart" (2000: 357). The insistence on the irrepressible movement of the proletariat that is captured in these phrases is a refreshing challenge to political thought on several counts, not least its eternal refusal of pessimism. However, the pivotal problem in this formulation is the inability to pose a critique of labour in either its immediacy – as work – or in its historically specific form within capitalism – as abstract labour and value. As a result, the very real contradictions, antagonisms, and affective experiences of work are marginalised if not erased completely by the claim of immeasurability and autonomous cooperation. Conflict, as an internal condition of the labour-capital relation all but disappears from the workplace and the broader conceptualisation of work. The assumption of autonomous cooperation articulated through knowledge and affect remains problematic, premised on the complete realisation of an affirmationist ontology of labour grounded in affective production.

4 From Class Composition to the Foundational Threshold of Political Ontology

Postworkerism's consideration of labour is founded in the inversion of the general intellect, whereby the affective, linguistic and intellectual capacities of living-labour assume the role of fixed capital. In the previous chapter we traced the steps through which this theoretical development took place. The reconstruction of the general intellect, whereby the content of fixed capital is expressed in the capacities of living labour rather than machinery, is in part carried out through a renewed approach to class composition analysis, to the point where the categories of analysis are fundamentally reworked or dispensed with. However, ultimately the categories of class composition play a secondary role to the reconstruction of labour as an expression of biopolitics. The postworkerist attempt to renew Marxian categories takes place through an encounter with the work of Michel Foucault, Gilles Deleuze, Felix Guattari, and a 'return' to Benedict de Spinoza. For postworkerism, the outcome of these encounters is a vitalist and affirmationist understanding of politics, in which labour and life constitute a singular, productive substance.

The affirmationist perspective of postworkerism has been identified and criticised by various authors. Benjamin Noys (2010: 106–133) notes the conflation of life and labour in Negri's thought and identifies this as the ontological foundation of Negri's politics. In a similar vein, Katja Diefenbach (2010: 63–95) presents a critical reading of postworkerism's theorisation of biopolitical labour. Diefenbach notes that within the framework of postworkerism, and as a result of the encounter I point to above, labour-power is "ontologised" (2010: 86). Both Noys and Diefenbach identify a political impasse within postworkerist affirmationism, which foregrounds the argument made throughout this chapter, focusing on the connection between the ontological turn within postworkerism and the critique of political economy.

The tendency toward a vitalism of labour, production and politics was already evident within the debates of the 1970s that lead to the development of postworkerism (Negri, 1989). The search for new analyses of class composition provided the general framework through which the tendency to vitalism moved. Much of this material I outlined in the previous chapter, where I showed that the subsumption of language, intellect and affect, that is the capacities of 'life', leads to the "incorporation of the mode of production in the body of producers" (Diefenbach, 2010: 86). While each theorist of postworkerism has pursued this intuition in their own way, a common experience was a passage through the Years of Lead via the encounters with Foucault, Deleuze and Guattari. For example, Marazzi noted that in light of the impasse of *opera-ismo* "Foucault seems to offer new material" (1979, cited in Wright, 2013: 389). Meanwhile the activism and thought of Franco Bifo Berardi became entwined with that of Guattari, and Deleuze (Berardi, 2008; Dosse, 2010 [2007]). While Negri's 'return' to Spinoza remains a prominent influence as philosophical foundation of postworkerism. It is through these encounters that the unique trajectories of the postworkerist theorists evolved into vitalist conceptions of labour and capital, where the category of labour is replaced by that of life.

Perhaps the clearest indication of the vitalist shift comes via the growing importance of Foucault's concepts of biopower and biopolitics in the post-workerist theorisation of capitalism and biopolitical production. In a series of lectures delivered in the latter half of the 1970s Foucault (2007) explored how 'life' and the 'biological features' of the human species materialised as the terrain of political and power strategies. Life and living are contested terrains. Biopolitics and biopower denote an array of historically specific techniques of discipline, security, control, and management that arise with modern politics. For Foucault, whilst power and life are what is at stake in the historical shift to biopolitics, they do not in any way represent ahistorical or transcendental categories. Power is not a particular force or object that operates upon a sep-arate object, it is rather an immanent and specific relationship within a given terrain. For example, Foucault argues that "there are not first of all relations of production" (or of family or sexuality) "and then, in addition, alongside or on top of these relations, mechanisms of power that modify or disturb them, or make them more consistent, coherent, or stable". Rather, "mechanisms of power are an intrinsic part of all these relations and, in a circular way, both their effect and cause" (2007: 2). The complex, though properly materialist, problem Foucault highlights here is that if one is to struggle, it is necessary to begin from the internal dynamics of the specific relations within which one finds themself.

The work of Foucault simultaneously resonated with the heretical Marxism of postworkerism, while opening a way out of the existing limits of *operaismo*, perceived or otherwise. However, and not uncharacteristically, in the hands of the postworkerists, Foucault's terms are significantly revised. This revision is clearest in the work of Negri, who insists that "the concept of biopolitics ... ultimately needs to confront and address the question of labour", and in doing so begin again with Marx (Casarino and Negri, 2008: 148). Lazzarato, for his part, argued that "Foucault needs a new political theory and a new ontology to describe the new power relations expressed in the political economy of forces" (2006: 12). Thus, for Lazzarato "biopolitics is the strategic coordination of these power relations in order to extract a surplus of power from living-beings". Negri's assertion that biopolitics needs to confront labour, that is needs to be thought from the perspective of labour, indicates the foundation upon which labour and life merge, becoming the basis for a new form of productivity. In the hands of Hardt and Negri, Foucault's analysis of biopower and biopolitics is transformed and inverted, such that the constituent power of labour becomes the origin point for any consideration of political conflict and transformation. At this point Hardt and Negri move from an analysis of biopolitics to the affirmation of biopolitical production: the production of social life itself. Hardt and Negri claim that it is the Deleuzian (Deleuze, 2006 [1986]) reading of Foucault and the work of Deleuze and Guattari that fully uncovers biopolitical production's "ontological substance of social production" (2000: 28).[4] In Hardt and Negri's formulation, biopolitical production is best understood in terms of "mass intellectuality", "immaterial labour", and the "Marxian concept of the general intellect" (2000: 29). More recently they write that "the biopolitical circuit is ... all contained in the production of the common which is also simultaneously the production of subjectivity and social life" (Hardt and Negri, 2009: 299). Thus, the ontological turn of postworkerism is incipient in the way in which they approach the work of Foucault.

The development of the common also plays a key role in defining the ontological status of labour within postworkerism. For example, Marazzi states that the common is the "entire knowledge, understandings, information, images, affects and social relations that are strategically subject to the production of goods" (2011: 119). While the common remains a somewhat ambivalent and contested concept within broader autonomist Marxist debates (see for

---

4   While Hardt and Negri develop a Deleuzian rendering of Foucault's concepts, there are notable divergences between Negri's and Deleuze's theorisation of Spinoza's conception of affect (see Ruddick, 2010) and between their approaches to politics. For example, see the comments on communication and speaking out (Deleuze and Negri, 1990).

example Silvia Federici (2012), Midnight Notes (1992 [1990]), *The Commoner*, Massimo de Angelis (2007)), a significant influence upon the postworkerist theorisation of the common comes via Spinoza and Deleuze. The distinctive element of the postworkerist theorisation of the common is that it is understood to be produced in the communicative, intellectual and affective relations between bodies. Negri's work on Spinoza and Michael Hardt's (1993) study of Deleuze illustrate the particular Spinozist inflection postworkerism imparts to the notion of the common. Deleuze reads Spinoza's concept of 'common notions' as "the representation of a composition between two or more bodies, and a unity of this composition" (1988: 54). While Hardt understands the 'common notions' to be a productive relationship, a physics between bodies, "not merely a chance composition, but an ontological constitution" (1993: 99). Finally, Negri entwines labour and affect, to the extent that they both express the idea that "labour is the power to act" (1999). It is in this vein that Hardt and Negri assert that they follow "Spinoza's conception of 'common notions', on the *production and productivity* of the common" (2009: 120–121, emphases in original). Thus, the thesis of the biopolitical production of the common is imbued with an ontological inflection.

It is worth pausing here to consider the critiques of constructing a foundational ontology that have emerged from within the postworkerist perspective itself. Negri argues that a "substantialist ontology" has "no place" in his politics, rather "the ontological aspects of subjectivity are established (or rather produced) through the formulation of points of view, the interlacement of orientations of struggle and the revelation of intentions" (1989: 128). Thus, "it is a very special form of ontology, one which we can here call a *constitutive ontology*" (1989: 128). Based in a Spinozist conception of affects and change, Negri's constitutive ontology claims to elude fixture and foundation. He states that "ontology is not a theory of foundation …[it] must be open to the production of the discontinuous, to the unforeseeable, to the event" (Hardt and Negri, 1994: 287). The political implications to this perspective are challenging, and not without internal inconsistencies.

Charles Wolfe (2007), follows the nuances of the development of ontology in Negri's thought, tracing the temporalisation of matter that defines Negri's materialist ontology. Wolfe argues that for Negri materialism is a *"theory of action … not a theory of science or of truth"* (2007: 218, emphases in original). Materialism as a theory of action implies the possibility of change and mutation, thus Wolfe also notes that for Negri the "ultimate concern is not to lose the political dimension, the possibility of change/innovation/transformation" (2007: 218). And yet the difficulty or problem that emerges here, is that of the "leap … from a materialist ontology to the assertion that the true 'base' of this materialist metaphysics is 'living labour'" (Wolfe, 2007: 216). The difficulty that Wolfe points to here, is close to the limits that I am tracing in postworkerist conceptions of the foundation of labour-value-affect and the common. Wolfe whittles Negri's central problematic down to the question of how can 'the new' appear, and correctly points to the limit in which Negri asserts that living labour *just is* capable of 'hybridisation' and transformation. Negri's materialist ontology is thus not fixed, but rather constitutive.

Retaining the political dimension, as Wolfe points out above, leads Negri to maintain that a materialist ontology must begin from the subjective viewpoint, which is ultimately expressed in the antagonism between living-labour and capital. On one hand, this makes sense, as demonstrated in the histories of constituent power (Negri, 1999). However, Negri's insistence on living-labour as an ever-productive constituent power draws him onto difficult ground when entwined with the existing labour processes of capitalist production. Negri rejects a simple naturalism and yet is inevitably drawn back to an eternal conception of living-labour as a productive and transformative substance. As we have already seen, Negri falls back upon notions of naturalism, whereby "the socialised worker produces value *naturally*" (1989: 79). At the threshold of Negri's political, anti-foundational ontology is the re-inscription of foundation in the alleged autonomy of affective production. Unfortunately, labour is far more fragmented, stratified and entangled in the reproduction of capital than the image of living-labour cast by Negri, and postworkerism more broadly, indicates.

Given the inability of Negri and postworkerism to overcome the tendency toward a foundational conception of affective production, Thomas Lemke is correct to point out that with the analysis of biopolitics "the problems with Hardt and Negri's argumentation are clearest" (2011: 74). Lemke argues that with Hardt and Negri "'life' ... is not ... configured as a social construct or as an element of historical knowledge; rather it figures as an original and trans-historical entity", which expresses the "ontological conception of biopolitics proposed by Hardt and Negri" (Lemke, 2011: 74). For Lemke, this conception of biopolitics leads to an unworkable, expansive and flattened conception of life, power and struggle, most clearly expressed in the formulaic construction of the multitude versus Empire. In Lemke's words, "the vital and autonomous multitude struggles against the unproductive, parasitical and destructive Empire" (2011: 74). Lemke identifies as the key limitation in Hardt and Negri's biopolitics their political expression of the Multitude against Empire. This limit finds its equivalent limit in the formulation of labour as a self-organised form of common cooperation pitted against capital as a parasitic, external force. These limits have clear consequences for the consideration of labour, exploitation, and accumulation.

5   The Character of Labour in the Becoming-Rent of Profit

Theories of rentier capitalism draw a line of analysis that identifies the proliferation of forms of rent across all aspects of social and economic life. In the context of rentier capitalism, economic power emerges out of "what you control" or "have", rather than "what you do" or "produce" (Christophers, 2020: xviii). In general terms, the dynamic of accumulation shifts from one of exploitation to one of extraction or rent seeking. The theorisation and analysis of the role of platforms in contemporary capitalism has also generated important debates about rent, exploitation, and accumulation. In the following comments I do not mean to dismiss the importance and insights of the analyses and theories of contemporary forms of rent. Rather, I draw attention to how the postworkerist perspective on contemporary rents is anchored in their theorisation of the character of labour. The novelty of the postworkerist iteration of rent is anchored in the autonomy of production. The postworkerist theory of rent is unique in its emphasis upon a specific conception of labour as autonomous cooperation. Nonetheless, the postworkerist attention to rent forms a part of important considerations of contemporary wealth accumulation.

For postworkerism, the common, value and rent are mirrored reflections of each other. The ontological turn of postworkerism can thus be located in the very premise of cognitive capitalism. For Vercellone, the

> capital-labour antagonism increasingly takes the form of antagonism between the institutions of the common as the foundations of knowledge-based economy and the logic of expropriation of cognitive capitalism that develops itself under the form of rent.
>
> 2010: 92

According to postworkerism, the common expresses a form of post-capital labour in the present. Vercellone expresses this perspective clearly when he argues that the structural forms and institutions of the knowledge economy "we could define, at least potentially, as a post-capitalist exterior" (2010: 95). The common is thus an ambiguous and yet highly significant concept for postworkerism. Similarly, Hardt argues that in cognitive capitalism, the capitalist remains external to productive activity, and rent becomes the mechanism to "cope with the conflicts between capital and the common", a mechanism through which "finance expropriates the common at a distance" (2010: 351).

Vercellone has argued that Marx's analysis of rent in *Capital volume III* brings Marx to the point of theorising the becoming-rent of profit. A significant aspect of Vercellone's claim is found in Marx's comments that not only does the capitalist as a personification of capital step to the side of production, but so too does the superintendent, the paid manager. For Vercellone this condition represents the simultaneous realisation of the autonomy of labour, as well as the tendency of profit to be articulated as a form of rent. The argument is vague but runs as follows: now that the capitalist brings nothing directly to the table (or the shop floor), including a manager, it follows that the productive function of the capitalist is exhausted. Labour is thus autonomous, and the exploitation of this autonomous labour, given that it is not 'direct', manifests as rent. Thus, the disappearance of the capitalist and the superintendent leads to the becoming-rent of profit.

As we noted above, Marx is speaking of the 'productive capitalist' in *Capital volume I* when he states that "the cooperation of wage-labourers is entirely brought about by the capital that employs them" (1990 [1867]: 449). Some limitations to the postworkerist argument about cooperation were outlined above, but it is useful to approach the issue from yet another vantage point. In *Capital volume III* Marx presents a more nuanced analysis of this question, once he has zoomed out from the 'hidden abode of production'. Marx (1992 [1894]: 512–514) certainly writes of the disappearance of the capitalist from the factory floor, but not in any such way that it transforms capital, or the labour-capital relation. The chapter on the 'Trinity Formula' (954–970) also provides a clear indication that value is a relation beyond the immediate appearance of revenues. And while it is true Marx argues that the productive capitalist becomes increasingly superfluous as does the superintendent in the oversight of forms of production, there is no indication that the superfluity of the capitalist and manager on the shopfloor presents a crisis for the form of value.

A further issue with the postworkerist narrative concerning the tale of the productive capitalist pertains to the image of a more noble form of exploitation that lends itself to productivist against parasitical narratives. That is, the postworkerist critique of rent along this path recapitulates a productivist foundation of politics and struggle. Caution is necessary here, insofar as a certain moralistic productivism haunts all theories of rent, whereby anyone who receives an income without working can be posed as a parasitic rentier on the productive good. In other words, not just the landlord but the welfare recipient. As Melinda Cooper has pointed out,

> any political movement that begins by distinguishing between the productive worker and the unproductive rentier runs the risk of scapegoating those who, through a history of dispossession, have always been relegated outside the sphere of formal waged labour.
>
> 2024: 393

Not all theories of rent succumb to this risk, and I don't mean to imply that postworkerism scapegoats those "outside the sphere of formal waged labour". Indeed, the postworkerist notion of labour has sought to incorporate all activity as an undifferentiated productive activity. Nonetheless, a reversion to productivism as a foundation of sound value is critiqued throughout this book. In any case, it is certainly true that the accumulation of wealth and its transmission today is often facilitated through forms that can be described as rent, and that this structure of accumulation articulates the organisation of some forms of labour exploitation (Christiaens, 2022). However, the postworkerist theorisation of labour via the lens of rent misarticulates persistent dynamics of exploitation and commodification of labour.

For the postworkerists, moreover, the process of financialisation is directly linked to post-Fordist capitalism and the forms of labour involved. As Marazzi argues, it is necessary to see

> financialisation as the other side of a process of the value *production* affirmed starting from the crisis of the Fordist model, from the capitalist incapacity to suck surplus value from immediate living-labour, the wage labour of the factory.
>
> 2011: 48

Thus, '*financialisation is not an unproductive/parasitic deviation ... but rather the form of capital accumulation symmetrical with the new processes of value production*' (Marazzi, 2011: 48 emphases in original). What characterises this shift, is a

> transformation of valorisation processes that witnesses the extraction of value no longer circumscribed to the place dedicated to the production of goods and services but extends beyond the factory gates [and] enters directly into the sphere of the *circulation* of capital.
>
> MARAZZI, 2011: 48

Accumulation, then,

> no longer consists, as in the Fordist period, of investment in constant and variable capital, but rather investment in *apparatuses* of producing and capturing value produced outside directly productive processes.
>
> MARAZZI, 2011: 48

Thus, for Marazzi, value extraction takes place from a position of externality, and the apparatus forms the channels of rent that constitute this form of expropriation.

The theorisation of autonomous production and rent is symptomatic of postworkerist productivism. Labour is conflated with life as the basis of a productivist ontology of the common, and it is ranged against a parasitic and passive form of capital in rent. While Marazzi ostensibly rejects the idea that finance is parasitic, he nonetheless offers a passive form of capital against a productivist image of life. Pietro Bianchi has argued that in the work of Marazzi, not only has capital breached the sphere of production into circulation, but what is now at stake is "that life itself, in its most universal generality, becomes a source of value-production". The result of which is a portrayal of "a contemporary finance capital that is entirely passive, no longer able to create surplus value" but must pursue the "becoming-life of labour" (2011: 49). Even Marazzi, in this instance, evokes a productivist notion of life to make sense of contemporary capitalism.

It is worth insisting that Marazzi's argument here is directly connected to the problem of value and substance, as well as to the problems of ontology in postworkerism. Marazzi (2014; 2014a) has battled with the problem of substance, labour and value in two recent texts. In one instance, Marazzi argues that the contemporary forms of production, finance and rent have led to the "*de-substantialisation* of the value of goods" (2014a: 6). In the second instance, he agrees with this assertion, but claims that we need to find a new substance of value and labour. The problem that Marazzi misses here is that the assertion of labour as autonomous production in the common has already rendered the postworkerist conception of labour as a new form of substance. As Diefenbach has pointed out, in the final consideration, the so-called autonomy of production wielded through labour's control of the general intellect actually "means that labour is substantialised, capital desubstantialised – it is no more than a parasitical mechanism that appropriates inventive productivity" (Diefenbach, 2010: 89). In this way, the thesis of the becoming-rent of profit encapsulates all the limitations of postworkerist theorisations of labour, value and class composition.

The theorisation of exploitation as a relationship of rent is problematic in several respects. It presents the relationship between labour and capital as being directly between labour and rent. The conditions that are outlined in the postworkerist argument come very close to Marx's presentation of labour and money rent in feudalism.[5] The reversion to a theory of rent places the

---

5   The postworkerist hypothesis of the common is reminiscent of Marx's analyses of feudalism. For example, Richard Miller (1984) draws attention to the political determinants that shaped

productivist foundations of postworkerism in sharp relief. The lament for the productive capitalist, and the resentment for the rentier "who earns without working" (Negri, 2009), is the mirror image of the valorisation of the productivity of all forms of activity. As Roggero has put it,

> Even when we talk about the 'capture of the common', we must not mean the transition to a parasitic capitalism: the company must organise the work of the capturers. Social cooperation is therefore not exclusively self-organised, just as it is not organised exclusively by the master. Capital, in fact, is a social relation: since cooperation is located within this relation, freedom and autonomy are always at stake and never given as a starting point.
>
> 2020, 163

Thus, the ontological, transhistorical and productivist conceptions of labour are necessarily implied in the reversion to rent as the principal dynamic of labour exploitation.[6] As a result, postworkerism also avoids and is incapable

---

the extraction of money rent from independent labour. Marx, in *Capital volume III* argues that 'it is evident that in all forms in which the direct labourer remains the "possessor" of the means of production and labour conditions ... the property relationship must simultaneously appear as a direct relation of lordship and servitude' (in Miller, 1984: 199). Miller draws attention to this quote commenting on Marx's analysis of feudalism and rent in relation to labour. He notes that,

"by 1600, corvée labour ... had been extinct for about two centuries. Even rent in kind had largely been replaced by money-rent ... what we see is an economy dominated by production under long term leases, in independent workshops, or in cottage industries catering to merchants. An impossible beast, feudalism without feudal lords." (199)

The point of interest here is that rent in this case represents an extraction of surplus from a condition of labour that is the 'possessor of the means of production,' and has capacity for self-subsistence. That is, the labour in question is ostensibly autonomous in the form of its organisation. Postworkerist arguments concerning the general intellect are reminiscent of Marx's analysis of feudal labour, although their tone is affirmative rather than critical. Ultimately postworkerist analysis of labour looks forward to a future in which the autonomous condition of the general intellect will generate a supposedly higher level of self-subsistence, through independently cooperative labour and biopolitical production.

6   Tim Christiaens (2022) offers a very interesting critique of digital labour and its relationship to postworkerist theories of labour, value and rent. On the one hand, Christiaens is able to both ground and critique the postworkerist perspective on rent and value in his analysis of digital platform labour. However, at the same time, he recapitulates the postworkerist problems of the theory of value when he argues "Most forms of immaterial labor are, in a traditionalist sense, unproductive. People working in advertisement, research and development, care, or transportation, are all unproductive in the labor theory of value, but these sectors form the motor of the post-Fordist economy ... If one thus applies a theory of exploitation that derives value from the production of material commodities, one is stuck with a theory blind to major

of posing the problem of the value-form as a terrain of critique. However, if value is a historically specific form of mediation and domination, the form of rule in a commodity society, then the moral dimension of the postworkerist argument is exposed. In other words, value, productive labour, productivism need hold no inherent dignity. They are rather historical concepts within a particular set of historically specific relations. Moreover, the postworkerist theory of autonomous production – and it is necessary to be clear that the hypothesis of autonomous production is not the same as the proposition of the autonomy of workers' struggle – sidesteps the difficult questions of how the relationship between the wage, remuneration, the contractual forms of such, and work, are defined. In sum, the critique *of* labour within capitalism has largely been replaced with a perspective that seeks to valorise a perceived post-capitalist form of labour within, and yet somehow beyond, the present relations of capitalism. From this perspective, the mode of encounter between labour and capital becomes one of rent. The positive or affirmationist inflection of contemporary postworkerist theorisations of labour replaces the critique of work, the commodity, the persistence of exchange, and the condition of labour as variable capital. This inflection effectively collapses the *critique of labour* into an *affirmationist political ontology*. In order to see how deep these limits run, it is useful to look further into the arrangements of post-Fordist labour and its relationship to value.

6   Fragmentation and the Persistence of Mediation

The processes and tenability of measure are significant for the post-workerists. The crisis of the law of value for them in fact signifies a crisis of a particular apparatus of measurement that was 'operable' in a specific historic context of capitalism. The displacement of this arrangement is understood to lead inexorably to the crisis of value. It is not clear, however, that this displacement should warrant the turn to ontology that postworkerism has undertaken. It is evident, and uncontroversial, that crisis is inherent to the dynamic of capital (Mattick, 2019). Crisis, and the double movement of capital, materialises as a struggle that continuously destabilises and restores norms of (re)production (Cooper, 2012). The crisis of measure is inherent to such a process, regardless of how its appearance and manifestation may shift. The apparent novelty of

____

changes in the global economy since the 1970s" (2022: 44). As we saw in Chapter 2, the character of a commodity's relationship to value is not dependent upon whether it is material or immaterial, but its integration to the circuit of capital.

cognitive capitalism, namely the immeasurability of value and the incommensurability between forms of biopolitical production and capital, which is so pivotal to the perspective of postworkerism, can be approached differently if we do not understand Fordism to be the historical fulfilment of the 'law of value', or measure as applied to concrete labour as the process by which labour is extracted.[7]

As Postone points out, the grounds for commensurability "are historically specific and social" (2012: 247). It is value that brings about this commensurability, which is to say a

> historically specific form of wealth that has nothing to do with their [commodities] properties, whether material or immaterial, but is the crystallised expression of a historically specific form of social mediation that ... is constituted by a historically specific form of labour.
>
> POSTONE, 2012: 247–248

However, the coordinates of the historically specific form of labour shift, and thus "the trajectory of value is such that it becomes anachronistic, and, yet, at the same time, is reconstituted as necessary to the system" (2012: 248). In developing this perspective, it is possible to approach the problematics raised by the theorists of the becoming-rent of profit, but with a more rigorous critique of labour. To demonstrate this, I offer below a counter-reading of the categories that are involved in the theorisation of the becoming-rent of profit.

Despite the postworkerist argument that there was once a period of clearly quantifiable units of labour and thus value, for Marx the question of measure was always tenuous and contingent. Marx's perspective on this is evident on at least two levels. The first I pointed out in Chapter 2, in Marx's (1868) argument to Kugelman that there is no way to quantify exchange-value except as it works

---

7 The work of Phoebe V. Moore is interesting on this count. Moore (2018) picks up the theories of affective labour, value and measure in the analysis of the agile workplace and the quantified self. Moore develops an insightful and thorough critique of how self-tracking technologies applied to modes of affective labour constitute a new form of measurement. However, despite the depth of analysis into new forms of measure and management, Moore's argument that these technological modes of measure open a new context by which "concrete labour is made abstract" (2018: 28) also mistakes value, abstract labour, as something produced in the process of measuring concrete labour within the labour process. However, as we saw in Chapter 2, abstract labour and value does not arise in the specific forms of measure of concrete labour but the level of social totality mediated by exchange. Nonetheless, despite this small disagreement on the character of value, Moore's work is extremely important in dynamics of contestation within the technical composition of class. I return to Moore's work in Chapters 5 and 6, in my critique of the affective sciences within the managerial and technological mediation of labour.

out as a blind average, after the fact. The second level is that of the wage, insofar as it articulates the conditions of work and reproduction. Given that the wage remains a mechanism in the internalisation of labour to capital, rendering labour as variable capital, it is of particular significance for the critique of the so-called condition of autonomous production, and thus the postworkerist theorisation of rent.

In the chapter on time-wages in *Capital volume I*, Marx states, after having already considered the effects of overwork on the worker, that there are conditions which expose the "sufferings which arise for the worker out of his being insufficiently employed" (1991: 686). Marx continues that:

> if the hour's wage is fixed in such a way that the capitalist does not bind himself to pay a day's or week's wage, but only to pay wages for the hours during which he chooses to employ the worker, he can employ him for a shorter period than that which was originally the basis of the calculation of the wages for the hour, or the unit of measurement of the price of labour.
>
> 1991: 686

In a situation such that "the working day ceases to contain a definite number of hours", then "the connection between paid and unpaid labour is destroyed" (1991: 686). There is no agreement that capital will pay for the reproduction of the worker. Rather, "the capitalist can now wring from the worker a certain quantity of surplus labour without allowing him the labour time necessary for his own subsistence". The capitalist can thus "annihilate all regularity of employment, and according to his own convenience, caprice, and the interest of the moment, make the most frightful overwork alternate with relative or absolute cessation of work" (1991: 686). Indeed, while legal limitations on the length of the working day remain in place, the ever-present need to be on-call or prepared for work that is characteristic of neocontractualism effectively transforms non-working time into a form of working time (Mitropoulos, 2012, Mitropoulos, 2005). As Mitropoulos put it,

> the perpetually irregular work of post-Fordism might, though not necessarily, decrease the actual amount of time spent doing paid work, it nevertheless enjoins the post-Fordist worker to be continually available for such work, to regard life outside waged work as a time of preparation for and readiness to work.
>
> 2005: np

However, more specifically in terms of the limitations of the postworkerist argument concerning the measurability of value, it is clear that at least as far as Marx was concerned, the operability of value was never contingent upon a formalised external standard of measure, and this remains the case for labour-power through wages as well as any other commodity.

Indeed, Jamie Peck and Nick Theodore (2012) present a picture of underemployment and contingency which recalls the dynamic of the wage outlined above by Marx. While the struggle against Fordism involved the refusal of factory labour and innovative struggles of non-standard labour (Cooper, 2015; Mitropoulos, 2005; 2006 and 2011), the "unruly 'transition' from New Deal to postwelfare modes of regulation ... is also a story of the contradictory expansion of a patchwork of localised regimes of labour regulation" (Peck and Theodore, 2012: 747). Peck and Theodore continue that "this shifting landscape of labour (re)regulation runs the gamut from pockets of hyperexploitation to enclaves of resurgent community-labour politics" (Peck and Theodore, 2012: 747). The "structural expansion" of contingent work sees a process in which "the generation of short-term, insecure, high-turnover jobs ... meshes with the desperate need for work among underemployed workers" (2012: 747–748). The question of the wage remains pivotal in this situation which sees the increase in "street-corner labour markets and other informal hiring sites, the growth of day labour temp agencies and the proliferation of various forms of labour subcontracting" (Peck and Theodore, 2012: 748). As a result, there is a tendency that "extends managerial control over job tasks and the pace of work ... and pushes wages and workers back out into competition" (2012: 748–749). That is, contingency does not decentre the wage as such, but rather rearticulates it.

Marx's comments above are made in the context of a discussion of time wages. However, his consideration of piece-wages also contains striking resonances with the contemporary moment of neocontractualism. The example of piece rates is of interest because labour operating at piece rates does often satisfy the conditions of 'autonomous production'. Moreover historically, piecework also challenges the narrative according to which productive cooperation could not take place without the 'productive capitalist'. Marx's analysis of the domestic industries in the 1860s, the vast majority of which were not covered by the factory acts, unsettles the image of the factory as the sole productive site. The domestic workers Marx is referring to work either from home, carrying out finishing or mending, or from what were called 'mistresses houses', or small workshops. These workers constituted the vast majority of lace-making and straw plaiting (140000 of 150000 workers), and most of them worked at piece rates. As George Caffentzis (2011b) has argued, the postworkerist analysis of rent conflates Marx's categories of 'wages of supervision' or 'superintendence' and 'profit of enterprise'. While the relationship between these categories is analysed in *Capital volume III*, Marx's comments on piece-wages in *Capital volume I* provide a useful lens for a consideration of post-Fordist arrangements of work, and in turn the postworkerist analysis of rent.

Marx's analysis of piecework introduces a degree of complexity into the narrative of cognitive capitalism outlined by Vercellone. Piece-work already offers an example of a mode of production where the superintendence of labour has become redundant. Marx argues that "since the quality and intensity of the work are here", in a context of piece work, "controlled by the very form of the wage, superintendence of labour becomes to a great extent superfluous" (Marx, 1991: 695). As I pointed out above, for Marx this is a condition that is exemplified in the "so-called domestic industry" of the 1860s. Thus, it is not a condition he was on the brink of theorising but unable to due to a lack of conditions. It is the condition of that day. Caffentzis' (2011b: 45–47) critique of cognitive capitalism also draws attention to Marx's comments on piece-wages and the "bitter autonomy" they provide. Caffentzis (2011b: 46–47) draws an explicit connection between the production of subjectivity produced by the conditions of piece-wage workers in the 1860s and that of the cognitariat today. Marx argued that piece work develops "the wider scope" of "individuality, and with it the worker's sense of liberty, independence and self-control" so too does it create the "competition of workers with each other" (1990 [1867]: 697). Caffentzis argues there is a parallel in the "divisive individualism" that characterises the employment experiences of, for example, the piece-rate workers Marx discusses and the conditions of the cognitariat.

The parallel Caffentzis draws is also identified by Sergio Bologna's (2010 [2007]) analysis of workers' responses to post-Fordist conditions of work. Bologna analyses what he calls "free expressions of rage" which all expose "work [as] the central theme, the impending problem that shapes or deforms rhythms of life, human relations, places that we inhabit, family relations and so on" (2010 [2007]: 170). Based on online testimonies, Bologna argues that while in the Taylorist era:

> there was a timekeeper following you, today you are followed by one of the many hierarchical figures of the company, an expert in the thousand shortcuts to manage flexibility, substituting an unlimited term contract worker with a short-term contract worker, and then this with a temporary worker, further with an external worker, then with an independent self-managed worker.
>
> 2010 [2007]: 172

While Vercellone (2010) contends that "rent has always been the other side of the common", the arguments of Caffentzis and Bologna above, show that a dispersal in the organisation of labour is the other side to so-called autonomous production. Indeed, Bologna argues that:

> it even seems that the main feature of the current management system of work is to create the conditions of difference in such a way that each [worker] perceives, in the first place, the *non-affinity* with the person he or she works with.
>
> 2010 [2007]: 173

This is not to say that cooperation as a mode of solidarity among fragmented workers does not exist, only that it is not a given in the labour process itself. Bologna's considerations of the challenges for cooperation and autonomy among hybrid workers outlines the difficulties faced in developing this type of cooperation.

The issues of class fragmentation outlined above have implications for the consideration of cooperation. The postworkerist definition and consideration of autonomous cooperation is unclear and tends to obscure or ignore the ways in which the imperatives of capital are still engaged in the mobilisation and mediation of labour and cooperation. For example, postworkerism has identified Toyotist models of production as representing a break with Fordist regimes (Marazzi, 2011 [1994]: 17–27; Negri, 2013 [1995]: 87–94; Hardt and Negri, 2000: 289–290). While postworkerism is critical of the character of precarious employment, and wider factors associated with lean production, they have also emphasised the cooperative elements of Toyotist and post-Fordist arrangements of production. It is worth noting, however, that the cooperative character of, for example, Toyotist forms of decision making are widely overstated (Angry Workers, 2020: 301. See also Smith, 2000 for a critique of lean production and Toyotism). Matt Vidal, in a thorough analysis of post-Fordist management practices, argues that Toyota's early

> consensus building process (*nemawashi*) largely excludes shopfloor workers: supervisors and middle managers informally discuss their proposals with higher-level managers to obtain feedback and consent before formal meetings take place. While workers can propose ideas to supervisors via quality circles, it is only supervisors or higher managers who can formally submit proposals for refinement and approval.
>
> 2022: 46

While Toyota's model relates to manufacturing processes, indeed Vidal's overall study does too, similar issues regarding decisions, cooperation, and power within the workplace can be extended to the service sector.

Lean or just-in-time service provision often involves the technological mediation of cooperation in a range of affective and service modes of production (Canel et al., 2000). As Vidal suggests, "today lean is increasingly being adopted in healthcare, banking, insurance, civil service, education, software, airline services, legal services, telecom, mass merchandising, and restaurants" (Vidal, 2022: 5). Bologna draws attention to the implications of lean production in service arrangements and their impact on forms of cooperation. For Bologna, "it appears that the post-Fordist system wants to leave behind the idea of cooperation, destroying it systematically" (2010 [2007]: 175). A further example of the technological mediation of shopfloor cooperation can be found in data management and scheduling techniques (Kesavan et al., 2022; Lambert et al., 2019). Staff scheduling software such as Kronos or Muse map sales, delivery and staffing details to create optimal, lowest-cost staffing rates for managers. While cooperation as an autonomous capacity of labour would imply a degree of control over the conditions of cooperation, staff scheduling software creates algorithms to which flexible labour is subject.

Madison Van Oort (2023) provides important insight into how cooperation is mediated in the retail sector. Van Oort notes that "along with just-in-time inventory, fast-fashion retailers have harnessed digital technologies to achieve just-in-time labour" (2023: 36). In Van Oort's telling, workplace management algorithms articulate the organisation of labour on the shopfloor. An exposé on the use of Kronos by Starbucks shows that even though the actual labour process of coffee-making involves minimal technological processes and a high degree of interpersonal labour, the question of cooperation remains inherently contested (Kantor and Hodgson, 2014). Indeed, the cooperation between workers is closely mediated by staffing technologies. The various successes of Starbucks workers in industrial struggles in the early 2010s is indicative of the fact that workers do cooperate in their own interests, though this is an example of cooperation as a mode of conflict with the mediated forms of cooperation in the labour process (Roggero, 2023). Cooperation remains contested as an element in the technical composition of class.

One of the implications of the postworkerist reconsideration of cooperation is the removal of conflict from the labour-capital relation. Gigi Roggero (2023) has criticised the political limitations in postworkerism by drawing attention to the problems of the general intellect and cooperation. While the affective, intellectual and linguistic characteristics of labour are now integrated with commodity production and circulation, the relationship between labour and capital cannot plausibly be reframed as an ontologically productive common opposed to an external apparatus of capital as rent. To do so removes the dynamic of exploitation and conflict within the labour-capital relation. For Roggero, postworkerism rejects the possibility of the antagonistic cooperation of workers in solidarity and struggle with one-another against capital, in favour of a "glorification of cooperation within the labour process" (2023: 135). Further, for Roggero the formulation of labour outlined in postworkerism posits "capital ... [as] a parasitic shell over a cooperation that was already free and autonomous ... as if technical composition was ... immediately translatable into political composition" (2023: 135). Against the image of autonomous cooperation, labour in fact remains enmeshed within the regulatory apparatus of capital. In other words, cooperation, even in its affective articulation, is managerially and technologically mediated. In the following two chapters I critique the mobilisation of the affective sciences within the managerial and technological mediation of labour, demonstrating that the organisation of cooperation and exploitation remains central to the critique of work, and internal to the labour-capital relation of immaterial production.

7   Conclusion

The argument throughout this chapter identified the core limits of postworkerism in the relationship posited between immaterial labour, autonomous production, and value, arising from a productivist ontology of labour-value-affect. The postworkerist theorisations and analyses of immaterial production tend to occlude tension, difference, and contradiction within the organisation of work, and as such flatten the analysis of contemporary class composition in both its technical and political iterations. The occlusion emerges in the ontological reading of affect and labour that postworkerism develops. The limitations of the postworkerist position can be summed up in the shift from a critique of labour via the categories of class composition and value, into a political ontology that valorises existing labour processes. The ontology of labour-value-affect, precisely because it is constructed as immediately social, autonomous and cooperative, amounts to a weak position from which to generate a critique of labour in the present. The political impasse of postworkerism finds its clearest expression in the assertion of the productivist ontology. In doing so it neglects the contested character of affective production, the processes by which affective production is rendered internal to the labour-capital relation, and thus postworkerism cannot articulate the contested character of class composition. In order to address these issues, we need to take up a consideration of the technical composition of affective production.

The following chapters reinvigorate the analysis of class composition through a critical analysis of contemporary processes of management and technologies. Crucially, what is exposed are the ways in which the affective sciences, in contrast to the Spinozist inflections of affect, have been directly integrated into the techniques of management and technological mediation of labour. Affect is thus a heavily contested character that is mobilised through the labour-capital relation. Chapters 5 and 6 analyse how the affective sciences have been integrated into the managerial and technological imperatives for the valorisation, measure, and modulation of labour, and the implications this holds for theorising class composition today. It is only through the critical consideration of affect as a component of the technical composition of class and capital that it is possible to plot the coordinates for the refusal and negation of this condition. The following chapter begins to undertake such a task, in identifying and critiquing the ways in which affective management functions in the contemporary workplace.

PART 2

Contested Terrains of Affect

The Affective Sciences and Managerial Practice

1   Introduction

Tracing the historical imbrications of the affective sciences and workplace managerialism, this chapter argues that affective modes of management are best understood as fundamental components of the technical composition of class. Contra postworkerism, the present chapter argues that the entanglement of labour and affect in late capitalism does not automatically escape the problem of management and measure. Indeed, the integration of the affective sciences into managerial technique marks a direct incorporation of bodily affect as a component of both workplace organisation and capital. That is, 'affect' is internalised within the labour-capital relation in terms of both the labour and valorisation processes, rather than signifying an automatic autonomy of labour from capital. My analysis of the relationship between affect and labour as a problem of management allows for a critical destabilisation of the ontological foundations of postworkerism and opens new areas for the analysis and critique of labour. While employee productivity remains a key objective of managerial practice, the integration of the affective sciences in a context of immaterial production brings into play the management and cultivation of affective states, events, and episodes within the individual and organisation. Therefore, affective management is concerned with the variability of affective states, rather than job attitudes, when considering employee productivity. The chapter establishes how the deployment of the affective sciences within management impacts labour and functions as a component in the technical composition of class.

Work has always had an affective and emotional dimension to it, insofar as it is experienced emotionally and affectively by workers. This is true of work that directly involves aspects of emotional and affective labour, as well as types of work that do not require such forms of engagement as part of the labour process. It is also true in turn, that management has always been attuned to these aspects of working life and their impacts on employee performance (for early examples of this see Hersey, 1932; Fisher and Hanna, 1931). As such, management has always sought in various ways to address these aspects of employee life as an object of managerial intervention. Nonetheless, the contemporary turn to the affective sciences among management specialists introduces new problems in understanding the relationship between affect, work and management. In particular, the attention to affect among managers and management specialists has shifted from a concern with a worker's *attitude toward* their job, and to the management *of employee affect within* the job, as an element of the work itself and as a measure of performance. This shift is particularly pronounced in immaterial and affective modes of production. Situating the emergence of contemporary forms of affective management alongside the persistence of established modes of management helps to understand the role of the affective sciences in the composition of capital and class.

Critical Management Studies (CMS) have contributed significantly to the theorisation of management practice and managerial objectives in changing workplaces. The first section of the chapter analyses CMS and its engagements with affect theory in management, work, and organisational contexts. The dynamic interaction between CMS and labour process theory (LPT) is also important for the argument developed in this chapter. Both CMS and LPT have provided invaluable illuminations of work and management in late capitalism, however it remains the case that within the literature of CMS and LPT there is little direct engagement with affect as a technique, medium, and object of management. Therefore, it is important to open with an engagement with the insights of CMS for conceptualising management, labour, and capital in the contemporary analysis of service work, before identifying the under-theorisation within CMS of affect as a component of managerial technique.

The second section of the chapter critically considers what scholars across a variety of disciplines have taken to calling affective capitalism (Lee, 2023; Reber, 2012; Sampson, 2014). Affective capitalism is a term that denotes the merging and mobilisation of theories of affect within the reproduction, circulation, and valorisation of value. As indicated in Chapter 1, I do not consider immaterial/affective labour to hold a hegemonic position in contemporary class relations, to mark the opening of a new periodisation in capitalism, or to have shifted the foundational elements of the labour-capital relation. Similarly, I do not think that we have entered a new historical phase of capitalism that could best be described as specifically affective (Best, 2011). Nonetheless, the questions being addressed by theorists under the rubric of affective capitalism are useful for the critique of immaterial/affective modes of labour, and grasp something important about the role of affect in relation to labour and capital today. My engagement with the notion of affective capitalism lies in a critical analysis of workplace managerialism and class composition.

To clarify what is at stake in the internalisation of affect within the labour-capital relation via the affective sciences, I outline two prominent fields in affect theory: on the one hand, a Spinozist/Deleuzian field of affect, and on the other a field of affect theory embedded in psychology, psychoanalysis, and biological considerations of the affective architecture of the body (Gregg and Siegworth, 2010a). Both fields of theory influence the understanding of contemporary workplace dynamics. However, the way in which the second, psychologically and physiologically based field informs affective management techniques is of particular interest. I argue that this is a fundamental dimension to what is being named in the concept of affective capitalism. Framed in this way, the notion of an affective capitalism helps to illuminate some of the shifting coordinates of contemporary class composition.

Moving into the critique of management science proper, the third section of this chapter analyses the specific integration of affect theory with managerial technique. This section engages with Affective Events Theory and related approaches to workplace motivation as cases that demonstrate the integration of affect with managerial theory and technique. Motivation studies and considerations of emotions in the workplace have long been present in the history of organisation studies and industrial/organisational psychology. However, the most recent return to theories of affect within these fields marks a novel recentering of the affective sciences within management and organisation studies. Several striking convergences can be observed between affect theories, the affective turn in the neurosciences, and the changing techniques of managerial practice.

The affective sciences, particularly as developed in the fields of psychology and psychoanalytic theories, have come to inform affective modes of management. In turns recapitulating, modifying, and completely breaking with classical Taylorist time and motion studies, affective management techniques operate as a complex through which the emotional and affective capacities of labour are entwined with the imperatives of capitalist reproduction and valorisation. Importantly, while the measure of productivity and time management remain crucial (Kelly, 2024; Gregg, 2018), in many circumstances these objectives are increasingly bound to notions of variability in affective intensity, expressed for example in motivation and effort, and articulated through the different affective states of employees. Affect, as a notion of intensity that is quantifiable as per the affective sciences, thus lends itself readily to problems and objectives of productivism measured in, for example, motivation. The integration of the affective sciences within managerial technique thus reflects, in part at least, a grappling with the challenges to the measurement of productivity posed by labour processes with immaterial outputs.

After considering how the affective sciences have been directly incorporated into the techniques of management to elicit affective intensities, the chapter concludes by considering how life experience is also framed as an affect to be drawn on in production. From a certain managerial vantage point, employee biography, such as life events of hardship, transform into a reservoir of affective experiences translatable to work through the concept of emotional mining. The transformation of the cumulative affective experiences of one's own life into productive capacity expresses the historically determined gendering and racialisation of affective labour. In this section it becomes clear that the post-workerist historiography of affective labour is poorly equipped to grapple with how the gendered and racialised structures of affective production become the very foundation of management, motivation, and productivism. Finally, I close the chapter by arguing that the affective dimensions to management practice are best understood as a component of the technical composition of class. I return briefly to the categories of class composition analysis as theorised by the *operaisti*, to demonstrate that the categories of class composition need to be revised considering the critique of the affective sciences.

2   Critical Management Studies and the Problem of Affect

The critique of work inevitably confronts the problem of management. Management as an ensemble of techniques for the coordination, articulation, disciplining and measuring of labour, marks a dynamic of conflict within the labour-capital relation. Analyses of both the labour and valorisation processes help to trace the combined historical development of management theory and practice in the context of struggles within, and transformations of, the organisation of work. Since the beginning of the 1990s, Critical Management Studies (CMS) has come to name a heterogenous collection of scholarship that cracks open and critiques management from a range of divergent perspectives that nonetheless retain a certain commonality. Departing from a common analysis of management as a "pervasive institution entrenched within capitalist economic institutions", CMS is engaged with "the study *of*, and sometimes *against*, management, rather than with the development of techniques or legitimations *for* management" (Alvesson et al., 2009: 1). As a field of analysis and debate, CMS invites an ongoing engagement with shifting forms and patterns of management. It is unsurprising then, that CMS has been attuned to the problems of organisation, productivity, and management in post-Fordist organisational contexts. Canvassing the contributions of CMS helps to complicate postworkerist conceptions of immaterial and affective labour.

The initial theorisations of immaterial labour developed by postworkerists were informed by analyses of shifting patterns in work organisation. That is, the theory of immaterial production emerges from considerations of change in the forms of concrete labour which are put to work in the labour and valorisation processes of contemporary capitalism. During the 1990s, Maurizio

Lazzarato and Antonio Negri (1991) analysed emergent forms of post-Fordist management as techniques of power. Noting the differences between Taylorism and new managerial techniques, such as Total Quality Management, postworkerists drew attention to forms of 'participative management' and teamwork characteristic of the 'new economy'. These participative managerial techniques are said to draw from and function through an organisation of labour that is in turn said to be creative and cooperative (Dyer-Witheford, 1999: 223–230). Nick Dyer-Witheford argues that "if new production systems are the objective side of capitalised general intellect, then the work team represents its subjective side, in cellular form" (1999: 223). Virno (2004) has also drawn attention to these characteristics of labour with a particular attention to linguistics, represented in the compulsion to speak and communicate within the labour processes of post-Fordism. More recently, Hardt and Negri (2017) returned to a consideration of affective labour, management, and class composition. But while a consideration of managerialism and the labour-capital relation have continued to inform postworkerism, its analysis and understanding of the contested nature of affect, and indeed of management, as a feature of labour-capital contestation in post-Fordism remains undeveloped.

CMS theorists have taken up the implications of postworkerism in turns both sceptical and sympathetic. For some, the postworkerist perspectives on immaterial production throw fundamental aspects of management orthodoxy into crisis, undermining its key foundations of workplace organisation, human resource management, and other areas of management and organisation (Hanlon, 2007). Gerard Hanlon (2007) argues that the conditions of immaterial production, which is to say its inherently cooperative and self-managed character, render management and HRM redundant. Hanlon argues that "work is fundamentally changing" based on the conditions of "immaterial labour" (2007: 273). Continuing, Hanlon states that "central to this change is the notion of the interface – workers increasingly interface between work teams, customers, hierarchies, functions, technology, and so on" (Hanlon, 2007: 273). The interface, for Hanlon, is the articulation of the autonomy of labour. Further, for Hanlon "immaterial labour is thus changing work because firstly, innovation stands outside of capital and capitalist organisations respond to this and try to control or manipulate" (2007: 274). In this instance, Hanlon is credulous in the face of the claims made by postworkerists regarding the inherent productivity, collectivity, and autonomy of immaterial labour.[1] As a result, Hanlon does not consider how affect itself emerges as a terrain of management.

---

1   In Hanlon's critique of the history of management theory he presents important insights
    into the various adaptations of management to the changing patterns of labour. This history,

Similarly, Peter Fleming and Matteo Mandarini (2009) explore the implications of immaterial production for CMS. For these authors, immaterial production read through the thesis of the social factory re-centres the need to analyse work, but also challenges the conventional metrics of labour and productivity. In alignment with the general postworkerist thesis, here the cooperative and autonomous character of immaterial labour underpin the subversive potential of these types of work. Usefully, Fleming and Madarini (2009: 340–341) point to three conditions of emancipation that emerge from the challenge of immaterial production to conventional metrics of productivity: freedom in work, freedom through work, and freedom from work. However, even though Fleming and Mandarini situate their discussion of immaterial production within the framework of the social factory and connect their analysis to a program of emancipation, they do not comment on how affect itself is mobilised as a resource for managerialism in conditions of immaterial production, and thus do not consider what implications such an incorporation might hold for their three-front program of emancipation. Elsewhere, Fleming (2014; 2015) has addressed the frameworks of motivation and passion as the managerial regime of late capitalism, noting this regime is less a realised state of affairs than an authoritarian command made of labour. While Fleming's argument concerning the ideological function of motivation in the workplace is important, and I return to the refusal of this command in Chapter 7, here I want to emphasise an element missing in Fleming's account. Namely, that from the managerial perspective, motivation and passion are not reducible to the job attitude of an employee or how they feel about their job. As we will see below, what is novel about the integration of the affective sciences is the ways in which variable affective states becomes the medium through which management operates.

Also in dialogue with the postworkerist perspective, a more nuanced appraisal of the role of affect in contemporary management relations is found in another thread of CMS associated with Rick Iedema and colleagues. Iedema et al. (2005 and 2006) have taken up the question of the management of affect and labour in terms that directly reference postworkerist theories of immaterial production and affective labour. In two separate articles, these authors consider the implications of immaterial labour to workplace management and change. They raise two relevant points for the discussion here: firstly the 'affectualisation' of work (2005), and secondly teleo-affective volatility within contemporary workplaces (2006). Affectualisation refers to the capturing of

---

told in large part through the critique of Mayo, traces the ends to which management as a discipline has gone in recuperating labour to the valorisation process. See Hanlon (2016).

"body feelings, emotions as well as socio-personal judgementality" in the rear-rangements of post-Fordist labour, suggesting that organisational change must be seen as more than just a knowledge shift (2005: 333). Teleo-affective vola-tility is similar, in that it refers to "that dimension of social-organisational life where people sense and dynamically negotiate their own and others' goals, actions, expectations, needs and feelings" (Iedema et al., 2006: 1112). The atten-tion to volatility acknowledges that these factors "remain volatile in the face of management practice" (Iedema et al., 2006: 1112). In each of these cases, there is a positioning of the negotiation of work and workplace management by workers. Interestingly, and as I will explore below, this particular perspective is compatible with the framework of Affective Events Theory, and thus points to the ambivalence of affect in the contemporary workplace.

Working across the fields of CMS and LPT while charting new directions in research, Phoebe Moore (2018) has illuminated historical intersections of affect studies, affective and immaterial production, and managerial tech-niques. Moore also draws attention to and complicates the narratives of postworkerism. The foundations of LPT are found in the work of Marx in his exploration and critique of the labour process, and later developed through the work of Harry Braverman, (1974; see also Knight and Willmott, 1990). LPT, while travelling various lines of inquiry, commonly politicises work and its inherent power relations expressed through the technical make-up of the labour process. Moore (2018: 37–65) provides a useful overview of the history of LPT in relationship to work design. Work design encapsulates, in short, the nature of tasks and their organisation within a workplace and the labour pro-cess (Moore, 2018: 41). Moore constructs a historical schema to outline the waves of work design, corresponding to articulations of the labour process.[2]

Moore coins the era of Agile Systems Management to characterise the period of 2001–present, bringing up to date the theorisation of LPT and work design in her critique of the 'agile workplace' (2018: 44). Moore's notion of the agile workplace corresponds to, and engages with, many of the claims made within the theorisation of immaterial and affective production. Agile work names the compulsion to be responsive, always on, flexible, and engaged in a permanent condition of self-quantification. Subjecting the formerly invisi-ble labours to persistent quantification is a condition of management, often self-administered, in the age of agility. However, even here in Moore's work,

---

2 The first wave is Industrial Betterment (1870–1900); second wave is Scientific Management (1900–1923); third wave is Human Relations (1925–1955); fourth wave is Systems Rationalism (1955–1980); fifth wave is Organisational Culture and Quality (1980–ongoing); sixth wave, coined by Moore is Agility Management System (2001–present). See Moore (2017: 41).

while affective labour is critically considered within the architecture of myriad measures, affect as the method of management is largely absent. The concept of mood is the closest we get to the critique of affect as the measure itself of motivation and productivity. The affective sciences are left unconsidered within Moore's historical schema (2018). It is worth noting that Moore, while complicating and extending the postworkerist consideration of affective labour, measure, and value, essentially recapitulates that the relationship between concrete and abstract labour is articulated through measure. As Moore understands this relationship, it is through measure that "concrete labour is made abstract" (2018: 28). Moore's theorisation of the relationship between value, labour, and measure does not consider the implications of the critique of the value-form and misarticulates the relationship between concrete and abstract labour. In any case, as I argue below, coming to terms with contemporary class composition requires a critical consideration of how the affective sciences are integrated into managerial technique, and Moore's work is important for this, though my argument draws a different but nonetheless related emphasis.

Beyond the direct engagements with postworkerist conceptions of labour evidenced by the above theorists, the linguistic and affective turns within CMS offer some insight into the argument pursued in this chapter, while also highlighting the limitations of considerations of affect within CMS. Marianna Fotaki et al. note that "critical theorists of organisation have only started to integrate and explore recent developments in affect theory from diverse fields including cultural studies, feminism, queer theory and psychoanalysis" while drawing attention to the fact that "affect permeates organisations profoundly, influencing people's motivation, their political behaviour, decision-making and relationships with leaders and followers" (2017: 4). Indeed, as I show below it is precisely these variables of intensity that affective management practices seek to harness. However, in order to demonstrate how affective intensity is understood from the perspective of management, it is necessary to clearly delineate how the affective sciences become imbricated with managerial technique. In other words, it is necessary to read affect within organisations and workplaces from a class composition perspective.

Currently, within the parameters of management and organisation studies, affect is approached from a range of perspectives, but rarely from a class perspective. As a result, while the rich engagements with affect in organisations via CMS, which spans psychoanalytic iterations of affect theory, I/O psychology, and psychosocial considerations of affect, through to Spinozist and Deleuzian conceptions (Kenny and Fotaki, 2014: 18; Hunter and Kivinen, 2022: 3–4; Slaby et al., 2019), provide fertile ground for academic debate, much less is offered in terms of affect as a point of class contestation in the workplace and beyond. In other words, CMS has provided a framework to interrogate the changing dynamics and emphases of management and managerial practice. However, to date CMS has had little to say explicitly on the specific ways in which affect has become a component of contemporary workplace dynamics internal to the labour-capital relation, through both the labour and valorisation processes, or in terms of the composition of class. However, if we turn our attentions to theorists and scholars in the fields of industrial and organisational psychology, the significance of affect in management and organisation studies becomes clear. More importantly, the dynamic of affect as a field of contestation and class composition is illuminated. The following section of the chapter presents a cartography of affect theory to demonstrate how affect can be read as a point of class contestation in the workplace.

3   Affective Capitalism and the Theorisation of Labour and Capital

Affect theory and the affective sciences, in their origins and development, have no fundamental or immediate relationship to work and management. However, as Luc Boltanski and Eve Chiapello suggest:

> forms of capitalist production accede to representation in each epoch, by mobilising concepts and tools that were initially developed largely autonomously in the theoretical sphere or in the domain of basic scientific research. This is the case with neurology and computer science today.
>
> 2005 [1999]: 104

It is my contention that this is also the case for affect theory and the affective sciences. The process is made evident in the movement of the affective sciences from the academy, the laboratory, and the clinic to the workplace, in all its contemporary diffusion (Dror, 2001). In the past decade, the theory of 'affective capitalism' has gained increasing currency in academic circles as a means to grapple with this process.

Theorists of affective capitalism analyse the mobilisation of affect as a political and economic relation through the various imbrications of affect, labour, value, production, consumption, and circulation (Lee, 2023; Andrews and Duff, 2020). For example, the "Affective Capitalism Symposium" sought to explore how affective capitalism "merges with established therapeutic discourses and blurs the limits of intimacy at work", while "transform[ing] us into assets, goods and services by appealing to our desires, needs and social relationships, or by making us act on a mere gut-feeling" (2014: np). Dierdra Reber argues that affective capitalism marks "the radical apogee of an epistemic shift from reason to affect", which has only become visible in late capitalism (2012: 63). For Reber, affective capitalism is a "headless capitalism" reflecting the shifts in arrangements of production, circulation, and consumption, illuminating and complicating the role of desire, passions, the body and subjectivity as forces of both reproduction and antagonism. Meanwhile, Hangwoo Lee, has argued that "affective capitalism transforms the population's everyday bodily experiences into quantitative metrics that can be observed, measured, and processed" (2023: 4). Across these efforts to define affective capitalism, we find important steps in grappling with the novelties of late capitalism, but there is room to push the concept further.

While not employing the term affective capitalism, Beverly Best draws attention to the connection between the "social dynamic of affect" and conditions outlined in Deleuze's society of control (2011: 60–61). In itself, Best's observation is uncontroversial, given that Hardt and Negri (2000) themselves make this point explicitly. However, Best makes the important argument that the predominance of affect is a continuation of a dialectical mode of mediation. Drawing on Frederic Jameson's dialectic, Best argues that the affective politics of the present are in fact the latest regime of historical mediation. The significance of this argument is found in its reintroduction of antagonism into the consideration of affective politics, which poses a challenge to the ontological foundations of postworkerism explored in Part 1 of this book (Best, 2011: 62). The dynamic of mediation outlined by Best is important for understanding the tension between the categories of affect and emotion, which I return to in the following chapter. The emerging analysis of affective capitalism clearly overlaps with those of affective, immaterial, emotional, and intimate labour. The contribution I make to the critique of the affective turn, is to develop an under-theorised aspect of the internalisation of affect within capital, manifest in the connection between affect theory, managerial science in post-Fordism, and the analysis of the technical composition of class.

Affective capitalism, as a field of theoretical inquiry and a concept, is predicated on the broader turn to affect of recent decades. The affective turn is marked by a growing attention to the analysis of affect and emotion across various academic disciplines since the 1990s. At its broadest, the affective turn draws from an array of conceptual lineages, which run through the work of Benedict De Spinoza (1996), Gilles Deleuze (1988; 2005), Brian Massumi (2002), and Antonio Negri (2013); via William James (Redding, 1999), Melanie Klein (Sedgwick, 2007), Silvan Tomkins (1962), Antonio Damasio (1994; 1999; 2003) and Adam Frank and Eve Sedgwick (1995), amongst others. In various ways, all of these authors have influenced or given some kind of expression to the affective turn. Some, such as Marguerite La Caze and Henry Martyn Loyd argue that reference to an 'affective turn' was restricted primarily to cultural studies and critical theory (2011: 2). Others, such as Athena Athanasiou et al. (2008) point towards a broader epistemic shift, principally within social sciences, but also within psychology, and neuroscience (see also Greg and Seigworth, 2010; Clough and Halley, 2007). Clare Hemmings (2005) offers a critique of the ontological implications associated with the general turn to affect. Constantina Papoulias and Felicity Callard (2010) provide a thorough analysis of the various ways in which affect theory intersects with biology and theorises the body. Papoulias and Callard map the divergent ways in which affect theorists present an anti-foundational theory of the body and biology, which becomes significant when considering the affective sciences as incorporated into management, explored below. I will not retrace in detail the nuances of the affective turn here. I simply outline two prominent vectors of affect theory in recent decades, particularly as they pertain to the problem of work: a broad affective sciences theoretical vector and a Spinozist-Deleuzian vector (Gregg and Siegworth: 2010). To develop a compositionist analysis of the affective turn it is necessary to outline its prominent theoretical foundations and demarcate the key vectors of analysis, in order to demonstrate how the affective sciences have come to inform managerial theory and practice in the context of post-Fordism.

As Melissa Gregg and Gregory Siegworth (2010a) note, 1995 marked an important year for affect theory. That year saw the publication of Massumi's *Autonomy of Affect* and Sedgwick and Frank's *Shame in the Cybernetic Fold*, both of which are key reference points within the affective turn. For the purposes of my argument here, these two essays are also important insofar as each belong to distinctive lineages in the development of affect studies. Massumi's (1995; 2002) work resides within the Spinozist and Deleuzian lineage of theories of affect. Sedgwick and Frank (1995) fit within the lineage of psychology, drawing in particular from the work of Silvan S. Tomkins and Melanie Klein (Sedgwick, 2007). Gregg and Seigworth (2010) identify seven specific lineages of affect theory, grouped within these two primary strains of research and scholarship. The demarcation I point to corresponds to their analysis of "two dominant vectors of affect studies in the humanities": the psychobiological, deriving largely from the work of Silvan S. Tomkins, and the Spinozist and Deleuzian lineage focusing on bodily capacities. Donovan Schaefer marks a similar genealogy of affect, traced through the histories of the humanities and the sciences (2019). In contrast, Ruth Leys argues that the affect/emotion distinction that is key, for example, in the work of Massumi (2002) is weak and that in fact there is a strong compatibility between Tomkins' "emotional architecture" and the "intensity-relation" Spinozist-Deleuzian view (2011: 442). However, the two prominent fields of affect theory are of particular interest when analysing the imbrication of affect and work. What I am here calling a compositional critique of affect theory, in connection with labour, work and capital, corresponds to the two dominant vectors identified by Gregg and Seigworth, and Schaefer. A compositional analysis explores how these vectors, now with a particular focus on the affective sciences, become implicated in the problem of work, management, and technology.

The affective sciences emerge from diverse lineages across cognitive psychology through to biopsychology, neuroscience, industrial and organisational psychology, and theories of emotion in the workplace. The definitive commonality across this field of theory is the notion that affects are innate to or inscribed within a body such that they can be considered biologically prefigured. Affects and emotions are mobilised and expressed in individual responses or actions caused through emotional cues and feelings. In other words, an event or stimuli of a given nature triggers an affective response from the individual. Affects, from this vantage point can thus be triggered, provoked, managed, and indeed measured. An ontology of affect and emotion that assumes their biological prefiguring allows for the development of mechanisms to categorise, manage and measure affective responses to stimuli, events, and environments. A clear difference with respect to the Spinozist-Deleuzian theory of affects is apparent here. While the Spinozist-Deleuzian perspective understands affects are of the body, they are not reducible to it – affects express and compose relationships between bodies but are in no way biologically prefigured – there is no affective script that is foundational to the body. By contrast, within the broad perspective of the affective sciences, affect and emotion are very much inscribed within the body. This distinction carries important consequences when we begin to analyse the role of affect in the management of labour.

Wittingly or not, theorists of affect within the fields of psychology lay the foundation upon which modes of affective management are built. Silvan S. Tomkins (1962), for example, analyses and describes affect in terms of scripts, emotional architectures, motivation, and motivational systems. As Donovan Schaefer (2019) points out, Tomkins modified the evolutionary psychology notions of affect as expression, into a theory of motivation. This modification is particularly pertinent to how the affective sciences have formed a foundation underpinning workplace affective management and can be explored in the theory of basic emotions. The notion of an embedded script of affects within the body, which can be triggered, forms an affective core that can be activated and then managed. Schaefer demonstrates the biological foundations of this element of Tomkins' work, explaining how Tomkins draws from Darwin's theories of the expression of affect in animals, "but shifts the frame from a focus on expression to motivation" (2019: 35). Schaeffer's insight here is very important, as it highlights the affect system as more foundational to activity than the drive system of Freud. In Schaefer's reading, for Tomkins the "affect system was the more foundational structure", constituting what might be considered a position of "affect foundationalism" (2019: 35). Tomkins and theorists such as Paul Ekman and Donald Nathanson who draw from his work, identify a specific number, often nine, affects of the body (Leys, 2011: 437). These nine affects form part of a "genetically hardwired" affective script, or emotional architecture that is triggered by objects in the world, but which has no knowledge of the objects in the world that trigger it; affects are "non-intentional, bodily reactions" (Leys, 2011: 437). Importantly, the affective structure of a body as theorised by Tomkins and others, is qualitatively different to the cognitive structure and the process of rational thinking. Affective psychology is thus distinct from the cognitive modes of analysis and decision making. The affects and emotions are triggered through relations, but the site of analysis is the individual body. This is, then, a fundamental core of affects distinct from a hard cognitivism, embedded in the biological composition of the body. One of the implications of this perspective is that affect is in principle open to quantification.

There is nothing inherently problematic about the affective sciences and the social turn of cognition studies, with its focus on measure and biology. Indeed, as Sedgwick and Frank argue, the turn to affect via Tomkins was important in queering and destabilising the various "teleological presumptions ... historically embedded in the disciplines of psychology" (1995: 7). Charles Wolfe (2010) has also re-opened an interesting thread in analyses of the brain directly via Spinoza, which revived an analysis of the affective brain that is not reducible to practices of cognitive psychology. However, as I noted earlier in this chapter via Boltanski and Chiapello, in my analysis of the affective sciences, I am interested in the degree to which concepts, theories and techniques developed in a given disciplinary area become bound up with the organisation of work, specifically in relation to forms of management and measurement.

The theorisation of affective capitalism, particularly when analysing the specific configurations of work, management, and organisation, must be attuned to the nuances and contradictory implications of affect's divergent origins and trajectories. As I will show below, the affective sciences associated with biology and psychology tend to inform managerial technique. It is therefore essential, if we want to understand the contested character of the labour-capital relation in terms of its affective iterations within post-Fordist work settings, to incorporate each field of affect theory into our critique of class composition. It is only in this way that we can properly come to terms with the technical and political composition of class in relation to affective labour. One of the fundamental aspects of the incorporation of affective relations into capital is found in the complex of affective management techniques. The following section critically engages the incorporation of the affective sciences into management discourse and practice.

4 The Affective Sciences and Management

At the academic level, we can see that an emergent technical apparatus of affect is informed by such theoretical interventions as Affective Events Theory (AET), emotional mining and emotional capital, and the integration of organisational psychology research into workplace management (Weiss, 2002; Weiss and Cropanzano, 1996; Latham, 2007). The research carried out in management theory has encompassed a range of other 'on the job' practices such as World Class Customer Service (WCCS), Total Quality Management (TQM), Interpersonal Emotion Regulation (IER), and Appreciative Leadership and Management (ALM). In this section, I analyse how contemporary examples of managerial theory and practice engage with and incorporate the affective sciences. I will focus on Affective Events Theory (AET) as an explicit example of how the theorisation of affect informs managerial and organisational imperatives in the context of work; the reworking of theories of motivation through an affective lens; the analysis of core affect as a measurable unit of performance, and emotional capital and labour as a material of affective management. Through a critical analysis of these categories and examples, I show that the integration of affect theory into managerial practice should be considered a factor in the formation of contemporary class composition: an emergent apparatus drawing upon affect theory and the affective sciences for the measurement, modulation and containment of labour.

While this apparatus of affective management repackages and deploys practices that could be described within the terms of Taylorism applied in a new context (see for example Gregg, 2018; Moore, 2018; McNally, 2010), such an approach does not grasp in full the qualitative shifts that are taking place in managerial practice. For example, Gregg (2018) has written an important analysis of managerialism's persistent attention to productivity concerns via time management within immaterial modes of production. However, what is also significant about contemporary managerialism is the emphasis upon positive and negative affective states articulated to motivation and engagement as objects of management for purposes of job performance and productivity. For Gary Latham and Craig Pinder, motivation is "a set of energetic forces that originate both within as well as beyond an individual's being to initiate work-related behaviour and to determine its form, direction, intensity and duration" (2005: 486). They continue, that motivation is a "psychological process resulting from the interaction between the individual and the environment" (2005: 486). As a result, the problem is not only one of understanding how time management has adapted to service contexts or the proliferation of modes of measurement beyond the workplace, though these are certainly important too. Instead, it is of how the modulation of affective states of workers has become entwined with performance and productivity measures, and how affective states are engaged through processes of temporal and contextual organisation (Spector, 2020). It is necessary therefore to critique the specific ways in which the affective sciences are being integrated into methods for managing post-Fordist labour.

In drawing attention to the problem of affective management, I am taking a cue from critical management theorists Helle Bjerg and Dorthe Staunaes (2011), who draw together Tomkins', Deleuze's and Massumi's theories of affect to develop an analysis of Appreciative Leadership and Management (ALM). Bjerg and Staunaes note that managerial techniques and technologies are increasingly "designed to energise the register of affectivity" (2011: 139). These technologies, they continue, concentrate "on the production and formation of intensity rather than identity" in such a way that "the subject is managed ... through offers of being moved by a special affectivity or intensity" (2011: 139). They argue that, through the turn to affect, "management of self-management works through complex interactions between reflexivity and affectivity, within an ambiguous affective economy of both negative and positive affects". They conclude that "affects and affectivity are not simply by-products or something to be overcome, but the core matter to be managed by and through" (Bjerg and Staunaes, 2011: 139). Bjerg and Staunaes point to a shift in understandings of what is to be managed and how, and their emphasis on the notion of "by and through" points to the issue at hand, namely how affect is constructed as the medium through which management occurs. As Bjerg and Staunaes astutely note, "management, in the sense of making employees do your exact bidding, is impossible. Only the relation, not the subject, can be governed" (2011: 144). Affective management is thus "a strategic action on the intensity of relations and, thereby, a strategic action on the capacity to affect or be affected" (2011: 144). Building upon the comments of Bjerg and Staunaes, this analysis of affective management can build and extend a useful critique of class composition.

Management science, such that it is, has a long history of concern about and engagement with the problem of workplace motivation (Latham and

Pinder, 2005). Issues that fall within the scope of management science include the relationship between motivation and productivity, and the impact of job attitudes on both motivation and productivity. As Lane Dorian puts it, in an analysis of the relationship between affect, goal setting and productivity, "lack of employee effort is a control problem that management accounting research seeks to understand and resolve" (2021: 618). While a specific occupation with affect as developed within the affective sciences is a more recent development within the field, there is much to learn from the history of motivation and attitude studies in the workplace. The interrogation of workplace motivation and attitude has produced a range of theoretical lenses and concepts that can help to understand the novelties of contemporary approaches to workplace affect in relation to management. These include "job satisfaction, morale, commitment, involvement, engagement, work subjective well-being, and work affect" (Judge et al., 2017: 357). The prominent disciplines that have given expression to these ideas and inform managerial discourse and practice include Industrial and Organisational Psychology (IO psychology), Organisational Behaviour (OB), and Human Resource Management (HRM), among others. Before interrogating the contemporary iterations of the affective sciences in management, a brief overview of the history of emotion in workplace psychology provides a useful context for understanding the novelties of the present moment.

Theories of workplace emotion, affect, motivation and performance have always accompanied managerial interest in the lives and activities of workers. In one sense, there is a generic interest in the problematics of motivation and workplace affect that can be traced through the history of organisational psychology in relation to managerial imperatives. However, the specific iterations of affective management change with the transformations in the organisation of labour. In other words, the managerial approach to workplace affect, and indeed how affect is understood as both an object of and means through which to manage, changes over time as the character of work itself changes. For example, Judge et al. propose 6 epochs of "job attitude studies": the world war era; the post-war era; the cognitive era; the behavioural era; the dispositional era, and finally the affective era (2017: 359). An attention to and concern with worker performance, commitment and motivation is common throughout each of the apparent eras, but the specific iteration of this concern changes in each case. For example, early studies, such as Rexford Hersey's (1932) *Workers' Emotions in Shop and Home: A Study of Individual Workers from the Psychological and Physiological Standpoint* or V.E. Fisher and Joseph Hanna's (1931) *The Dissatisfied Worker* both demonstrate an attention to issues of motivation and the affective experiences of the worker in relationship to job performance and productivity in the context of industrial production. In these texts dissatisfaction on the part of the worker is linked to the desire to quit, which in turn becomes the object of management and intervention – there is something wrong with a worker who would want to quit. But the subsequent eras propose more nuanced approaches to worker affect, such that affect itself becomes a variable and terrain of management, not only an indication of poor attitudes on the part of labour. Affect is internalised to the organisation of work.

Following Timothy Judge et al. (2017), the cognitive era was characterised by a calculative perspective on emotion as pertaining to job performance. The calculative approach implied mathematical engagements with and representations of job satisfaction. One of the important areas of research in the behavioural approach raised the issue of organisational commitment, with the aim of demonstrating that organisational commitment, influenced by job satisfaction, would in turn impact performance at work. For the purpose of my argument, the transformation in the approach to affect studies between the cognitive and affective eras is of most significance. Within the fields of I/O psychology and management theory, the hold of the cognitive approach to workplace emotion was powerful enough that the turn to affect within these fields followed on the heels of the development of sociological theories of emotional labour. Citing the influence of Arlie Hochschild's work on emotional labour, Daus et al. highlight that the "the revival of the study of affect first came not from psychologically oriented researchers, but from sociology" (2020: 5–6). The attention to theories of emotional labour continue to inform contemporary affective management theory (Zapf et al., 2020; Grandey et al., 2020; Brotheridge and Grandey, 2002).

The shift from calculative and cognitive into affective approaches to management, job performance and satisfaction, crystallised a thread that had long been present in organisational psychology and management science, insofar as considerations of affect had been implied and present in all the earlier approaches. But the explicit turn to affect marks a unique period in the theoretical scaffolding of management science. Central to the consolidation of an explicitly affective approach to management science is the reengagement with the measurability of affect within the individual. Affect is constructed in relation to work motivation and performance, as well as in terms of job satisfaction and disposition. Secondly, the identification of the relationship between changes in the affective state of a worker's body and events in the workplace that impact the affective state of employees, has created a new field of managerial intervention. In each of these dimensions, affect is framed as a codified and measurable element of the biologicaln make-up of the body, and in turn posited in relationship to issues of work performance and productivity. Affect becomes the object of management, a terrain of managerial intervention, and the relationship through which management takes place.

As outlined in earlier sections of this chapter, the contemporary construction of affect as a terrain of management arises from the affective sciences (Weiss, 2002; Li et al., 2020). The concept of affect as scripted in the body, both biological and quantifiable, lends itself to the imperatives of the management of and through affect (Yang et al., 2020). In a comprehensive analysis of the terrains of emotion and affect theory that have come to inform organisation and workplace psychology, founder of Affective Events Theory, Howard Weiss (2002) outlines how the affective sciences are at stake in managerial imperatives. Weiss argues that researchers in the field of industrial and organisational psychology and related fields, have worked with a limited notion of affect, and encourages a broadening of engagement with affect theory. In doing so, he points to three primary lineages of affect theory to inspire such a renewal of engagement, namely the evolutionary, the cognitive, and the physiological traditions of affect and emotion studies. Ekman's (1992) studies of affect expressed in facial emotions and Tomkins' (1962) studies on affective scripts, among others, underpin the new approach to affective management suggested by Weiss. Relatedly, Gary Latham (2012) has shown that the problematics of job performance, motivation and satisfaction are cornerstones of the above disciplines, which calculate job performance as 'ability × motivation'. In a more specific sense, accompanying the general attention to performance and motivation, there is a long and varied history of studies that focus on emotion and motivation within the workplace (Latham, 2012; Payne and Cooper, 2001). While this specific history is peripheral to the affective turn as such, the affective turn has influenced contemporary forms of managerial discourse and practice in two ways. On the one hand, in recent decades organisational theorists have engaged more deeply with questions of affect in connection with job performance and motivation, indicating a move away from cognition and reflexivity towards affectivity (Seo et al., 2009: 951; Bjerg and Staunaes, 2011: 139). On the other hand, some of these same theorists are now drawing directly on theories of emotional and affective labour (Daus et al., 2020; Newman et al., 2007; Ashkanasy and Daus, 2002). Both Neal Ashkanasy and Catherine Daus (2002), and David Schweingruber and Nancy Berns (2005), draw directly from Hochschild's seminal work on emotional labour. Ashkanasy and Daus have pointed out that the managerial techniques geared around questions of affect are most applicable and effective in scenarios where a high degree of emotional labour is at stake. That is, at both the theoretical and shop floor practical level, theories of affect, emotional and affective labour have exerted a growing influence on those working within a managerial perspective.

Howard Weiss and Russell Cropanzano's (1996) development of Affective Events Theory (AET) offers a specific framework for analysing the affective states of employees. Their contribution to IO psychology is to isolate affect as a variable within workplace settings that impacts job performance and satisfaction (1996: 2). This represents a novel contribution in that, unlike previous theories which conflated motivation, performance, satisfaction and emotion, it separates these with a focus upon affect. Specifically, AET seeks to inform analysis of the causal factors of the affective states of employees, and to offer ways of understanding the relationship of these states to job performance and satisfaction. AET thus introduces a framework for identifying affect as a variable in workplace settings and correlates changes in this variable with job performance. Weiss and Cropanzano point out that previous cognitive models of analysis within IO psychology automatically equated satisfaction with affect and job performance (1996: 1–10). That is, as a general formula, job satisfaction was equated with positive affect and higher rate of job performance. However, For Weiss and Cropanzano, "affect is not job satisfaction" (1996: 65; see also Weiss, 2002); indeed, they insist that affect, job performance and job satisfaction are all independent. Weiss and Cropanzano (1996) argue that the perception or judgement an individual makes concerning job satisfaction is ultimately based upon a cognitive and rational evaluation. More specifically, Weiss and Cropanzano (1996) demonstrate that there is little evidence of a causal or correlative relationship between satisfaction and performance. The significance of this claim is to shift attention to affect. In particular, they argue that while satisfaction is a cognitive evaluation, job performance is affective. As a result, affect becomes the prism through which job performance is evaluated and measured.

Locating affect as the pivotal factor in workplace management introduces several degrees of nuance into the analysis of job performance. For example, much like those working in the area of the psychology of affect and emotion, such as Tomkins or Ekman discussed above, Weiss and Cropanzano list affects as a spectrum or script within the body. Thus, they identify positive and negative affects that move between sadness, happiness, anger, fear, and joy (1996: 22). Rather than delving into the controversy within psychology over whether cognitive appraisals of affect result from a separate structure or are hardwired into affective scripts,[3] Weiss and Cropanzano simply insist that for any given affect to be appraised, it must be the result of an event within an individual's context or environment. Weiss and Cropanzano are not concerned with whether a separate cognitive structure within the brain interprets affects, or if the process of appraisal occurs with the affect itself. In other

---

3   See for example Ekman's (1992) argument which distinguishes from Freudian psychology.

words, the focus of AET is upon the causal relations involved with affective states, and the relationship between affective states, activity and perception. Weiss and Cropanzano focus on the relationship between event and affective response. In this way, the relationship between events and affects is delimited as the terrain of management: the cultivation of affective states with positive work outcomes can be managed through the management of events. Finally, Weiss and Cropanzano introduce the analysis of duration into the scrutiny of the relationship between affect and job performance. Rather than limiting the analysis of the relationship between work performance, emotion and affect to single events or points in time, AET argues that there is a cumulative or inverse dimension to affective experience over time. The question of duration, affect and performance is characteristic of AET.

AET has not only contributed to opening up the analysis of affect within the workplace, it presents an experimental approach for the ongoing development of managerial techniques tuned to the question of affect. A significant conclusion that emerges from studies of AET, is that there exists no inexorable correlation between positive affect and performance. Theories of AET diverge from perspectives that identify and aim for simple positive affective states to improve job performance by arguing that various affective states can impact upon work performance in different ways. As a result, for AET, various affective states, such as anxiety, are not understood to be inevitably detrimental to work performance (Schmitt, 2020). A typical example to demonstrate this point is the timing of deadlines, the impact of deadlines on positive and negative affect, and how both positive and negative affect can be harnessed to productivity. However, the analysis carried out by Bjerg and Staunaes (2011: 144–151) discussed above also resonates with this aspect of AET. In particular, Bjerg and Staunaes point to the role of shame as a focus of affective management within appreciative leadership and management (ALM). Bjerg and Staunaes argue that the emotional component of work, from a managerial perspective, is most often bound to motivation and satisfaction, that is to say a positive affective or emotional state. However, they note that in the work of Tomkins positive states of interest and desire are "closely connected to the cultivation of potential shame" (2011: 145). The implication here is that the spectrum of affects can be mobilised in different settings in order to influence job performance. AET has thus opened up a complex rethinking of workplace affects, motivation and job performance.

Affective management theory illustrates how the elicitation of labour is articulated through affective intensity (Weiss et al. 2018). The curation of goals is one key way in which affective management is implemented. As Plemmons and Weiss (2012) outline, affect is relevant in terms of goal outcomes and choice of goals. Writing for the *Institute for the Study of Labour*, Lorenz Goette and David Huffman (2005) outline a model of affective motivation that illustrates the complex way in which affect is mobilised in goal orientation in the workplace. Goette and Huffman (2005: 2), paralleling the discussion above, note a shift in focus from the cognitive to the affective in studies of motivation. Through a case study of bicycle couriers, Goette and Huffman outline a dual model approach to labour supply, or work effort and motivation, to isolate and emphasise the significance of the affective drives, mobilisations and motivations of the employee in relation to productivity. They state that "the standard economic model of labour supply assumes that a worker decides how hard to work and when, based on a purely cognitive calculation of costs and benefits" (2005: 29). However, they insist that the affective dimension is an important but marginalised area for consideration.

Given the common piece-wage arrangement of courier work, whereby the daily rate is determined by the amount of jobs a worker obtains, Goette and Huffman (2005: 28) investigate the significance of the affective dimension of motivation. They suggest, based upon interviews with couriers, that there is a minimum amount that couriers say is necessary to make coming to work worth it, and an amount (generally higher than the necessary amount) beyond which the urgency to earn another dollar declines. The significance of this finding lies in their argument that there is an affective relation between the worker's effort and the meeting of the performance goals at intervals throughout the day. As a goal approaches, affective drive increases and therefore so too does labour supply. However, once a goal is reached, labour supply declines. That is, the affective dimension of labour-supply can be managed through measuring and timing goals. They go on to argue that "from the perspective of the employer, affect can be productive if it leads to greater motivation than is achievable by financial incentives alone". At another level, low indicators of affective engagement on the job constitute a problem for productivity: when a

> worker's goals are not ambitious enough, affect can be counterproductive. Thus, our findings suggest that it is in the interest of employers to identify and perhaps influence the goals and affective engagement of workers.
>
> GOETTE and HUFFMAN, 2005: 31

Affect is identified here as a significant factor in labour supply. An economy of positive and negative affects informs the analysis and management of motivation, task setting and labour.

Uta Bindl and Sharon K. Parker (2012) similarly present an analysis of "employee proactivity" in relation to affect and workplace goals. Bindl and Parker note that

> employees more than ever are required to not only comply with broader goals that are set by their organisation, but also to be self-starting in shaping their own careers and initiating improvements in work practices and procedures.
>
> 2012: 227

Their notion of proactivity refers to the way in which employees take up these tasks, and they identify three pathways of employee proactive motivation: "can do", "reason to" and "energised to" (2012: 227–228). Bindl and Parker identify the last of these three pathways as under-theorised and pertaining to the question of affect. They suggest that individual affectivity of either negative or positive valence influences identification and innovation within the workplace. What is significant in the framework provided by Bindl and Parker, is that the key variable for negotiating this new condition of employment is the affective relationship between the worker, the organisation, and the future. Kibeom Lee and Natalie Allen (2002) present an interesting parallel analysis, which examines not only the question of identification with the organisation or workplace, but also the role of affect in workplace deviance behaviour and its management. In each case, the affective state of the worker is the object of management.

Assuming the containable and readily mapped body, the application of affective science to the workplace often relies upon the management of 'core affect'. Core affect is said to be the unit of analysis for understanding "momentary, elementary feelings of pleasure or displeasure and activation or deactivation" (Seo et al., 2009: 952–953). Put more succinctly, core affect is that which needs to be managed when measuring and regulating workplace motivation. Core affect is connected with three primary areas of workplace motivation, each of which has varying impacts on performance and implications for measurement and management. These are a generative orientation (the mobilisation of "behaviours such as exploring, innovating and risk-taking"), effort (which is also called intensity) and persistence. What is of interest is that these three areas of analysis for core affect break down into three axes through which management of and through affect can take place. Taken together, for management theorists these elements constituting core affect provide an experimental terrain for management technique.

A number of correlations can be made between the management of labour through core affect and the attempt to locate emotional intelligence within the workplace. In a similar fashion to the hypotheses posed concerning core affect, an individual's emotional intelligence, and his or her position in the labour process, is said to have an effect on work performance. For example, various attempts have been made to construct a demonstrable relationship between emotional intelligence, emotion recognition and productivity. A clear example of this can be found in the retail industry and in particular in the role of salesperson. EI is thus understood to have direct, moderating or indirect effects in the workplace. Bechtoldt (2008) and Byron et al. (2007) provide examples of how such effects might actualise at work. Byron et al. (2007) analyse the effectiveness of retail sales persons in recognising non-verbal emotion in customers and relate this to the success (productivity) of the worker. Bechtoldt points to how workers in "service lines of business" might use their own EI to better handle interactions with customers or how workers might manage their own emotions to better handle stress at work. From a manager's perspective, EI emerges when a supervisor is "able to manage their employees" emotions' and thus better maintain enthusiasm and team performance (2008: 127). Theories of EI are thus mobilised as further material for the practices of affective management.

The analysis throughout this section has identified affective management, as informed by the affective sciences, as a component in the technical composition of immaterial and affective forms of labour. While work and management have always had an affective and emotional dimension, affective management as I have explored above provokes new areas for consideration in the relationship between work and management. Time and motion studies, scientific management, and their bearing upon labour and productivity persist (Kelly, 2024; Gregg, 2018). But the integration of the affects of the body and affective events, as both terrains and techniques of management marks not only a specialisation in how affect is understood by management theorists, but produces new variables through which the disciplining of labour is being articulated and imposed.

5   Affect as Material of Service Labour and Management

The conflation of labour and life that I have explored in previous chapters tends to pose the attributes of immaterial and affective labour as natural characteristics, divorced from historical consequence or specificity. A problem that has often emerged in postworkerist considerations of affective labour is mistaking historically determined forms of work imposed on particular bodies as natural capacities organised horizontally across the social body. Affect becomes a generic, ahistoric quality of activity, rather than a historically specific determination of labour. It is by now well established that the requirement to perform affective labour is not a call that exists outside of, for example, gender and race. Angela Mitropoulos puts it as follows: "it is not ... authentic human sociability that is valorised in affective labour, but the apparently genuine circulation of affect *as if it is not work*" (2012: 174). Thus, while affective modes of labour appear natural and thus function as a pool of surplus labour to be drawn on within and beyond formalised economic relations (Mitropoulos, 2012: 106, 164, 174), the critique of affective labour/capitalism cannot begin with an uncritical acceptance of such appearances. Mitropoulos further notes that the problem of the appearance of naturalness is also one of how "property and labour mesh with an inseparable complex of gender, sexuality, class and race" (2012: 185, see also Mitropoulos, 2009, 2008 and 2012a). Patricia Chong (2009) has also drawn attention to the complex interactions that take place between emotional labour, race and gender, particularly in terms of expectations about who is supposed to perform such labour, and how.

In Chapter 3, I noted the existence of tensions between the classical perspective and that of the workerist-feminists within the development of *operaismo*. These tensions have been remade in various ways in the present context. While postworkerists claim to valorise the myriad forms of labour that make up the present social world as ontologically, politically, and economically productive, their arguments have often removed nuance rather than amplified it. This is a particularly telling shortcoming given that postworkerist theories of immaterial production are characterised, at least tacitly, by forms of labour and cooperation that are 'low-end' in the labour market. The composition of domestic, service, and caring work continues to be organised globally by gender and race. As Premilla Nadasen (2024) demonstrates, the historical composition of caring labour is enmeshed with gender, class and racial capitalism, which challenges the postworkerist historiography of affective labour. It follows that affect is not a generic category, but rather, as an artefact of labour, is mobilised across demarcations of gender and race which are historically determined, contested, and transformed through the struggles of those who perform this labour. The boundary at which informal service/care work and the formal economy meet is a contested one, oscillating between efforts to incorporate such labour within capital, or to deny, marginalise and/or naturalise its economic role (Glenn, 2012; Nadasen, 2015; Cooper, 2017). For these reasons, the composition of caring labour is articulated through the technical, social, political, and affective modes of composition. It is important to critique how management theory attempts to capitalise on these dynamics.

Evelyn Nakano Glenn (1992; 2010) provides an analysis of service work in the twentieth century that weaves together race and gender, rather than analysing them as separate categories. Glenn's work is important in pointing to how divisions of labour and constructions of skill form along race and gender lines. She also points to the relationship between the public and the private that characterises the exploitation of service work. For example, Glenn points out that "the service worker also often performs in a public setting the same sorts of tasks that servants did in a private setting", and that "the situation of women as unpaid reproductive workers at home is inextricably bound to that of women as paid reproductive workers" (1992: 22, 31). Glenn also demonstrates that "the division between skilled and unskilled jobs is exactly where the racial division typically falls" (1992: 37). Mitropoulos (2012) has traced the genealogy of servitude to service work in a critique of the contract. For Mitropoulos, the significance of service is that it is imposed as

> the foundational gift of a naturalised servitude ... the surplus labour that is always outside the remunerative, measured and reciprocal logic of the wage contract as such, but which is nevertheless crucial to its reproduction.
>
> 2012: 32

Indeed, "far from being marginal to the extraction of surplus labour, this expectation of a labour freely given has always been central to capitalist re/production" (Mitropoulos, 2012: 164).

David Staples' (2007a) analysis of the work, organisation and struggles of US home-based labour, and Encarnacion Gutierrez-Rodriguez' (2010) decolonial approach to migration and domestic work, both take up the question of biopolitical and affective labour raised by postworkerism, but with different inflections. Both authors develop close analyses of two examples of home-based service work in the contemporary context, specifically in relation to the question of affective labour. Staples shows that in the US context, home-based service labour necessarily "takes on the appearance and characteristics of traditional, that is to say modern, women's work: literally 'worth-less' and bound to the household" (2007a: 23). Staples continues that:

> the contradiction of 'own account' and self-employed, as well as exchanged and subcontracted labour which resists being monetised ... presents capital in particular, and the state in more nuanced ways, with a uniquely exploitable ... supply of surplus labour.
>
> 2007a: 23

For Staples, what is at stake here is a question of biopolitical control, a governance of life (2007a: 111). He notes that "what makes political subjectivities

in this space flow ... are the highly controlled technologies of 'sex' and 'race'"
(2007a: 113). Gutierrez-Rodriguez' analysis of the affective labour and value
of domestic work echoes Staples' insights. Gutierrez-Rodriguez suggests that
while it may be the case that "affects constitute the social and cultural fabric
from which *living labour* and its productive power stems", in terms of domestic
work, "within the chain of value coding, this labour is marked by the absence
of its affective productivity" (2010: 140, emphases in original). Both Staples and
Gutierrez-Rodriguez insist on bringing the question of biopolitics to bear upon
labour, but the result is very different to Negri's understanding of biopolitics
which I discussed in the previous chapter. There is no expectation that labour
will automatically affirm its productive autonomy in the above examples.

Although the technical composition of class appears to be abstracted from
the lived stratifications discussed above, in the context of affective techniques
of management they tend in fact to become interlaced. In a case study of
door-to-door salespersons at 'The Enterprise Company', Schweingruber and
Berns, outline the "emotional mining" that is implemented in the management and self-management of these workers (2005: 681). Emotional mining
refers to the process of finding experiences, which form emotional capital,
in the workers life or biography, but which had not yet been considered relevant to the labour process of sales work. The objective of emotional mining
is to tune the memory of those experiences to improve the individual worker's emotional management and thus emotional labour. Schweingruber and
Berns state that "we use the term *emotional bridge* to describe how this new
emotional capital is used to connect the worker's previous self to the new self
that is being developed on the job" (2005: 681). These comments parallel those
of Foucault, when he stated that the Chicago school theory of human capital
implies that "this machine", that is a worker, "has a lifespan" (2008: 225). I would
also point out that this approach to emotional mining complicates the future
orientation that is often ascribed to post-Fordist economies. While Adkins
(2005; 2012: 625–627) has argued that post-Fordist conceptions of the commodity labour-power involve a future orientation rather than retro-activation,
Schweingruber and Berns indicate that another temporal orientation reaches
into the biography of individual workers lives. Schweingruber and Berns'
analysis of the mining of emotional capital illustrates a direct link between
practices associated with human capital, and the deployment of affective
sciences within managerial practice.

There is a close proximity between the techniques of management discussed
above and the attributes of immaterial and affective modes of labour. Not only
do researchers in and practitioners of affective management draw increasingly from theories of emotional and affective labour, but such techniques

tend to be applied most specifically to forms of emotional and affective labour in lower end service and care work. Moreover, not only do these techniques focus most intensively on these sectors of the workforce, they also intersect with the racialised and gendered characteristics of affective labour. As such, there is an interlacing of the historical characteristics of affective labour and the specific managerial techniques discussed above. As an example, to add to those already outlined, the analyses of emotional capital and emotional mining that are discussed by Schweingruber and Berns (2005: 690) draw from the racialised and gendered histories of sales workers. Given the racialised and gendered composition of low-end service work, the affective economies mobilised in affective management and emotional mining intersect with the personalised narratives of service workers. As Schweingruber and Berns put it, "it was not obvious to college students ... that an inspirational relative or a dramatic experience like escaping your native country in disguise can become a reason to sell books door to door" (2005: 690). Further, they argue that "enterprise managers help dealers turn these sorts of experiences into 'emotional purposes' (also called 'emotional incentives')" (2005: 690). While it appears somewhat absurd to entertain the notion that managers would draw such threads between a personalised narrative and the job of sales work, it nonetheless indicates the terrain of emergent managerial practice – not only affect and emotion but affect and emotion in their historically contested dimension. For this strand of management thinking, the experiences of migration and poverty constitute the raw material from which one is expected to improve oneself, particularly in the context of service work. In other words, the historically contested and demarcated attributes of affect – that is the non-generic character of this labour – are what managerial techniques come to draw upon. One clue emerges here to the shift in managerial technique and measure, from standardised time, motion and output to the complex temporalities found in the narratives and affective experiences of life that weave from one's past through their present and into their future.

6   Conclusion: Affective Management and the Technical Composition of Class

The analysis of affective capitalism, affective labour and the emergence of affective management techniques presented in this chapter can be connected to the theorisation of the technical composition of class. When considered alongside Chapter 3's exploration of class composition, we begin to see the context for the development of new and affective forms of management. This context is in part defined by the conflict between the emergence of affective and communicative forms of labour, and the need to contain or mobilise such labour within the valorisation process. These arrangements comprise a series of intensive forms of measure, mobilised across the historically sedimented demarcations of service work. The managerial response to the diffuse workplace of post-Fordist forms of labour has been to shift from a standard time-motion form of measure to an approach that intersects directly with the affective relations of work and life. As explored in Chapter 3, the categories of class composition analysis are in dynamic relationship with each other. The relationships of social and class conflict within and beyond the workplace can shape the organisation of production and reproduction, while the technical arrangements of production and reproduction in turn shape the forms of social contestation.

In workplace affect studies, the theoretical articulation of affect and emotion as innate biological traits effectively gives rise to the technical framework for the regulation and measurement of affect and emotion. The affective sciences tend to construct the body as an affective architecture or script that can be mapped and read in certain controlled ways. This conception of the body as a measurable terrain of various intensities informs the development of specific techniques aimed at the management and measurement of labour. While this understanding of affect is in some contradiction with the Spinozist and Deleuzian conception of affect that has been taken up by the postworkerists, it nonetheless forces us to consider the contradictions of affect in the workplace. Far from suggesting the automatic autonomy of affect as ontological force of production, the deployment of the affective sciences in the context of work complicates the politics of affective labour. The materiality of affective labour involves the measurement, management and modulation of affects as labour. It does not translate immediately or automatically into a form of ontological resistance.

It is therefore not controversial to argue that the relationship between labour and value, its organisation in time and space, has remained a key problematic for the management of living-labour. Labour remains that subjective dimension of (re)production and accumulation that capital cannot do without, and which it can yet never contain. The shift to the post-Fordist economy has added a further twist to this problem, insofar as the communicative, affective, emotional and cognitive dimensions of labour are now subject to transactional and exchange relations, and thus increasingly drawn into (re)production and circulation in one way or another. Moreover, these dimensions are not drawn into motion just as they are, but expressly for the purpose of the circulation and accumulation of value. This involves the construction of a 'space' through which the modulation, refraction and measure of affect and labour can take place. Such a space need not be read as necessarily physical (although certain architectures, may operate as such an intensified space), but rather as an organisational force that compels the body to act in specific ways: technologies that compel or extract affects from within specific labour processes. It is here that we can locate the most acute possibilities of conflict within capitalist social relations focused on the production of affect. The following chapter expands the analysis of the technical composition of class and affect through a consideration of affective and emotion recognition technologies in the workplace.

Affective Capital, Labour, and Emotion Recognition Technology in the Workplace

1 Introduction

Recent developments in the workplace have seen the intensification of methods to elicit and capture value within and across the affective encounter, notably through the introduction of technologies that seek to measure the production of emotion by service workers.[1] While this tendency was already evident over the past decade and more (Gawne, 2012; Moore, 2018), with the experience of the pandemic and its impacts on worker monitoring, there is now an "acceleration in the demand for AI that can sense, read and evaluate a worker's emotions" (Mantello and Ho, 2023: np). This phylum of technologies incorporates affective computing and machine learning. A survey of patents on workplace affective technologies undertaken by Karen Boyd and Nazanin Andalabi (2023), highlights the sharp increase of these technologies being developed for workplace use in the years leading up to 2020. Picking up on the themes explored in Chapter 5, the aim of the following analysis is to build a dual critique of the trajectories shaping the development of affective technologies in relation to work, as well as specific affective technologies deployed in the workplace. This chapter identifies a technological nexus that entwines affect and labour in contemporary forms of work. The technological nexus, expressed in the insertion of affective and emotion recognition technologies in the workplace provides a crucial insight into the technical composition of capital as it relates to affective labour.

The argument developed in this chapter follows two entwined lines of critique drawn from the analysis of technological infrastructures that compel and apprehend the production of affect. One line of my analysis explores the inscription of the affective sciences, specifically via a consideration of the design and use processes of affective computing, Human Computer Interaction (HCI), and machine learning within emotion recognition technologies deployed in the workplace. I argue that the rendering of affect as 'emotion' within emotion recognition technologies represents one fundamental way in which affect

---

1 Sections of this chapter were previously published in Gawne (2012).

can be understood as a component of the technological composition of capital and class. Emotion recognition technologies are constituted through the codification of affect as an identifiable, quantifiable, measurable, and manipulable artifact of activity. The process of codification marks an engagement with affect as a productive intensity but also acts as a reduction and fixing of affect to a reproducible unit or action. There is a fundamental contradiction at play here, implied in the rendering of affect as emotional script. But it is precisely this contradiction that opens into class compositional critique of affective technologies in the workplace. As the codification or script of affects is fixed within the emotion recognition technologies, affect is simultaneously reified while becoming a structure through which labour is mediated. Once deployed in the workplace, such emotion recognition technologies illustrate how affect, via the affective sciences, is further integrated into the composition of capital.

The second line of analysis explains how, once affect is fixed within capital, emotion recognition technologies are put to work arranging, compelling, and ordering the actions of affective labour. That is, the fixing of affect within emotion recognition technologies leads to the modulation and ordering of the affects of the user, in this case the worker. While the 'turn' to affect in computing and HCI design has opened up a vast field of research with multiple potential applications (see for example the collection Tao and Tan, 2009; Richardson, 2020), this chapter focuses on just one of these applications – namely emotion recognition technologies that seek to subordinate user affect to the imperatives of capitalist valorisation (productivity, rapid circulation and accumulation). In so doing, I aim to identify how, within HCI, certain technological assemblages come to submit the body of the worker to a particular *ordering of affect*. The ordering of affect occurs both in the design process and as the effect of the use of particular affective HCI technologies in the workplace. In other words, the ordering of affect aims to produce an affective state in the worker, which in turn is meant to shape the affects produced by the worker. In pursuing this line of inquiry, we will be better placed to understand contemporary elements of the technical composition of affective labour.

Theorists and critics of affective HCI have laid some of the foundations for the argument developed in this chapter. For example, Eva Hudlicka (2003: 3–6) provides a useful overview of the potential applications of HCI technologies. Within a larger taxonomy of applications, she identifies one phylum of technologies that aim to sense, recognise and modulate user affect. In Hudlicka's words, such technologies might be deployed, amongst other possible uses, for *"maintaining a particular user state for a particular task"* and for *"inducing"* a particular affective state in the user (2003: 5; emphasis in original). Both applications are characteristic of the use of emotion recognition technologies in the workplace and the monitoring, modulation and ordering of affective labour. More recently, the work of Edward B. Kang (2023) provides critical insight into the process through which affect is rendered within emotion recognition technologies. Kang's argument concerns the reduction of affective complexity in the construction of codes and datasets that allow emotion to be recognised and measured by various technologies. As is indicated in the work of Hudlicka and Kang, the development and applications of emotion recognition technologies point to the tension that exists between affect and emotion within affective computing and AI.

As explored in this chapter, there is a consequential epistemological and ontological contradiction in terms of how affective and emotion recognition technologies construct the categories of affect and emotion, and in how they interact with labour. For the purpose of my argument the contradiction is a productive one: the machinic embodiment of affect and emotion illustrates the fixing of the affective sciences within the technological composition of capital, and thus within the technical composition of class. This chapter begins by rearticulating the tension between affect and emotion for the purposes of illuminating how this tension plays out in the context of affective technologies. Once this tension is established, the chapter considers how issues related to affective machines have been addressed by postworkerism to date. Following this, I turn to consider the affective iterations of human-computer interaction. Based upon this consideration of affective HCI, the chapter develops a critique of how affective scripts and datasets are rendered within affective technologies, and how this process impacts the theory of affective capital and labour. The affective technologies explored throughout the chapter are significant in terms of the articulation of labour and capital, and thus important in terms of the technical composition of class. However, as a means of addressing the problems of productivity within the service sectors, the impact of these technologies is less clear. The chapter concludes by considering the relationship between affective technologies, the augmentation of labour and the terms of surplus-value creation. While some look to the potential of affective technologies to boost service sector productivity, I find that the impacts are primarily at the level of articulating the labour process, not intensifying the production of surplus-value.

2   Affect and Emotion

Debates over the relationship between affect and emotion as distinct and discrete categories continue to characterise scholarship in the fields of philosophy, psychology, and computer science, among other fields of research. This tension is characteristic of affective technologies developed for workplaces. It sometimes appears as though the various theorisations of affect have in common an understanding of affect as a bodily and relational force, while emotion is an individualised feeling. Yet, as explained in the previous chapter, in certain fields of study 'affect' and 'emotion' can be used interchangeably, while in others there is a fundamental distinction between them. Moreover, each concept is internally variegated and contested, and debates over the definition of what constitutes an emotion, for example, play out in the scholarly field of human computer interaction and affective computing. It is therefore useful to clarify how the differences between these categories and their inherent ambivalence are navigated, particularly as we are coming to terms with the process of modulating and ordering affective labour through the uses of HCI and affective technologies at work.

The engagements with affect and emotion used throughout this chapter traverse the various lineages of affect and emotion theory. I engage the contested notions of affect through a class composition lens, which is to say I seek to identify how different lineages of affect have been inscribed in the labour-capital relation to contradictory ends. The Spinozist (1996), Deleuzian (Deleuze, 1988; Massumi, 2002) and Negrian (1999) theorisations of affect are drawn upon to highlight how labour is impacted by affective technologies. At the same time, the construction of affect as biological, physiological and behavioural, as found in the work of Silvan S. Tomkins (1962) and Paul Ekman (1992) is essential to understanding how affect is rendered technologically. Finally, the theorisations of core affect (Russell, 2003) are also at stake in the debates regarding the design of affective technologies. Read through the lens of class composition, it becomes apparent that the affective sciences have been drawn upon and inscribed within affective technologies to mediate, modulate and order affective modes of labour.

To briefly reiterate the distinctions outlined in Chapter 5, Deleuze defines affect as an intensity of feeling that runs across, between and through bodies, but which cannot be captured within an individual body. The necessity of affective relation is thus never closed. Affects cannot belong to or be arrested within a subject but must exist as a flow of intensity between bodies expressed as passion or action. As Brian Massumi suggests, emotion will necessarily emerge from an affect, but it is effectively objectified and possessed by an individual. For Massumi, "emotion and affect are of different orders" (2002: 27). Emotion becomes the individual's, the subject's expression of feeling. In this respect, emotion represents the reduction of affect as open flow to something that is quantifiable, fixed and exchangeable. Affect is apprehended, or put into a freeze frame, in the moment of exchange (Best, 2011). In this way, the categorical tension between affect and emotion is mirrors the tension within the labour-capital relation.

Affective and emotion recognition technologies crystallise this dynamic tension between affect and emotion technologically. But in order to do so, they must draw not from the Spinozist field of affect theory, but rather that of the affective sciences. For Tomkins (1962) and Ekman (1992), the concept of discrete or basic emotions predominates, simplified as the physiological inscription of affects within the body. It is this notion of affect that is most readily drawn upon in the codification of affect within affective and emotion recognition technologies. The notion of 'core affect', which I/O psychologists have drawn upon and informs managerial science as discussed in the previous chapter, is relevant to the debates regarding affective technology even as it tends to elude incorporation within the designs of HCI. In short, posed from a class composition perspective the affective sciences are drawn into the logic of management and capital as they become the functional core of emotion recognition technologies.

The literature and discussions of affect and emotion informing HCI, affective computing and emotional/affective technologies straddle the tension between defining, differentiating, and classifying emotions and affects. In a similar way to how the affective sciences inform affective management theory and practice, an inherent ambivalence between affect and emotion is present within affective computing. This ambivalence is internal to the affective sciences. Indeed, within affective computing there is "no universal consensus on how to classify emotions" (Richardson, 2020: 79). Instead, there are two primary approaches to the basis of classification. The first approach emphasises a discrete set of categories of emotions (Ekman, 1992), while the second approach that measures affect/emotion along two interacting dimensions, one of valence and one of arousal, similar to that of AET outlined in the previous chapter. These two approaches sit alongside each other, at times in tension, opposition, or entwined together. It is my contention that this very tension between emotion and affect, and its embeddedness in the technological nexus of affective labour, is characteristic of the technical composition of affective capital and reflects the particular form of mediation of both labour and affect in conditions of capitalist production. The epistemological challenges at stake within the affective sciences in both managerial and technological iterations (see for example Kang, 2023), are secondary to the fact that they form part of the technical composition that shapes the activities of affective labour.

It is worth opening a further inquiry into how affect and emotion can be read through the lens of class composition analysis, as this illuminates what is at stake in the debates regarding affect, labour and capital. The tension between affect and emotion reflects the concepts and categories of labour and labour-power. In *Post-cinematic Affect* (2010), Steven Shaviro makes the argument that affects bear the same relationship to emotion as does labour to labour-power. The first in each of these respective relationships, affect and labour, can be described as the open intensity, and the non-containable force. Labour is the form-giving fire of human creativity; affect is the open intensity of relation that cannot be individualised and objectified (Marx, 1993 [1939]: 361; Spinoza, 1996). In contrast, the categories of emotion and labour-power can be understood as the objectified form of the creative intensities from which they emerge, and which they represent. Emotion is a contained, scripted, and personalised manifestation separate from affect; while labour-power consti-tutes the captured, commodified expression of labour (Massumi, 2002; Marx, 1951: 74–97). Building upon this distinction, we come to the following prob-lem: if the exchange of labour-power represents a necessary objectification of labour within the social relation of capital, which in turn distorts the pro-cess of affective production, then an aporia emerges when we talk of affective labour within the valorisation process. The aporia lies in the contradiction that emerges in the deployment of the affective sciences within the technological nexus of work. Moving through this contradiction involves locating the con-tradiction in the basis of the labour-capital relation and a consideration of the categories of class composition. The inscription of the affective sciences within the technological nexus undermines the Spinozist iterations of affec-tive labour that characterise postworkerism. In other words, it is only through the critique of mediated affective labour that it is possible to move beyond this contradiction.

Paying attention to the uses of HCI in contemporary labour processes, I look to a dynamic interaction between affect and emotion that mirrors the tension and contradictions between labour and capital. Emotion recognition technol-ogies, through the affective sciences, arrest the Spinozist notion of affect and reduce it to a unit of order that is measurable, reproducible, and quantifia-ble. These later conditions are imposed upon the practices of affective labour. In this sense, affective and emotion recognition technologies form a point of mediation and refraction that articulates affective labour (or the affects of the user) in a similar way as a prism impacts upon light waves: shifting their flow, direction, and speed. As labour confronts emotion recognition technol-ogies in the workplace, workers remain engaged in the production of affects. However, this production is mediated and ordered through the affective scripts fixed within the technological nexus. Although refraction does not change the substance of affect, it does alter the rhythm of movement and the perception of the flow. In other words, both the commodity-form and the technological nexus mediate the conditions in which, and the reasons why, affective production is taking place.

In this respect, we can engage the problem of affective labour and technology in the Spinozist terms of movement and rest, speed and slowness, and its contradiction with the affective sciences fixed in emotion recognition technologies. Tension emerges as affect qua activity (as labour) moves through different spaces, constituted by different logics and codes: value's organisation of labour expressed through its technical composition, determines a degree of movement or rest of a body and affect particular to the imperatives of valorisation. The tension shapes, in more simple terms, how the body works. This tension can itself be understood as a dynamic of class composition. While labour and affect have an open quality, their apprehension via the commodity and the technological nexus reduces labour to its commodified expression and affect to a scripted and quantifiable code embedded in the machine. Here the deployment of a technological infrastructure to induce and maintain an affective state in a worker, mobilised within the logic of valorisation, forms the prism that compels and bends the affective encounter.

3   Affective Machines and Problems of Composition

Theorists of affective labour have identified the need to consider the problem of immaterial production. However, there remains an under-theorisation of how and in what ways the contemporary organisation of capital has also taken up and incorporated the problem of affect managerially and technologically.[2] The complexities that emerge when we consider the technological nexus that mediates the production of affect warrant a more nuanced and critical consideration. The implications for how the technological nexus articulates labour are found in call centres, hospitals, retail outlets or any other customer service floors. Following the insights of early compositionist critiques of class and work, the point of departure for such a task involves a specific focus on the technical, including the technological, organisation of labour. The critique of affective HCI developed in this chapter thus aims to situate emotion recognition technologies as an element within the structural organisation of the labour process and within the critique of class composition.

---

2   Matteo Pasquinelli is the closest later generation postworkerist to have most systematically taken up the technological implications of AI, immaterial labour and the general intellect. His most recent book *The Eye of the Master* provides insight into recent debates on this question.

Postworkerism presents an analysis of contemporary class composition that tends toward the conflation of the technical and the political. I emphasised in Chapters 3 and 4 that this conflation is evident in the postworkerist analysis of language, affect and labour which culminates in the productivist ontology of affect. Specifically, the analysis of affective and linguistic production, for postworkerism, sees an inversion of the category of fixed capital such that machinery is emptied of social knowledge as productive force, and instead the general intellect is now located in the faculties of living labour (Hardt and Negri, 2017). The critique of the affective sciences, affective computing and emotion recognition technologies, challenges the image of labour presented by postworkerists. Indeed, the re-inscription of affect within technologies of work fixes affect within the logic of valorisation and mediates the process of affective labour. However, in recent decades debates within postworkerism have seen a certain divergence of perspective on the role of technology in relation to affective capitalism. I will develop my analysis of affective technologies below, but it is first useful to address the debates within postworkerism concerning technologies of affect, and to touch on related perspectives on the quantification of affect.

In recent years both Bifo and Lazzarato have outlined critical perspectives on the general intellect that problematise the technological question. Both theorists have drawn substantially on the work of Felix Guattari (1995) and Deleuze and Guattari (2009; 2004). While certain tendencies within postworkerism have assumed a specifically accelerationist inflection (Pasquinelli, 2014; Negri, 2014), Bifo's thought in recent years has emphasised slowness, exhaustion and depression (2012; 2013; 2014; 2024; see also Eden, 2012). One of the central sources of ambiguity, and indeed pessimism, that emerges in Bifo's thought is his sense of the increasingly high-strung tension between the general intellect and the 'body' of labour. Although Bifo shares the analysis of the transformations of labour and value developed by theorists such as Negri, not only is Bifo's political interpretation of these transformations far more pessimistic, so too is his understanding of the relationship between labour and the general intellect. In short, for Bifo, the general intellect has escaped the democratic control of labour. The general intellect valorises information and affect, but in a way that immobilises the political capacities of labour. The regime of 'semiocapital', the term Bifo uses to denote the contemporary condition, mobilises the intellectual, affective, attentive and linguistic capacities of labour, but it does so through the imposition of a radical separation that rearticulates a conception of alienation more in line with Marx's original formulations (Marx, 1961; Berardi, 2009). Bifo's analysis of the technical components of cognitive and affective labour draws attention to, and is itself emblematic of, the limits of postworkerism concerning the question of technological composition.

Disagreement on the character of fixed capital in late capitalism also defines contradictory perspectives within postworkerism. Lazzarato notes that for Marx machinery is the "most adequate form of fixed capital" (Marx, 1993 [1939]: 694 in Lazzarato, 2014). However, while Lazzarato is generally credited with coining the term immaterial labour, he has now moved beyond his previous analyses of immaterial production and the general intellect (Lazzarato, 2023: 216–217). Distancing himself from the concept, Lazzarato now argues that contemporary arrangements between labour and capital are characterised by "machinisms" or assemblages that "have invaded our daily lives" (2014: 13). More specifically, and closer to the argument I develop throughout this chapter, Lazzarato insists that these machinisms now "assist" our ways of speaking, hearing, seeing, writing, and feeling by constituting what one might call "constant social capital" (2014: 13). This is a somewhat different perspective on the machine than that presented in Marx, but it is useful for clarifying some aspects of my argument in this chapter.

Lazzarato argues that today "machines ... *suggest, enable, prompt, encourage, and prohibit certain actions, thoughts, and affects or promote others*" (2014: 30, emphasis in original). For Lazzarato, today workers "constitute mere inputs and outputs, *a point of conjunction or disjunction* in the economic, social, or communicational processes" (2014: 26). This is a fundamentally different position to Marx's image of the scattered intellectual organ and automaton presented in Marx's *Grundrisse*, or indeed any notion of the individual: "intelligence, affects, sensations, cognition, memory and physical force are now components whose synthesis no longer lies in the person but in the assemblage or process" (Lazzarato, 2014: 27). As I will show below, there is a certain convergence between the perspective Lazzarato develops here and my analysis of the interaction between HCI, affective technology and labour.

Outside of a specifically postworkerist framing of the issues of quantifying affect, the work of scholars such as Nick Dyer-Witheford (1999; 2017) and Phoebe Moore (2018; 2021) offer a useful consideration of technology, work and the quantification of affect. Moore's work is of particular importance, in that it explores the attunement to affect of contemporary managerial and technological imperatives. The approach to affect in late capitalist conceptions of work and productivity that Moore outlines is articulated through 'the quantified self' and management of the agile workplace. For Moore, agility incorporates conditions of precarity and the harnessing of affective intensity within workplaces, as well as the quantification of non-work activity within the logic of productivity. Pitts (2023; 2022) has addressed issues of measurability of immaterial modes of labour that touch on both the managerial and technological imperatives of late capitalism but does not directly address the implications of the modulation of affective labour via HCI. Cecchinato et al. (2021) engage directly with HCI in the workplace. However, their focus lies in a consideration of how workers make use of platforms to their own ends, which I will pick up and address in the next chapter. For now, it is necessary to develop the critique of affective HCI and AI as elements of the technical composition of class.

4   Human-Computer Interaction and Affective Capital

Rosalind Picard's (2000) work on affective computing opened a field of enquiry which has subsequently been taken much further by researchers and designers in the field. Recent trajectories in HCI, drawing from work in affective computing, have sought to emphasise the affective state and expression of users in the design of interactive technologies and to develop the capacities of machines for affective display (see Zeng et al., 2007; Gunes et al., 2004; and Truong, 2010; Richardson, 2020). The variety of innovations emerging from affective computing and HCI is vast and include eye-tracking instruments, devices which interpret the emotional significance of physiological data such as temperature and heart rate, as well as emotion and gesture recognition technologies, to name just a few (see Gunes et al., 2004; Lao and Kawade, 2004; Zhao et al., 2003; Jaimes and Sebe, 2007). The significance and importance attributed to these types of designs has only grown in recent years, as the attempt to manage and monitor work motivation and performance took new turns during the pandemic experience (Mantello and Ho, 2021). The sheer diversity of these applications indicates the scale of the general 'turn' to affect in computing and interactive technologies.

While the turn to affect in computing finds a clear expression from the mid-late 1990s and early 2000s, there are important precursors in the history of computing and interactive technologies. For example, Elizabeth Wilson (2010) draws attention to the importance of affect in Alan Turing's thinking on artificial intelligence. Wilson uncovers an often-neglected history of computing that situates affect as an early, pivotal question in terms of concepts, design and index of intelligence. Wilson (2010: 58–82), further demonstrating the relationship between the affective sciences and computing, identifies an encounter of Turing's early investigations into AI, and the affect theory of Tomkins and other psychologists of emotion. Based on this reading, a minor, though nonetheless direct dialogue between the affective sciences and computing is evident since the 1950s. Considerations of affect are also present within early interaction design aesthetics, preceding the specific emergence of affective computing. It remains the case, however, that despite this minor tradition, until very recently cognitive and calculative, as opposed to affective, models have by and large constituted the index against which intelligence is measured.

HCI, understood as a broad field of research and development, focuses on the improvement of the relationship between users and computers. However, the engagement with affect in recent decades has contributed much to expanding this field. Prior to the affective turn, most research in HCI was concerned with the logical and calculative powers of the computer, while studies in human-machine interaction focused upon the adaptability of the user to the computer. Here, it was assumed that it is easier to get a person to adapt to the rigidity of a machine/computer than to get the computer to learn and adapt to the user (Raskin, 2000). More recently, as Noam Tractinsky et al. (2000) have demonstrated, researchers have uncovered empirical correlations between designs that address the affective dimension of an interface and its perceived usability by humans, constituting evidence that challenges the previous wisdom of function over form. These increasingly sophisticated engagements with affect are productively complicating the frameworks through which computer and interface design and development is thought. Not surprisingly, in the relatively short period of time in which affective computing and technologies have emerged as a field worthy of serious consideration (Hudlicka, 2003; Sengers et al., 2002; Boehner et al., 2005; Partala and Surakka, 2004), numerous divergences have emerged. These divergences reflect the difficulties inherent in the very definition of the concept of affect and cognate understandings of interaction.

Some of the initial engagements with affective computing approached the problem of the direct relationship between an individual user and his or her computer. Picard (2000: 1) defined affective computing as a form of computing that either relates to, influences or arises from emotions. This implies that the computer should be able to recognise and respond to emotion in the user, and in other cases, that the computer itself possesses emotion of its own. In a chapter linking affective computing and HCI, Picard (1999) identified four areas of development: reducing user frustration, communication of user emotion, developing the means to handle affective information, and finally, development of social-emotional skills. In each case, the aim is to improve the fluidity of the relationship between an individual user and a computer through a direct attention to the dimension of emotion in computing.

Picard's conceptualisation of a one-to-one affective relationship between user and computer reveals a number of practical and theoretical limitations. In the first instance the slippage in terms from affect to emotion opens the way for a conception of affect as a quantifiable substance which can be measured, interpreted, learnt and directed. Following the argument of Kirsten Boehner et al. (2005), what we have here is an example of an informational model of emotion. In their words,

> emotion, in the informational model, is a dual of cognition, but it is nonetheless the same sort of phenomenon – an internal, individual and delineable phenomenon, which acts in concert with and in the context of traditional cognitive behaviour.
>
> BOEHNER ET AL., 2005: 59

Thus, the potential for opening a deeper affective engagement within the confines of this informational model is limited by this reduction of affect to a quantifiable unit. This, in fact, has reproduced some of the very problems that advocates of affective computing had identified and critiqued in the cognitivist approaches to artificial intelligence.

A further limitation can be identified in the personal nature of the relationship between user and computer. The construction of the concept of affect, emotion and relationship here effectively reduced these terms to fixed possessions held either by the user or the computer. The affective relation is therefore understood as an interchange of fixed units of emotion, determined through the reading of indicators on the body, or in the expression of the computer. Affect itself is defined as a fixed possession or inherent feature, of a person, precluding any understanding of its social, cultural or political dimensions (Sengers et al., 2002). To counter this notion of affect as information, Boehner et al. (2005) develop an interactional model as a way of constructing a more complex framework through which to approach the question of affect and emotion. Within the interactional model affect is not reduced to either a possession of the individual or a characteristic that can be fixed within a computer. Rather emotion and affect are placed in a social and cultural context, and as such are seen as dynamic arising from action and interaction. Within the interactional model we can see affect as a form of intensity produced in the relationship between the user and computer.

The theoretical limitations of affective HCI, evident in the preponderance of the informational model, has led others to push the potential of interactive design in the direction of constructing environments or spaces of 'becoming'. Jonas Fritsch (2009) draws on Massumi's theorisations of affect to deepen the prospects for affective engagement in HCI. As is well known, and pointed out above, Massumi develops the Deleuzian and Spinozist theory of affect through a discussion of how a body, already constituted by various intensities and potentials, is in turn affected and thus moves to a higher or lower capacity to act (Massumi, 2002). Affect is a pre-personal potential and intensity, which is irreducible to the level of the personal or individual. Affect is inherent to and mobilised in experience and event, that is to say, affects move and reconstitute given bodies. To affect or be affected is thus to be within a process of becoming, with a greater or lesser capacity to act. Fritsch discusses these theories of affect in the context of a public interactive installation called *Touched Echoe* by artist Markus Kison. I draw attention to Fritsch's discussion of the public installation simply because it provides an example of affective technology oriented to the amplification of affective interaction, or what Fristch calls affective engagement. The installation creates an open affective engagement through the orientation of the interaction and the transformation of the physical space in which it is installed (see Fritsch, 2009: 6–7). What is significant in Fritsch's discussion is his focus on the installation's production of an amplifying and expansive affective encounter. Fritsch's contribution to the field pushes the conception of affect within interaction design to another level, beyond models of emotion and information.

Based on the above discussion of tendencies within the development of affective technologies, it is possible to make a qualitative, yet fluid, distinction within the field. On the one side are located those innovations that are designed to amplify affect, and on the other are technologies for the ordering of affect. The demarcation is fluid insofar as the distinction between amplification and ordering could shift depending on where and how a given technology is mobilised within the materiality of social relations. Yet it is useful as it allows us to problematise the relationship between technology and affect, and further, to grapple with the tensions involved in this relationship. Technologies of amplification can be defined as those infrastructures that aim to create an expansive affective engagement and environment, as discussed above in the works of theorists such as Fritsch (2009) and Boehner et al. (2005). Here we encounter an affective resonance opening out to processes of becoming, akin to Spinoza's concept of common notions, expressed in the productive resonance of ideas and action. The interaction that occurs through the affective technologies are oriented to the amplification of affective experience. By contrast, ordering technologies function not through resonance and expansion but act as a directive force upon a body's behaviour. We now turn our attention to examples of the latter technologies.

5   Technologically Fixed Affects, or the (Re)Inversion of the General Intellect

Affective computing and HCI are increasingly employed in the development of workplace technologies for the modification of labour (Boyd and Andalibi,

2023). In order for emotion recognition technologies to identify, modulate, mediate, and respond to user affects, they must first be able to recognise them. However, the technological recognition of user affect in turn requires a reduction of the complexity of affect to a delimited and fixed script. The process of rendering affect/emotion as a recognisable unit within affective technologies is not uncontroversial epistemologically, ontologically, or as I will argue, politically. Viewed politically, which is to say from a perspective combining the labour-capital relation, the labour process, and the composition of class, the rendering of affect as fixed technology is a key point of contradiction and mediation between labour and capital. In the following comments I turn to examples of speech emotion recognition (SER) and facial emotion recognition (FER) technologies as they relate to the augmentation of affective and emotional labour in the workplace. Through a consideration of how affect and emotion become codified and scripted within affective technologies, and how this codification in turn mediates labour, I demonstrate that the technological nexus of affect is now a key component of the technical composition of class.

A significant literature has grown around the critique of AI, including a specific consideration of affective AI, in terms of its surveillance qualities. However, while surveillance is a very real concern, my interest is more directly upon the issue of how these technologies articulate labour. As Kat Roemmich et al. (2023) have also argued, while the uses of emotion recognition technology and affective AI are often geared toward surveillance, this is not all that is at stake. Indeed, the "purpose of workplace monitoring is not simply to monitor employee behaviour and activities, but to also *shape* them" (Roemmich et al., 2023: 2). Having interviewed workers regarding their experience of affective AI in the workplace, Roemmich et al. (2023) draw attention directly to what I am defining as the modulation and ordering of affective labour. For example, the modulation of affective labour takes place when emotion recognition technology intervenes in customer service calls to instruct workers to be more "perky" (Roemmich et al., 2023: 7). Importantly, this leads to a situation in which "emotion AI-enabled surveillance and the information asymmetry it generates, workers may assume the need to constantly practice the emotional labour they perceive is expected of them" (Roemmich et al., 2023: 8). The compulsion to perform emotional labour indicates the ordering of affective labour as articulated through emotion recognition technologies.

This critique of emotion recognition technologies sheds light on a deeper complexity involved in the contemporary production of affect and emotion than that which is generally considered in theories of affective and immaterial labour. Specifically, emotion recognition technologies set in motion a triple dynamic in the production of affect and emotion. The first of these is expressed in the production of the code or script of affects embedded in the affective or emotion recognition technology, such that it can recognise affect/emotion in the user. The second is found in the impact of these technologies once they are produced and put to work within a given labour process. In the later instance, the labour producing affects is mediated, modulated, and ordered through the encounter with the emotion recognition technologies. The final dynamic occurs after the encounter with emotion recognition technologies, which in turn modulates how workers produce affective relations at work. In other words, these technologies modulate how workers come to produce affect. The practical materialisation of this triple dynamic, anchored to the fixed code of affect that shapes the labour of the worker, constitutes the technological nexus as a component of the technical composition of class.

Identifying affect as a component of capital can first be demonstrated in a consideration of how emotion and affect are produced and rendered as a static index within emotion recognition technologies. There is a growing literature on a new hidden abode in the production of affect and emotion, located in the process of defining, measuring and embedding delimited notions of affect as code within emotion recognition technologies (Crawford, 2023; Kang, 2023; see also the Knowing Machines Project). Edward B. Kang (2023) provides a fascinating account of the production process of the emotions that become the index of measuring emotion/affect in speech emotion recognition technologies (SER). Taking a critical approach to the construction of emotions within SER, Kang draws attention to the epistemological and ontological implications of machine learning processes in producing emotions. Kang demonstrates that "for the purposes of developing an AI speech emotion recognition (SER) system … emotion must be defined, bounded, and instantiated as ground truth in the training data", which leads to the prioritisation of "particular emotional ontologies" over others "in the construction of SER datasets" (2023: 455). In this, affective and emotion recognition technologies recapitulate the epistemological and ontological tensions between affect and emotion explored in the previous chapter. But for my purposes, it is Kang's insight into how affective scripts are produced as datasets and the double dynamic of the production of affect that is most important, and indeed central to how we can conceive of the formation of affective capital.

Alongside the discussion in Chapter 5 regarding managerial technique, it is important to highlight the direct mobilisation of theories of affect and emotion as developed by the affective sciences, within emotion recognition technologies. The codification of affects in emotion recognition technologies is based on the discrete or basic emotions theory that characterises tendencies within the affective sciences. Kang (2023) draws attention to the tension between discrete emotion theory and core affect theory in the development of affective computing and the categorisation of emotions for the purposes of emotion recognition. All the decisions as to what constitutes an emotion, what to include as an emotion, and how to classify emotions, that are necessary for the constitution "ground truth", pose several problems ontologically and epistemologically.

The establishment of discrete emotions as the archetype in emotion recognition makes evident the relationship affective technologies have with the work of Tomkins (1962) and Ekman (1992). Theories of affective scripts that are characteristic of the psychological theories of Tomkins and Ekman rely upon numbered sequences of affect. As Kang (2023) illustrates, the implementation of discrete emotions within SER also reduces affective conditions to a numbered script, and affects are embedded in the affective technology in the form of a numbered script. In other words, SER design incorporates a process classifying various emotions according to primary categories arranged numerically. The numerical register parallels the theory of affect as embodied script found in the affective psychology of Tomkins and subsequent theorists. Affective technologies thus express an ontological prioritisation of a particular theory of affect and emotion in their design.

The implications of this prioritisation of limited notions of affect and emotion are not merely academic. Beyond the ontological and epistemological controversy noted above, it is important to highlight the political consequences as they play out in the context of affective labour. The implementation of affect or emotion as number allows for the translation of affects into statistical and measurable models (Kang, 2023; Dror, 2001). As Otniel Dror puts it, the numerical script "sanctioned an economy of emotional exchange and affective communicability" (2001: 359), that has ultimately been incorporated into the development of various emotion recognition technologies today (Kang, 2023: 457). The above tensions in defining affect and emotions for recognition purposes help to illuminate the character of the labour-capital relation in service contexts. While Kang is not concerned with the question of class composition or the labour-capital relation as I am approaching it in my argument, instead focusing on SER as a disabling technology, his work is crucial in demonstrating how affect/emotion come to be fixed and function as an element in the technical composition of class.

To reiterate, there is a triple element in the production of affect/emotion and its relationship to the technical composition of class/capital: emotion/affect functions as a component of the technical composition of capital insofar as it is codified as data in the SER technologies. In other words, the benchmark against which the act of performing affect in the labour process is measured is a fixed form of codified emotion. The command to produce affect in the act of labour is the secondary dimension in the technical composition of affect. In the later iteration – the act of producing an emotion that matches the codified forms in SER, apprehends the affective elements of production and contains them in an instance of emotion – the production of an affect of 'joy', benchmarked to the numerical representation of 'joy' in SER's dataset is not a universal articulation of joy, or something that can be considered joy outside of that measure. Moreover, the command and character of affect produced is fixed within the datasets and numerical sequences of the affective technology. This is instead, a mediated performance of affective labour.

The relationships between affective/emotional labour and concepts of performance have been extensively theorised. Emotional labour as a form of deep acting is one clear example of this framing of this type of work (Hochschild, 2003 [1983]). However, affective technologies introduce an additional factor in the management and performance of affective and emotional labour, expressed through the design and construction of emotional scripts. In elaborating this point, Kang (2023: 457) identifies a fascinating history of emotion within animation which comes to illuminate the technological mediation of affective labour. Kang traces this history through one key study that has informed emotion recognition in speech, undertaken by Frank Dellaert et al. (1996). Dellaert et al. construct thousands of speech samples of the 'believable agent domain' as a basis for identifying the expression of emotions in voice. Following Kang, 'believable agent' is a term coined by computer scientist Joseph Bates (1994) and developed based on the philosophies of Disney animators on how best to have animated characters express emotions, namely "to construct self-animating creatures" or "believable agents" (believable agents are also called woggles) (Thomas and Johnson, 1981 cited in Kang, 2023: 457). Aaron Bryan Loyall defines believable agents or woggles as "a character [that] allows the audience to suspend their disbelief and … provides a convincing portrayal of the personality they expect" (1997: 1). As Kang highlights, Bates took three tenets from Disney animators Thomas and Johnston:

> 1. emotional states must be unambiguously defined so that viewers can attribute definite emotional status to the character, 2. emotions must be directly apparent in the action of the character, and 3. emotional expression must be accentuated through foreshadowing and exaggeration.
>
> 2023: 457

These types of emotional criteria were given to the readers in Dellaert et al.'s study when generating the data set against which the emotion recognition could be developed. This demonstrates a curious historical relationship between affective technologies and animation. But more significantly for my purposes, it also illustrates how emotion recognition technologies can come to mediate human labour, such that, to stretch the metaphor a little, affective workers are expected to function as woggles in the workplace, in the articulation of believable affect. The codification of emotion thus shapes the performance of the emotion – a complex interplay combining the construction of the dataset and the static form of the codified emotion, the operation of emotion recognition technologies, and the impact it has on the actions of affective labour now mediated by the technology. While Dellaert et al., and in turn Kang, are engaged in the construction and critique, respectively, of speech emotion recognition technologies, the element of performance also carries over into other modes of emotion recognition and affective labour.

Facial recognition technologies function by reading, categorising and responding to a person's face. When it comes to emotion recognition, it is a well-documented problem with FER that the accuracy of emotion detection is very poor. A lack of accuracy coupled with the codification issues outlined by Kang (2023) indicate that the effectiveness of these technologies is very low in terms of identification and classification of emotions or affects. While such an issue is a problem when it comes to the ontological foundations of the technologies, it is essentially secondary and even inconsequential to the argument developed in this book. These technologies still structure and mediate labour in the workplace, in particular the work of producing affects, regardless of the technical limits and ontological ambiguities that underpin them.

An early example of facial recognition in the workplace provides an insight into how emotion recognition modulates labour. In its 2009 annual report, the company OMRON provided a brief overview of one of its then most recent, cutting edge and "exciting" sensor technologies. The name of this sensor technology is OKAO Vision, commonly called the smile-scan, and at the time represented OMRON's most advanced model of a facial recognition technology. The senior manager of OMRON's sensing and control laboratory, Masato Kawade, has stated that "the technology has great potential for a whole host of applications from consumer electronics to healthcare ... Or what about a 'smile-checker' for people working in the service industry?" (cited in Control Engineering, 2007: np). Evidently, the software itself is quite versatile, and as such there are a number of applications for which the facial imaging and sensor technology can be used. In applications designed for the private consumer, possible uses range from hand-held photography cameras, video game applications, and the use of biometric logins in personal computers. In other instances, facial recognition technologies have been installed in public areas such as town squares or transport areas with high pedestrian traffic, for identification and surveillance, including the ability to identify individual faces within large crowds. However, of most importance for the present discussion was the use of the technology for commercial applications within the workplace.

In 2009, Keikyu Corporation installed OKAO Vision smile scans in fifteen of its transport stations (Negishi, 2013: 327). In each of these workplaces, the smile scan technology is in use for the purpose of training and regulating the bodily performance of workers at the station. Workers at the station undergo a smile scan at the beginning of a shift. The technology, as indicated above, measures and ranks the 'potential smile' of the individual as a percentage score. The point of this process is to develop in the worker the most perfect smile for the individual to perform while on shift. It is further reported that a printout of the smile scan is retained to remind the worker throughout the day. Each of these applications operates as a directive on the body of the worker to perform a repetitious but familiar appearance of intimate labour.

The basic steps of the operation include fixing an image, reading it and providing a feedback loop with the user. The software first fixes an image then detects the face within the image. The feature points of the face, eyes and mouth, for example, are located within the image. Once the computer has recognised and interpreted the configuration of the feature points of the face, it is in a position to assess the overall image. The process provides the foundation for the facial recognition of the user. The information accumulated from the individual user's face is compared against the database, which in turn informs feedback to the user, and can include an estimation of gender and age, as well as facial traits including expression, gaze, and finally a facial image optimisation (Lao and Kawade, 2004). For example, the smile scan follows much the same series of operations, but adds layers of detail along the way. The scan itself locates a larger number of points on the face, such as the tips of the eyes and mouth and points on the cheeks. Reading the individual's face and the position of their features, the software then constructs a model image, a three-dimensional configuration of the face, and compares this against a library of facial images in its database. Given the measurement of the face and the location and shape of the key features, the software is then able to provide feedback rating and assigning a value to the individual's smile, out of a potential score of one hundred percent. It does this through measuring the movement of the key features of the face as it smiles.

FER technologies in the workplace come to modulate labour and affect. Negishi (2012; 2013; 2016) has analysed the implementation and use of OKAO visions as an exemplary model of post-Fordist service work in its insistence on the performance of the smile and affect, and as a framework to problematise surveillance. While the objective of Negishi's inquiry into the use of OKAO

Vision diverges from mine, his analysis can inform the question of the relationship between this technology and labour. As Negishi points out,

> despite the corporation's statement that the smile-exercise facilitated by the Smile Scan is only intended to improve the standard of customer service ... a secondary function of the technology is for railway workers to actively work on themselves: to exhibit approved sentiments.
>
> 2013: 327

Negishi continues that OKAO Vision "prompts workers to distinguish a 'natural' face from an 'unnatural' face and to eliminate 'unnaturalness' in order to interact with passengers in more authentic and effective ways", thus "regulating flows of events and affective intensities" (2013: 227). Negishi goes on to connect the use of facial recognition technologies to the question of surveillance and social control, but he has also hit upon key issues in terms of the regulation of work.

There are in fact two interfaces at work in facial and speech emotion recognition technologies in the workplace. The first involves the relationship between the user (worker) and the technology. On first appearance this relationship functions within a closed circuit. The worker engages with the computer, which interprets, measures and feeds back information about the performance of the worker. However, given the fact that this circuit is designed to modulate the performance of the worker in a second environment, the shop floor encounter with customers, the closed circuit at a given point opens onto this second space. At this point, the body of the worker, having already been engaged, interpreted, and modulated/compelled in the engagement with the smile scan, becomes itself a second interface expected to produce a desirable affective encounter with those other bodies it comes into contact with while at work. In the connection between the time of the worker's first encounter with the emotion recognition interface, and the ongoing performance throughout the worker's shift, we witness the broader assemblage that modulates the form of affective labour carried out on the job. This larger procedure, consisting of the first encounter between user-computer and the opening of this circuit onto the second space of the shopfloor, situates emotion recognition technologies as a central component in the ordering and modulation of affective labour.

The ordering of affective labour has further detrimental effects on the worker. Technologies that amplify the compulsion to perform emotional and affective labour, and the disciplinary impacts of these technologies, are disproportionately felt by marginalised workers and undermines, and exhausts workers own emotions. It is useful here to situate facial emotion recognition devices alongside other examples of the use of affective technologies for the modulation and ordering of affect in the workplace. In a similar way to the smile-scan, the use of vocal emotion recognition technologies in call centres produces a relationship between user and computer that compels the performance of a specific kind of affective labour. Vocal emotion recognition technologies are used in the training of workers and at the point of interaction. For example, *Diverted to Delhi* (Stitt, 2002), demonstrates how HCI is used in Indian call centres. Interviews with workers illustrate how their training for interaction with international customers involves the performance of 'correct' communication with clients – that is, the requirement to perform particular affectations of speech and communication. The training process aims to monitor the pronunciation of words, to train accents to sound either neutral or 'native' to the country from which they are calling and/or receiving calls, and finally to control vocal pitch and tone. Vandana Nath (2011) has also analysed the aesthetic and emotional labour in call centres focused upon the work of performing accent and pronunciation. As is the case with OKAO Vision, the first circuit between the worker and the technology produces an affective performance, which the worker then repeatedly enacts in the encounter with other bodies when on shift.

The ontological and epistemological contradictions within both SER and FER technologies in the workplace recapitulate a false universalism as to the expression of emotions. The implications of such a false universalism are significant in the effect that they rearticulate long standing biases, forms of oppression, and exploitation along structural conditions that are gendered, racialised, and ableist (Kang, 2023; Crawford, 2021). These are important implications, the critique of which must be central to the development of emotion recognition technologies. Kalindi Vora's (2010; 2012) analysis of call center work illustrates the intersection between affective technology, labour, management and the stratifications of service workers. Vora illustrates how the affective labour of call center workers in India is integrated into a history of racial and gendered demarcations of labour. Vora argues that "in transmitting vital energy to US residents, they [call center workers] enter into a history of US capitalist accumulation in relation to conquest, racial slavery and immigration" (2012: 697). There is an evident parallel here with my analysis of the previous chapter, where I argued that affective techniques and technologies, in their deployment, modulate not an ahistoric condition of labour, but a historically determined form. Vora has also shown that "management and quality control technologies shape not only the culture of the workplace but also the very subjectivities of the call center agents" (2010: 35). Nath (2011) echoes this with her comments on identity formation in call centre labour. In particular, and I will return to parallel issues in the final chapter, Nath (2011: 711–718) draws attention to the affective experiences of shame, anxiety and stigma felt by the workers. In any case, the cumulative result of the above, for Vora, is "the devaluing of racialised and gendered service work" that in turn leads to an uneven transmission of care to white middle-upper class families in the US. For Vora, these are the dynamics that shape the technological articulation of the affective encounter in Indian call centers.

The dynamic between affective technologies and labour can take less direct forms than those of the speech and facial recognition examples above. To take the example of care work, Ariel Ducey points out that "the way in which objectualisation and affective modulation intersect with institutions and relations of caregiving is particularly important because care produces society itself" (2010: 29). As Ducey notes, the issue that arises here is one of authenticity in labour and affect. That is,

> when the processes of objectualisation and affective modulation change caregiving, it raises concerns about whether the 'care' produced is genuine or meaningful, and therefore capable of producing 'society itself'.
>
> 2010: 29

The ambivalence that Ducey articulates resonates with Mitropoulos' remarks noted in the previous chapter, namely that affect must circulate "*as if* it is not work" (2012: 174). Ducey states that "the 'technology' of affective modulation ... is troubling because it seeks to align care with bureaucratic and commercial ends, but it does not predictably produce superficial care compatible with profit making" (2010: 29). That is, affective modulation is troubling both for labour and for capital: the modulation of affect pulls labour into the valorisation process, however it can also "trigger new solidarities" in response. This is an important observation, that opens an inquiry into the ambivalence of affective politics, which I return to in the following chapter.

The character of affective and emotion recognition technologies, their logic of development and deployment in the workplace, challenge the foundational assumptions of immaterial production. As postworkerist theory goes to pains to emphasise, the embedding of social scientific and technical knowledge within the machine that occurred with the massification of industrial manufacture is said to have broken down. The knowledge and technics of production, in a condition of immaterial labour, are dislocated from the machine and found instead within the linguistic, cognitive, communicative and affective capacities of living labour, with "living beings as fixed capital" (Hardt and Negri, 2009:

132). But as the discussion of affective technologies so far demonstrates, such is not the case. From these foundations, affective technologies in the workplace challenge the ontological assumptions of postworkerist conceptions of labour.

The implementation of emotion recognition technologies in the workplace function through the measurement of the performance of an emotive display for the creation of an affective encounter: it creates the possibility for the indexing of the efficiency of affective performance. The notion of efficiency in service work often takes on new meanings, as it is difficult to subject practices such as care or attention to the usual standards of productivity and metricity. However, in a context in which relation, attention and emotion become key considerations of economic organisation, the modulation and intensification of affect is paramount within the standards imposed upon the performance of labour. In this context, affective technologies are linked to the effectiveness of the worker, and to this degree a conception of efficiency within the workplace. The application of emotion recognition technologies such as facial and vocal emotion recognition is already evident in some service industries involving human-human affective interaction and human-machine affective interaction, or both (see Omron, 2009; Vora, 2010: 33–47; Records et al., 2007). These workplace management technologies challenge the image of the general intellect proposed by postworkerists. Despite the limitations, inaccuracies, ontological and epistemological contradictions that underpin these technologies, their deployment in the workplace is often promoted as a method of augmenting labour to increase performance and productivity. But given the character of the industries in which they are utilised, questions remain as to the capacities of these technologies to address these economic concerns.

6　　Affective Augmentation, Productivity, and Surplus Value

The innovations in affective computing and their application within HCI are now critical elements of computer design. In the condition of ubiquitous computing, the importance of innovations in affective design of interfaces continue to grow. At the same time as this tendency develops, we see that the importance of affective HCI mirrors the dynamics and forms of technical composition of class today. Affective labour is mediated by the computer interface or an encounter with emotion recognition technology in many workspaces. The configuration of affect as a quantifiable substance (or emotion) to be modulated in the interests of, for example securing customer satisfaction and loyalty (Bromuri et al., 2021) is enabled by theories of HCI that focus on the instrumental relation between the user and the computer. In another respect, however, and returning to the conditions of post-Fordism and service production, it is important to pose the question of the emerging technological infrastructure as oriented to the production and circulation of value.

As outlined in Chapter 1, productive labour in the Marxian sense simply means to be formally subsumed within capitalist social relations or formally incorporated into the wage relation for the valorisation of value (Marx, 1996; Endnotes, 2010). In other words, to be integrated into the wage system for the production of profit. As such, the concrete form of the labour performed does not bear upon the question of productive labour, but rather the condition in which it is employed and whether the activity replenishes the fund of capital from which it was paid (Marx, 1975). Childcare, for example, can be performed and paid out of the employer's personal fund and be rendered unproductive – the employer does not make any money out of the employment of this labour. However, childcare can also be performed and paid out of a privatised company as part of a profit seeking service provider, and thus assume a productive character. Marx uses the school as an example of this point, arguing that whether a capitalist

> laid out his money in a teaching factory instead of a sausage factory, makes no difference to the relation. The concept of a productive worker therefore implies not merely a relation between the activity of work and its useful effect, between the worker and the product of his work, but also a specifically social relation of production, a relation with a historical origin which stamps the worker as capital's direct means of valorisation.
>
> MARX, 1996: 644

The challenges to productivity within the service sector are therefore not whether services can be productive of surplus value, but rather the rate at which surplus value can be produced based on the technical conditions of a given labour process. While affective technologies modulate labour and operate at the level of the production of affect, it is unclear that they will, or indeed can, have much of an impact at the level of reducing a firm's costs in terms of competition or socially necessary labour time.

It was in the context of widespread deindustrialisation that the theory of immaterial production emerged. Deindustrialisation sees the relative and potentially absolute decline in manufacturing employment as a portion of a given economy. In combination with deindustrialisation is the growth of the service sector as a key absorber of labour. What some call the long downturn in global productivity, is also the story of the rise of the service economy (Brenner, 2006; Benanav, 2021). Services are often broadly and poorly defined, in so far as the category is inclusive of such a wide variety of activities as to become unwieldly (Smith, 2020; Benanav, 2020). Moreover, forms of employment can be deemed services by the simple process of outsourcing formerly inhouse jobs (Smith, 2020; Ritzer and Lair, 2009). Nonetheless, employment trends in healthcare, education, food services, hospitality, among others, have grown substantially across much of the world economy in recent decades, and the service sector as a whole has continued to grow and absorb more labour globally (Benanav, 2020: 56–64). In this sense, services are contributing more to the 'productive', measured economy than they have previously. However, the service sector confronts limits in terms of intensifying surplus value production, limits that are elsewhere often overcome by technological innovation in production.

The problem of service labour productivity pertains in part to the challenges of surplus value production outlined by Marx. The opportunities to reduce socially necessary labour time in service contexts face challenges in overcoming the labour-intensive character of much of the work. As Endnotes have put it, "as the economy grows, real output in 'services' tends to grow, but it does so only by adding more employees or by intensifying the work of existing employees, that is, by means of absolute rather than relative surplus value production" (2010: 39). In other words, there have been persistent limits confronted to intensifying service production in such a way that the rates of productivity and profit grow, and technological innovation within services has offered little to date in addressing these limits. This barrier to productivity is widely recognised, and leading economics commentators today present their own version of productivity limitations. Saul Eslake (2023) argues that a key dynamic in productivity slowdown in Australia is at least in part attributable to the shift in employment towards services. The labour-intensive character of care, education, retail service, and other modes of affective production pose challenges for prospects of technological innovation to intensify productivity in terms of outputs. High labour intensity, low efficiency, and limited options for technological innovation mark a technical, though not a political, limitation in these sectors of the economy in terms of increased productivity, returns, and by extension wages and conditions.[3]

---

3   The technical limit can be posed from various economic perspectives, in neoclassical terms or even Marxist terms. But to see this technical limit as insurmountable misses precisely the contested character of the labour-capital relation and accepts the narratives of capital accumulation on its own terms. As Melinda Cooper (2017 and 2024) has demonstrated, it has been the struggles of workers bound by the technical limits of service work, and who for a time shattered this limit in wage and welfare struggles, that has sent capitalism into crisis and inaugurated a long counterrevolution.

Nonetheless, some continue to place hopes in the augmentation of service labour to kick start productivity gains in the service economy. Alexander Henkel et al. (2020) have sought to demonstrate how the use of AI can augment customer service labour to increase productivity of workers, amounting to a modification of "interpersonal emotion regulation (IER)" which would in turn translate into better customer service and therefore sales (Henkel et al., 2020: 249). Surveying the possibilities for service labour augmentation, Henkel et al. argue that affective AI can "contribute to increased effectiveness and eventually lead to service productivity gains" (2020: 248). Service augmentation would see the combination of affective AI and human labour, rather than the replacement of workers *tout court*. The authors point to possible productivity gains through labour augmentation in health care, hospitality and elder care. Here, a reduction in employees alongside affective AI will lead to "efficiency gains" as well as "increased sales and improved customer satisfaction" (Henkel et al., 2020: 249). However, beyond the vague allusions to efficiency, the prospects for augmented labour productivity remain unclear.

To the extent productivity gains are found in the services sector via technological innovation, it tends to be through employee reduction as algorithms assume certain job roles. Chatbots, self-service bots, data mining, and bookings systems in hotels and restaurants indicate some areas where technological change has had some impact in service labour organisation (Prentice et al., 2019). Jason Smith has demonstrated that while the proliferation of technologies and devices to articulate service labour has been clear and substantive, they "have had negligible effects on one key economic variable: labour productivity in the workplace" (2020: 11). Moreover, attempts to demonstrate how affective technologies have augmented labour in terms of productivity or profitability increases, rarely move beyond speculative forecasting (Ruel and Njoku, 2021; Prentice et al., 2019; Colbert et al., 2016). While affective technologies aim at the modulation and intensification of affective production, they do little to address the limitations confronted in the service sector in overcoming the inherent challenges to the production of relative surplus value.[4]

---

4   An interrogation of the production processes involved with producing datasets, ground truth codes, data mining and related productive practices and the yield of surplus value would be a fruitful line of inquiry to complement my argument here. Beverly Best (2024: 38–46) provides useful insight into the dynamics of surplus value production in relation to digital labour, identifying the work of data mining and the curation and creation of digital commodities out of the raw material of 'prosumers'. Likewise, Philip Jones (2021) demonstrates that the production of algorithmic intelligence is grounded in the exploitation human labour teaching the algorithm. It would be in these practices that the generation of higher degrees of surplus

There is little evidence that affective and emotion recognition technologies have led to significant increases in productivity in low-end service work. Nonetheless these technologies constitute a key element in the technical composition of class, in terms of how "time is managed or dictated ... in what conditions ... and what managerial or technological mechanisms mediate ... work" (Notes from Below, 2018: np). In a similar manner to the methods of affective management outlined in the previous chapter, affective technologies are best understood as marking a novel technique to manage productivity issues through new indexes of labour organisation. These indexes articulate labour performance in terms of affect, motivation, engagement, and emotion. Affective management in its technological guise is therefore not reducible to a form of Taylorism or neo-Taylorism (Mantello et al., 2023), but instead attempts to manage labour through the mobilisation of affective intensity, as opposed to output in given widgets. This complicates notions of efficiency. The relationship between affective labour and efficiency pursued by affective management techniques and affective technologies is concerned with worker performance of affect and, for example, the interpretation and development of indicators of sales rates of workers linked to affective engagement (Byron, et al., 2007; Bjerg and Staunaes, 2011). Affective management techniques thus work as elements alongside affective HCI in the workplace as an apparatus of compulsion and refraction, that concentrates "on the production and formation of intensity" (Bjerg and Staunaes, 2011: 139), that is to say the modulation and refracting of affective labour. Affective technologies impose a metrics and form of measure onto affective relations that generates a refraction of affect in the labour of the worker. The imposition of measure, and thus the transformation of affect into something quantifiable and reproducible, sharpens the relationship between affective labour and perceptions of worker efficiency.

7   Conclusion: Technological Determinism or Technical Ambivalence?

The use of affective technologies in the workplace functions as a directive upon the body to produce a particular affective performance. This performance in turn can be characterised as a modulation of affect on two levels, occurring simultaneously. Firstly, FER and SER technologies compel the worker's body to perform affect in particular ways. In other words, this is a modulation of

---

value in this field of services is located, feeding into the generation of value at the social level (Best, 2024; Mattick, 2018; Caffentzis, 2013; Rubin, 1973).

labour that compels the body to produce an affective intensity. The first element of the modulation of affect takes place in the circuit between the worker and the FER or SER encounter. The next element in the modulation of affect takes place in the second space of the shop floor, in the encounter between the worker and the bodies it engages. In other words, affective workers reproduce a particular form of engagement or relation with those they encounter, which has been impacted by the interaction with the emotion recognition interface. The labour they perform is certainly involved in the production of communication, relationship and affect. However, the organisation or the material constitution of this work problematises rather than confirms the literature concerning affective labour and affective or emotion recognition technologies.

Affective technologies cut against the ontological assumptions of postworkerism and the collapsing of the categories of life and labour, into a singular productive substance. However, a return to a compositionist analysis, which picks up on the emerging technological nexus involved in affective and immaterial labour, specifically affective HCI, provides a means to address these limitations. A compositionist approach allows us to situate affective computing and HCI, and emotion recognition technologies within a specific relationship produced by the valorisation process and in the workplace. Rather than a simple interaction between user and computer, in the context of the workplace, affective technologies can function as a directive upon the body of the worker in the first moment of interaction, which in turn produces a homogenous form of interaction between the worker (user) and those bodies it engages with on the job. By emphasising a compositionist approach, this chapter highlights the fundamental terms and limitations of the postworkerist theory of affective labour with respect to the technological organisation of affective labour.

As shown here, the use of emotion recognition technologies in job training and at work points towards a novel form of command in the workplace. The mobilisation of affect in management discourse and technique, specifically as a mechanism for intensified affective performance, couples with the deployment of affective technologies in the workplace. Taken together, these factors demonstrate the depth, breadth and direction of the integration of analyses of affect and the affective sciences into the objective command of labour. Emotion recognition technologies and affective management techniques, in this sense, represent an attempt to introduce/impose a form of measure in the production/circulation of affect in contemporary work arrangements, and thus to link quantifiable standards and notions of efficiency to the command of affective labour.

The critique of both affective techniques of management and affective technologies throughout Chapters 5 and 6, forces a reconsideration of the relationship between affect, labour, autonomy and capital. For postworkerism, affective or immaterial labour produces life itself, which is sapped by a form of capital external to productive relations. But the production of affect is the production of capital, not as a parasitic other atop the common of labour, but as directly implicated in the labour-capital relation. The technological nexus outlined in this chapter, illustrates how affect is internalised to the labour-capital relation. Further, the internalisation of affect to productive dynamics distorts and modulates affective labour. This said, we should be wary of a technological determinism arising from this nexus. The turn to affect as management and technology of work is in part a response to the recurring crises of motivation and engagement at work. At the same time, the widespread circulation of disaffection, resignation, refusal, exhaustion, and withdrawal indicate a counter politics of affect at work. Affective capital is thus characterised by a deep political ambivalence. The final chapter of this book will explore the implications of this notion of affective ambivalence in the composition of labour.

CHAPTER 7

Ambivalence and the Affective Compositions of Capital and Class

1   Introduction

Throughout this book, the affective compositions of class and capital have been traced through two tendencies. First, the Spinozist inflection of labour found in the perspectives of the postworkerists. Second, through the notion of capital as affect expressed through the affective sciences in both managerial and technological forms. These two iterations of affective production are in tension with one another while also fundamentally imbricated together. Given this contradiction, the question emerges of what it would mean to construct an affective politics of class composition without recapitulating the ontological presumptions of postworkerism, and while retaining a critique of the codification of affect as managerial and technological discipline upon labour. This chapter explores this tension through a return to the categories of class composition and the concept of affective composition. In doing so, I seek to offer a way to make sense and navigate the ambivalence of affective politics we confront today.

Theories of affect, and what can be termed affective politics, are entwined with the contradictory dynamics at play in the reproduction of capitalist social relations. Borrowing from Ajay Singh Chaudhary, affective politics are here taken to mean the myriad and often contradictory "*material* affects, feelings, passions and emotions all vital to political possibility" (2024: 131–132). Or as Lauren Berlant put it, to think affective politics is "to engage the affective aspects of class antagonism, labour processes, and communally generated class feeling" (Berlant, 2011: 64). As convergent crises intensify across the globe, affective politics are increasingly recognised as a significant terrain of contestation (Bosworth, 2022; Chaudhary, 2024; Thomas and Correa, 2015; Southall, 2024). Debates concerning the politics of work and labour constitute one key thread in the inquiry into affective politics (Read, 2024; Lordon, 2015; Thomas and Correa, 2015). This chapter theorises affective politics in relation to work through a critical consideration of contemporary class composition analysis. In terms of the managerial techniques and technological nexus of affect outlined in the previous two chapters, key elements of the affective politics of capital are constituted by motivation, engagement, and the modulated performance of affect as commands made upon labour. However, the labour-capital relation remains contested, the affective politics of capital are not absolute, and social relations are not technologically determined. Contradiction and antagonism are ever present conditions of capitalist production and reproduction, both within and beyond the workplace.

The widespread contemporary discussions of exhaustion, resignation, dissatisfaction, and disaffection at work have made visible the contested politics of affect. Affective capital has turned to emotional dispositions, motivation, engagement, and performance for the intensification of labour. However, this has been met with various iterations of labour withdrawal, which express a refusal of the affective regime of motivation and engagement. Viewing the labour-capital relation through the prism of affective politics helps to generate new insights into the antagonistic character of capitalist production today. Simultaneously, analysing the character of affective production within the labour-capital relation can illuminate the significance of affective politics in both the reproduction and refusal of capitalist social relations. In other words, the production of affect is marked by a fundamental ambivalence and contradictory character that assumes specific forms in relation to late capitalism's regimes of work.

The conceptualisation proposed in this final chapter builds upon the technical and political composition of class while also addressing social and affective composition.[1] Recent engagements with class composition analysis, in turns both scholarly and militant, have proposed the social and affective composition of class as categories in addition to the technical and political, thus widening the scope of analysis beyond the formalised workplace (Read, 2024; Notes from Below, 2018). The social composition of class draws attention to the dynamics involved in class contestation that take place beyond the workplace (Notes from Below, 2018; see also Cant, 2020: 9). The 'affective composition'

---

1   It is worth noting that the engagement with class composition analysis I present throughout this chapter is not a complete or practical one. While I am making an argument that the affective sciences constitute an element of the technical composition of class today, which in turn holds implications for the political, social and affective compositions of class, a key element of the political practice of class composition analysis is absent from my work. Namely, I have not undertaken any worker inquiries or militant research in writing this book. The political orientation of *operaismo* in tuning the analysis of class composition to practical outcomes informed by the subjective perspective of workers is of high value and importance in my view. Indeed, I would say it is fundamental to effective political work, and something I have sought to practice in my own political practice. However, this book remains an academic work that limits its contribution to a consideration of the technical composition of class through the critique of affective management and technology. This caveat is true of the present chapter and the book as a whole.

indicates that the labour-capital relation, its maintenance and contestation, involves an affective dimension across the spectrum of hope, fear, desire, pleasure, pain and so on (Lordon, 2015; Read, 2024; Fleming, 2015). The contribution in this chapter is to locate the contested character of affect, as articulated via affective labour and capital, as a key component in each of the iterations of class composition mentioned above. In returning to class composition analysis, I also draw attention to the insights of one of the original *operaisti*, Romano Alquati. Alquati's considerations of 'hyper-industrialisation' and 'ambivalence' as developed in his later work, are useful concepts for engaging the problem of affective and class composition today.

2   Class Compositions: Technical, Political, Social, Affective

As we saw in Chapter 3, class composition analysis is, in many ways, the enduring contribution of *operaismo* to Marxist and communist thinking and organisation. It presents an innovative reading of Marx, tooled specifically to the orientation of proletarian organisation within a dynamic historic process. Mirroring, in part at least, Marx's conception of the organic composition of capital, *operaismo* linked Marx's categories directly to a consideration of subjectivity and class politics. For Marx, the composition of capital was expressed in its value- and technical-compositions, with the impact of the latter on the former determining its organic composition (Marx, 1990: 762). The technical composition of capital is revealed in the relation between the means of production on one hand, and the labour power that is employed to work it on the other, within a given production process. The *operaisti* inflected this category with attention to the variable component of the composition of capital, in labour-power. As Steve Wright has put it, technical composition of class expresses labour's "material articulation within the organic composition of capital" (2002: 79). The character of the means of production and the production process, the position of labour within it, the tasks and elements of a particular labour process, are all part of the technical composition of class.

Without seeking to assert the primacy of the technical composition of class, in this section I re-engage the categories of class composition, including the social and affective dimensions, to highlight how these categories of analysis can be of use in understanding immaterial and affective production today. Importantly for the *operaisti* and in my argument, the technical composition of class marks the point of encounter between fixed and variable capital. However, the subjectivity of labour, the experience and behaviours of workers, forms a basis for organising class power in relationship to the technical organisation of work specifically, and to the social relations of capital in general. The technical composition of class, and thus capital, is always susceptible to disruption by the variability of worker activity. The form that worker organisation takes constitutes the political composition of class. Tronti's Copernican inversion of class perspective, namely that we must begin with the struggles of the working class, lent priority to the struggles of labour in shaping the dynamics of capitalist development. While this perspective can be caricatured as a simple rehashing of linearity in capitalist development, what stands out is the complex interaction between the technical organisation of production and reproduction processes, the dynamic formation of working-class organisation as subversive activity, and the organisational forms this activity takes over time.

The approach I take below diverges from that of postworkerism. In striking contrast with the analysis of class composition developed within *operaismo*, Negri (2013b) has clearly rejected the contemporary viability of any relationship between the technical and political composition of class. Negri has argued that "'doing politics today' is a project that cannot be legitimised ... simply by the use of workers' inquiry modelled on the twin elements of technical composition and political composition" (2013b: np). Politics, he continues, is no longer about "fiddling around between technical and political composition" but rather redefining what politics is (2013b: np). For Negri, within this redefined politics there is no longer any "recognisable technical compositions or political compositions, one being consequent on the other", but "rather a simplified composition and a real consistency". The real consistency is the result of living-labour re-appropriating fixed capital, a "continuous theft of machinic elements" – linguistic, affective, and intellectual – into the body of labour (2013b: np).

There are strengths to Negri's position outlined above. In part it addresses the critique of classical *operaismo's* formulation of class composition. This is evident at least in so far as Negri's above position rejects a reductionist relationship between the technical composition of class determining the political. He is correct to note that politics is not reducible to and exceeds the relationship to the technical composition of class. However, dispensing with the category of technical composition altogether risks losing important insights into the material articulation of labour, and thus working-class capacities to refuse labour. Where Negri does retain a consideration of the technical composition of class, it tends to be highly abstract or collapsed into the political composition of class. For example, Hardt and Negri argue that with immaterial production the "technical composition, far from the traditional asymmetry with its political composition ... approximates political experiences by proposing directly and explicitly the common" (2017: 238). Now, "the new technical composition and political composition are able to approach one another" (2017: 238). While this argument reflects postworkerism's insistence that each cycle of struggle elevates the socialisation of labour and class conflict to ever higher levels, the collapsing of the technical and political compositions of class, blunts the critique of labour in the present.

As we saw in Chapter 3, one of the strongest criticisms of the formulation of class composition analysis is the tendency to a determinate relationship between the technical and political composition of class. Related to this critique, is the fact that its conception of work is reduced to formalised workplaces and the terrain of struggle limited to that same sphere. In Chapter 3 the workerist-feminist critiques of these limitations were explored via a consideration of their radical break with classical *operaismo*. Informed by these critiques, and through a consideration of Marx's circuit of capital beginning with the formation of labour-power, the category of 'social composition' has been proposed by Notes from Below as a measure to address these limitations.

The category and lens of analysis found in social composition widens and complicates both the technical and political composition of class. As *Notes from Below* put it,

> Social composition combines with technical composition before the leap into political composition. Social composition is the specific material organisation of workers into a class society through the social relations of consumption and reproduction.
>
> 2018: np

And continuing,

> Social composition is primarily a way to understand how consumption and reproduction form part of the material basis of political class composition. It involves factors like: where workers live and in what kind of housing, the gendered division of labour, patterns of migration, racism, community infrastructure, and so on.
>
> 2018: np

Based on the above conditions, the framework developed by Notes from Below has sought to address the limitations of classical *operaismo* in identifying a terrain of struggle and composition beyond the formalised workplace. In contrast to postworkerism, the category of social composition addresses modes of social organisation and cooperation beyond the formal workplace while retaining the broader framework of class composition analysis and the critique of the labour-capital relation. This avoids both a technical determination of political class composition, and the ontological assumptions of postworkerism. Later in the chapter I return to the implications of the social composition of class, but first I turn to the consideration of affective politics and affective composition.

3   Affective Politics and the Affective Composition of Labour: Motivation and Refusal

There has been considerable attention given to affective politics in recent decades (Chaudhary, 2024; Bargetz, 2015). As the convergence of economic, political, and climatic crises continue unabated, a variety of counterposed forms of affective politics have emerged (Chaudhary, 2024; Read, 2024; Thomas and Correa, 2015; Mitropoulos, 2015; Gawne, 2020). While the catalysts for, and contexts in which affective politics take shape are varied, work and employment clearly constitute one of those conditions. Motivation, and related ideas of engagement and persistence, have been a central object of affective management. As both affective management and technology articulate an emphasis on motivation, attentiveness, and engagement, they become a part of the technical composition of class. But affective politics of refusal, withdrawal, exhaustion, and disaffection are prevalent factors in contemporary work and politics. This tension between motivation and refusal constitutes a key terrain of social and class contestation in contemporary capitalism. In this section of the chapter I will trace out an affective politics and composition of labour, built around the themes of motivation and refusal.

3.1   *Periodisation and Affect*
An attentiveness to the affective character of social and political contestation has long characterised political thinking and Marxism. Pointing to a range of Marxist theorists, from Walter Benjamin, Raymond Williams, Lenin to Luxemburg and Ruth Wilson Gilmore, Chaudhary argues that "not only is affect central – if often underplayed – in political theory ... it is far from alien to Marxism" (2024: 123). Theorising and identifying the relationship between affective relations and political movements, Chaudhary continues that, "immediate feeling must proceed into a more formally articulated grievance which must relate to material reality" (2024: 123). Chaudhary's point that the politics of affect become material through concrete articulation and action is important. It helps to understand affective politics as the articulation of both

grievance and negation on the one hand, and of affirming common objectives and increased capacities to act on the other. The dynamic between grievance, negation, and action forms a basis for thinking through affective politics.

Beyond the immediate grievance into action framework of affective politics, others have taken a broader, historical periodisation approach to thinking about capitalist history as a series of affective regimes. For example, Frederic Lordon (2015) offers a history of capitalism through a periodisation of affective compositions and economies. As Jason Read summarises, Lordon presents "three different regimes of capitalist exploitation, corresponding to the emergence of capitalism, the rise of consumer society, and contemporary neoliberalism" (2024: 59). Put differently, these correspond to the periods of primitive accumulation, Fordism, and neoliberalism. Each regime is anchored through dominant affects. For example, fear as driving force in the emergence of capitalism, frustration at work during Fordism that is exchanged for the pleasure of consumption, followed by pleasure in employment alongside indifference to the job in the era of neoliberalism (Read, 2024: 59–60). While Lordon's construction of historical affective regimes charts a terrain much wider than the present argument, his construction of the idea of an affective politics in relation to labour is important.

In contrast to Lordon's argument that the neoliberal era of capitalism is characterised by an affect of pleasure and indifference in employment, the Institute for Precarious Consciousness argues that anxiety characterises contemporary affect. The Institute for Precarious Consciousness (2014) (IPC) categorises and periodises the history of capitalist re/production around a series of what they call dominant, reactive affects: misery, boredom, and now anxiety. According to IPC, the period in which the dominant reactive affect was misery corresponded to the "modern era (up until the post-war settlement)" (IPC: np). The Fordist period was organised around the dominant reactive affect of boredom. The present, post-Fordist moment, IPC argues, is characterised by the affect of anxiety. The wider implications of historical periodisation via affective politics are not the concern of my argument. However, the IPC's insistence that a political engagement with affect must reflect the complex relationships between public affects (see Berlant, 2011), private affects and work is telling. By suggesting such a relationship, IPC outlines an image of post-Fordist capitalism that captures the ambivalent and contested nature of affective composition.

Within the postworkerist iteration of affective politics, Bifo's comments on depression, panic, anxiety, and the overstimulation produced by semiocapitalism resonate here. Bifo (2009a) insists that panic and depression are the characteristic affects and pathologies of late capitalism. For Bifo "the mind must go to work in conditions of economic and existential precarity" (2009a: 100–101). As a result, "the time of life is subjected to work by an action of fractalisation of consciousness and experience which breaks the coherence of lived time" (Berardi, 2011a: 200). The conditions of panic, anxiety and depression lead Bifo to argue that reactionary politics are the only foreseeable mode of composition in the current conjuncture (LaborInArt: 2014). Indeed, for Bifo:

> Depression implies a change of speed. Only if language, culture and politics can interpret and translate into signs the slowing down that is necessary and urgently demanded by the psychic and social organism, will depression be able to evolve towards a new, happy form of exchange of human and world.
>
> BERARDI, 2011a: 197

Bifo here departs from the accelerationist inflection of postworkerism (see Negri, 2014). However, there are two limitations in Bifo's articulation of affective politics above which are reiterated in his consideration of the pandemic crisis and its aftermath (Berardi, 2022). The first is that it is unable to articulate a mode of affective composition as an expression of class struggle. Second, that his consideration of affective politics recapitulates the separation of labour and capital typical of postworkerism, only this is inflected negatively.

A further consideration of a broad affective politics is found in Chaudhary's theorisation of exhaustion in the context of the climate crisis. For Chaudhary, "exhaustion is an affective matrix" encapsulating "the exhaustions of political forms; of and with whole ways of life; the exhaustion of living or resisting the 24/7 world; engineering, technical and even aesthetic exhaustions" (2024: 154). Chaudhary's articulation of exhaustion encompasses a wider set of concerns than my engagement with the affective composition of labour and does not engage with class composition analysis, but his commentary on work is still illuminating. The exhaustion of climate margins for addressing the crisis and the velocity of the extractive circuit, is linked directly to the proliferation of "hyper-work" and "the speed-up, the exhaustion" across various modes of labour (Chaudhary, 2024: 56). In defining exhaustion as the dominant affect of our time, Chaudhary states that "exhaustion is not some rhetorical gesture, discursive fiction, or new theoretical fantasy. Exhaustion outlines the historical bloc, the mass political subject of this conjuncture" (2024: 150). Indeed, "this life, this civilisation, is above all *exhausting*" (Chaudhary, 2024: 150). I will return to the considerations of indifference, anxiety, and exhaustion as pronounced affects of the present, but first the question of an affective composition of labour needs to be addressed.

3.2   *Affective Compositions of Labour*

Jason Read's (2024) construction of the affective composition of labour, developed in part through an engagement with Lordon and de Jour, helps to clarify the connection between immediate work experience and wider historical periodisation. Read argues that affective compositions are produced within a given work regime or firm, and within a wider historical context. However, one is not necessarily reducible to the other. Read argues that,

> every labour relation has its particular affective composition. The joy and sadness, desire and frustration, are two sides of the same relation. This affective composition can be understood in its broader, macro sense, in which early capitalism, Fordism, and neoliberalism are organisations of desire, or suffering. Or it can be understood on a smaller scale, as each job, each work situation, has its own affective dimension, its particular pleasures and frustrations ... As such, the affective composition of labour is both something orchestrated at the level of the firm and something that exceeds it.
>
> 2024: 63

Continuing, Read states that affective compositions arise within a given labour relation, while also expressing general orientations toward work as a whole:

> As much as there is an affective composition of labour, the organisation of the various affects in and through a specific workplace, there is an affective composition *toward* labour, as work itself is the source of common hopes and fears.
>
> 2024: 74

The notion of an affective composition of labour outlined above, is applicable to any kind of work. In other words, the affective composition of labour above does not imply that the labour process is engaged in any kind of emotional or affective labour (Read, 2024: 63). In this regard, an affective composition of labour is a "a particular articulation of fears, hopes, and desires, even when there is not a demand to embody or elicit any particular affect as part of the job" (Read, 2024: 63). While this broader condition of affective composition is important, a specific consideration that emerges in modes of affective production sheds a further light on the aspects of technical class composition.

To theorise the affective composition of labour as an element of the technical composition of class, it is necessary to critique how the affective sciences come to articulate labour. It is certainly true that an aspect of affective composition includes how

> appearing to love one's job becomes part of the job as motivation and professional attitude becomes the measure or standard of performance. One must constantly demonstrate one's commitment and passion to work for the manager or supervisor.
>
> READ, 2024: 64

Such a command upon labour may function as an empty ideology or generate genuine affective attachment (Read, 2024: 61–62).[2] It is worth noting that the need to perform commitment and motivation might better be summed up as what I/O Psychologists would call a job attitude – how does one feel toward their job. However, what is missing in either instance is how the affective sciences aim for affect to be the medium through which labour is managed, and not only a disposition towards a job or work. This distinction is in part captured by Read, when he states that "the demand to produce a particular affect ... often overlaps with the demand to embody a particular aspect, [for example] the willingness to commit fully to a job" (2024: 63). But as valuable as this insight is, even this articulation of the issue doesn't quite capture the implications of the integration of the affective sciences into management and mediation.

The novelty of affective management frameworks, as we explored in Chapter 5, is the identification of affect as a terrain of intervention and work arrangement. This is a different issue to that of whether an employee has a good or bad attitude toward their job or their performance of such. Instead, the focus is on acknowledging the changing affective states of workers over periods of time, and finding ways to articulate these flows in accordance with the objectives of work. The affect of motivation as a function of management is not only articulated in the imperative to act as if you are dedicated to the job or the company. It is also articulated by managerial efforts to stimulate activity through implementation of goal setting, structure of

---

2 See Jason Read (2024: 61–62) for a discussion on the contrast between Peter Fleming's and Frederic Lordon's views on affective management and motivation.

workday, and the incorporation of analyses of affective appraisal and valence into organisational settings. Affective management incorporates "the individual, organisational and transactional determinants of affective responses in the workplace and their relation to individual and organisational effectiveness" (Kanfer and Klimoski, 2002: 473). As explored in earlier chapters, this has located the affective states of workers, both positive and negative, as the field to address through performance strategies. Motivation, in this instance, is less about commitment to the job, but a variable to be managed in relation to performance measures and goals (Dorian, 2021). As a mode of management, this notion of motivation is not restricted to immaterial forms of production. However, it is particularly attuned to forms of labour with intangible outcomes and where the intensification of labour cannot be increased, for example, through mechanisms of assembly line speed up.

4   Affective Sciences and the Technical Composition of Class

To consider the technical composition of class is to draw attention to the organisation of work, the encounter between fixed and variable capital within a given production process, the technological mediation of labour, and the techniques of management confronted by labour. The design of work and organisation, the forms of cooperation, the mobilisation of the affective sciences within contemporary modes of immaterial production should be considered as elements in the technical composition of class. The affective sciences, as demonstrated in Chapters 5 and 6, function as components in both the managerial techniques and forms of technological mediation of affective labour. The critique of the affective sciences as components of the technical composition of class stands in contrast to the characterisation of affective production, cooperation, value, and measure as articulated by postworkerism. More significantly, the critique of class composition opens new lines of inquiry into the contested character of affective politics.

The mobilisation of affect in managerial techniques, when framed as an element of class composition, has significant implications for the contemporary theorisation of affective labour and cooperation. Affective management clearly identifies affect as a dynamic internal to the labour-capital relation. From the perspective of affective management, affect is not considered separate from the objectives of work and productivity. Indeed, as the discussions of affective management in Chapter 5 illustrated, affect is positioned as a key variable within the intensification of labour (Slaby et al., 2019; Roemmich et al., 2023; Weiss and Cropanzano, 1996). Affective management techniques aim to link affective labour directly to the efficiency of labour and are implicated in the organisation of cooperation in the affective production processes.

One of the key shifts that emerges with the integration of affect theory into management is the movement from an emphasis on the direct measure of output to a focus upon the management of intensity, effort and persistence via affect. The integration of affect theory into managerial technique rearticulates the concepts of intensity, duration and persistence as modes of measure. From the perspective of affective measurement and management, while output and productivity remain key objectives, the principal target of intervention is the affective state of the worker for purposes of motivation, engagement and persistence. As Jamie Woodcock, of *Notes from Below*, has demonstrated, there is a distinction between time and motion studies techniques of management in a manufacturing setting and management through the affective intensities of motivation that takes place, for example, in service settings. Woodcock elaborates this in his research in call centres. Importantly, each approach, that is of either time and motion studies or affective management, articulates an encounter between fixed and variable capital at the level of management, but in distinct ways (2017: 52–59). The shift toward affective management reflects not only a difference in the character of the production process between tangible and intangible outputs, but also the integration of the affective sciences in articulating new needs in the organisation of work (Woodcock, 2017). The character of affect is thus internal to the labour-capital relation – affect is a component of commodity production and a condition in the mediation of the labour that produces affect. The critique of affect therefore becomes important in the contestation of work and any consideration of the political composition of class in relation to affective production.

Techniques of affective management unsettle the image of the self-organisation of immaterial production as posited by postworkerism. Affective management poses the relationship between labour, affect and value not as something externalised or in the form of the expropriation of cooperation. Rather affect is situated as a dynamic and object within the labour-capital relation, and thus subject to contestation and bound to a relationship of exploitation (Woodcock, 2019). What emerges here is a very different image of how affect functions as a variable of labour to that which is theorised by postworkerism. Against the image of an automatic cooperative dimension to affective labour, affect here figures as the force through which individual workers are integrated into a team and subject to managerial imperatives (Slaby et al., 2019). The particular attention to the management of intensity and persistence, and the attempt to locate both negative and positive affects within theories of management and work performance suggests that affective management theory is opening a new direction in managerial practice.

A further illustration of how affect becomes internal to the process of both management and cooperation is offered in the concept of affective arrangements (Slaby et al., 2019). In defining an affective arrangement, Jan Slaby et al. "mean a material-discursive formation as part of which affect is patterned, channelled, and modulated in recurrent and repeatable ways" (2019: 5). My analysis of both affective management and technologies in the workplace correspond to this definition of an affective arrangement. Affective arrangements suggest that a particular approach to standardisation and quantification remains important in managerial approaches to immaterial modes of labour. The work-team is proposed by Slaby et al. (2019) as an example to explore how affect is channelled and modulated within an affective arrangement. Work-teams

> are local set-ups that work by targeting and harnessing the domain of personal and affective relations between individuals. Affective arrangements – such as teamwork settings in corporate offices – both generate, stabilise, and exploit affective relations; relational affect is what these constellations 'run on'.
>
> SLABY ET AL., 2019: 6

"Affective arrangements" constitute an infrastructure for the articulation of labour in a given work context. Slaby et al. (2019) argue that the form of the team as a management device is only part of the whole, and it is the affective dynamics between the team members once work is under way that really matters. Insofar as Slaby et al. emphasise a Spinozist theory of affect, this argument is an important rejoinder to psychological theories of affect in the workplace, as explored in Chapter 5. Nonetheless, from a class composition perspective, an affective arrangement is a mode of management through the affective relations of labour. As such, affect is further demonstrated to be internal to the labour-capital relation, the modes of organisation, and the forms of management that articulate labour. Which is to say, rather than marking a separation between labour and capital in the cooperative powers of work, affect is both a point of articulation and contestation.

The technical composition of affect can also be explored in the technological mediation of labour that is implemented through affective technologies. The mediation of affective labour via emotion recognition technologies can be articulated and understood simultaneously as being of the worker and yet produced/performed on terms imposed by capital. In other words, the internalisation of affect to the labour-capital relation does not, indeed cannot produce a complete separation between labour and affect. However, the imperative to perform affect, and the summoning of certain affects to be performed, takes place in an organisational context beyond the control of the worker. The deployment of affective technologies through which affective labour is expressed aims to produce a curated affective performance for the interests of the firm. Technologies that modulate and measure affect, effectively incorporate the production of affect into the imperatives of management and valorisation. The cooperative relations that are produced in such encounters are thus not automatically creative or outside of capital, but rather are expressed through it. Moreover, as we saw in the previous chapter, the very production of emotion and affect as indexes against which labour is measured, further articulates affect as a component of the technical composition of class. As a result, the production of affect is in practice a component of capital and the valorisation process.

From a labour process perspective, the standardisation and performance of correct emotional labour can be read as a further inflection of Arlie Hochschild's (2003 [1983]: 97–99) analyses of emotional labour. Hochschild notes the cultivation of correct emotional disposition or embodiment that occurs in the training and recruitment of airline hostesses. The use of affective and emotion recognition technologies in the training of affective performance adds a further dimension to the management and standardisation of affective labour. Affective and emotion recognition technologies aim for a standardisation of affective performance through, for example, the measurement of the physical features of the individual, calculating and processing the image to produce an ideal to be replicated. In this way the imperative in the use of the smile scan, or vocal training in call centres, is to standardise the individual performance of labour.

The discussion so far has outlined how the affective sciences, in combination with wider patterns of employment, challenge the postworkerist conception of affective production and cooperation. Framing the affective sciences as a component of the technical composition of class, helps to identify how affect is a contested dynamic in contemporary capitalism. To draw attention to an enduring relevance of the category of technical composition, is not to suggest the technical determination of labour. It is merely to highlight particular and potential points of contradiction in the labour-capital relation. In other words, the categories of class composition remain useful within the grammar of critique. Specifically, interrogating the character of work organisation, labour processes, techniques of management and technological mediation, provides insight to the potential forms of class movements. Moreover, in order to retain a critique of labour in the present, and avoid the ontological assumptions of postworkerism, it is necessary to view affective politics as internal, at least in part, to the labour-capital relation. In other words, it is possible to link the affective sciences to the material articulation of labour-power within the composition of capital (Wright, 2002: 78). As a result, rather than affective politics marking a fundamental separation between labour and capital as per postworkerism, the managerial and technological mediation of labour via the affective sciences indicates the internalisation of affect within the labour-capital relation, and the need to critique the implications of this condition.

5 On Ambivalence

Evident in the above analyses of class composition and the affective sciences, is a distinct tension in the expression of affective politics. The tension is most clear in the clash between the affective sciences as an articulation of capital both managerially and technologically on the one hand, and a condition of labour irreducible to variable capital even while rendered as such, on the other. It is useful now to restate the question posed at the outset of the chapter: how could an affective politics of class struggle form without recapitulating the ontological assumptions of postworkerism and while retaining a critique of the internalisation of the affective sciences as capital? This question can be addressed in part by an attention to ambivalence, the "elements that go in different and opposite directions within a phenomenon" (Roggero, 2023: 112). Before moving into a consideration of affective composition in the following section, it is useful to touch on Romano Alquati's articulation of ambivalence, to provide a backdrop against which affective composition can be considered.

Alquati was among the first *operaisti*, whose early investigations into class composition at FIAT and then Olivetti set the tone for his own unique trajectory within *operaismo*, while also producing the very tools that defined the tendency (Alquati, 2013 [1961]; Alquati, 2013 [1964]). In developing the practice of co-research and class composition analysis, Alquati's work contributed to the fundamentals of *operaismo* politically and methodologically. The richness of Alquati's life and work has been explored by Evan Calder Williams (2013), tracing out his particular style and contributions to *operaismo*. Here I draw attention to two concepts elaborated in his later work and adopted by his collaborators: hyper-industrialisation and ambivalence (Alquati, 2001; Armano and Sachetti, 2009).

Firstly, hyper-industrialisation can be helpful in thinking through the implications of immaterial and affective production explored in this book. For Alquati, hyper-industrialisation marks a condition characterised by "the unfolding effective subsumption of the whole of human experience to social reproduction" (Sacchetto et al., 2013: np). While at a glance hyper-industrialisation sounds like the postworkerist argument concerning the real subsumption of labour to capital, there are important differences in the framing and implications of the argument. For Alquati (2001), hyper-industrialisation leads to an ever-widening integration of social activity to the objectives of capital accumulation. Hyper-industrialisation can include the incorporation of forms of production into the circuit of industrial capital. For Marx, "industrial capital is the only mode of existence of capital in which not only the appropriation of surplus-value or surplus-product, but also its creation, is a function of capital" (1975: 135–136). But following Emiliana Armano, hyper-industrialisation is also "a transversal and extensive way of organising not only the serialised and proceduralised production typical of manufacturing, but all human action more generally, including the sphere of reproduction" (2024: 38). The patterns and modes of subsumption in each instance produce specific configurations of labour and specific questions about the composition of a production process. Hyper-industrialisation then, does not express or result in an ever-higher socialisation of class subjectivity, as found for example in Negri's notions of the socialised worker and multitude. Nor does hyper-industrialisation imply a dislocation of labour and capital as in the theories of cognitive capitalism, affective and immaterial production, or the autonomous common. Coming to terms with the implications of hyper-industrialisation is thus not, for Alquati, a "question of reversing technical composition into political composition", as those who emphasise the General Intellect suggest (2001: 203). Instead, hyper-industrialisation represents a proliferation of problems to be investigated, only after which is it possible to understand the dynamics of accumulation and the peculiarities of class composition across wider social terrain.

Turning now to Alquati's concept of ambivalence, while he rejects the argument concerning the socialisation of subjectivity that removes the intricacies of class experience, subjectivity remains crucial for his work (Sacchetto et al., 2013). In Alquati's view, labour remains internal to the capital relation and the encounter between fixed and variable capital remains an object of critique. Alquati recapitulates the variability of labour as capital, once theorised by Tronti (2019 [1966]) and explored in Chapter 3. The potential for workers to act against their condition as capital, and for productive materials to be used other than for the purpose of accumulation, remains central to his analysis. As Alquati puts it,

> ambivalence ... has its heart in the theoretical Marxian-Trontian knot of
> the double character of the use-value of the human-living-work-capacity,
> singular and collective, and not just [in] work, but [in] the worker them-
> selves ... [who] can stop working and even go against work.
>
> 2001: 39

Beyond this subjective iteration, ambivalence emerges as contestation between the contradictory potentials for "knowledges and activities [to bend] to the autonomy of subjects" or alternatively to "be expropriated within the codification of capital's formalised technical-scientific language" (Sacchetto et al., 2013: np). Alquati's concept of ambivalence thus articulates the tension between conditions and materials of a specific production process and the potential for their subversion. Ambivalence retains a critical perspective but without a certain rigidity that can emerge in strict categorisations of technical and political composition of class.

Returning briefly to the concepts of postworkerism can help to illuminate the importance of Alquati's perspective. Gigi Roggero has advanced the critique of postworkerism via the work of Alquati. Writing about the common, Roggero, drawing from Alquati, states that

> the common is rooted in a historically determined ambivalence: the
> cooperation that constitutes the material framework of the possibility of
> autonomy, is at the same time cooperation for capitalist exploitation.
>
> 2020: 163

Roggero's articulation of ambivalence informs my analysis of the kind of ambivalence at stake in affective production. For Alquati, a fundamental condition of ambivalence characterises the labour-capital relation and the forms of hyper-industrialisation. The hyper-industrialisation of affective production sees the application of managerial and technological methods of measure and production to articulate labour. However, ambivalence, expressed through the actions, decisions, behaviours, and repurposing of materials by labour, opens the possibility for a counter-politics of class solidarity and action.

The insights of Alquati on ambivalence have been taken up and developed in the context of post-Fordist, gig, tertiary, and precarious work (Leonardi et al., 2019; Murgia et al., 2017; Armano et al., 2024). Leonardi et al. (2019) explore ambivalence in the food delivery sector, emphasising how the same platforms that articulate the exploitation of labour, become a tool of self-organisation of the riders themselves. *Notes from Below* editor Calum Cant (2019), explores a similar dynamic in his work as a delivery rider.[3] Reporting on the labour process and cooperation in food delivery services, Cant found that "the stages of the labour process don't rely on the cooperation between one worker and another, they can have the opposite effect" (Cant, 2019: 37). Interestingly, this issue also undermined the capacity to manage through affective relations in terms of disposition toward the job:

> The 'black box' nature of the labour process actually undermines the potential for workers to have much buy-in or pride in their work. Commitment relies on links being built between workers and managers leading to everyone seeing the whole company as a happy family – and these links were exactly what the app prevented.
>
> CANT, 2019: 41

However, this blockage was overcome in the context of self-organised resistance. Cant's analysis of the processes of self-organisation among delivery riders that resulted in strike activity, provides a good example of the ambivalence of composition in this sector. As Cant puts it,

> Two strike movements had emerged in two supposedly unorganisable areas: precarious hospitality work, and precarious food-platform work. The crossover soon began to be solidified into practical cooperation.
>
> 2019: 97

In arriving at this point, the apps that articulated labour as a component of capital, and inhibited cooperation among workers while on the job, were repurposed in their self-organisation, such that "cooperation began with a group chat. Key organisers from a few different unions came together to discuss how this momentum could be converted into joint strike action" (Cant, 2019: 98). This reflects the findings of Leonardi et al. (2019) in the use of platforms and chats by workers to consolidate their forms of on-the-job cooperation in solidarity and struggle with one another. For Leonardi et al., ambivalence

---

3   Tim Christiaens (2022) provides a useful analysis of these same dynamics in the digital economy, further elaborating on the question of composition and autonomy in relationship to postworkerist theories of immaterial production. While Christiaens does not directly consider the notion of ambivalence articulated by Alquati, his discussion of Tronti and the critique of labour identifies a similar set of conditions as that expressed in ambivalence. Interestingly, and as I commented in an earlier chapter, Christiaens holds to a substantialist, embodied notion of value.

leads to the possibility of "how connectivity can open up the possibility of transforming logistical territories into trenches of resistance" and "workers' recomposition" (2019: 168). In these examples, labour as a "form of existence of capital" (Marx) remains the site of critique and negation. While the cooperation of labour for accumulation is articulated through capital as algorithm and platform, the exercise of ambivalence opens a counter, antagonistic form of cooperation to contest capital.

I suggest that the integration of the affective sciences into the imperatives of capitalist valorisation can be understood through Alquati's notion of hyper-industrialisation, producing new contours of class composition to be explored. But as we have seen above, hyper-industrialisation does not mark the erasure of class refusal. Alquati's perspective on ambivalence can express an affirmationist and negationist politics without collapsing one into the other. Affective politics can be read along such a definition of ambivalence. Therefore, we should consider affective politics as an element of both managerial and technological mediation internal to the material articulation of labour, as well as of political movement against capital.

6   Ambivalent Affects

Approaching the contestation of affective politics through a consideration of ambivalence indicates tensions, behaviours, and terrains of conflict that can be explored through, while also complicating, the categories of class composition. If we recall, ambivalence captures the tension between the use of techniques or forms of production that might be subverted away from the work logic ends of capital, and toward the formation of working-class practices of resistance. As Roggero puts it, "valorising one aspect of ambivalence is what enriches a process, against that aspect of it that supports what is hostile to us" (2023: 113). At the same time, the forms of affective production explored throughout this book complicate the idea of ambivalence, insofar as the instruments of production to be repurposed are not always clearly distinct from the body of labour. This implies that the subjective element of ambivalence is even more pronounced in conditions of affective production. The use of platforms in delivery riding, for example, demonstrates a clear exercise of ambivalence toward the practice of worker resistance with the repurposing of platforms and apps. But how this might look in the context of affective production can be less clear. In this final section of the chapter, various approaches to affective ambivalence in relationship to work are proposed. The examples explored below are not exhaustive. They are offered as indications of where shared grievances are taking shape which may indicate the initial stages of a collective formation of subjectivity, to illustrate in skeletal form methods of affective ambivalence, and to point to potential directions that the concept of affective ambivalence could be developed in future (co)research.

Within the contestation of the affective composition of labour, one element at stake is the negation of the affective regime of capital, namely motivation, engagement, and dedication in work. Viewed through a negationist prism, the affective politics of exhaustion, disaffection, indifference, and refusal in relation to work and capitalist reproduction, assume a clear inflection. In a context where motivation, engagement, and imperatives to perform affect are summoned "as if [they are] not work", then the refusal of this labour manifests in peculiar forms and unexpected ways (Mitropoulos, 2012: 174). In discussing her concept of the oikonomia, Angela Mitropoulos argues that:

> perhaps the oikos is haunted not by communism – at least not as it has come to be understood as party, or state or policy – but by disaffection, a detachment from the oikonomic that signals attachments otherwise, and for this reason, barely decipherable by conventional political analyses.
>
> MITROPOULOS, 2012: 174–175

The emphasis on disaffection that Mitropoulos points to is a useful way of framing a refusal of the affective regimes of capital. Moreover, the idea of the illegibility of disaffection by conventional analyses, resonates with the sentiment of early *operaismo* in looking for "workers' informal and often non-verbalised transmission of behaviours antagonistic to the logic of valorisation by means of the 'cooperative' structure they were forced to endure" (Wright, 2002: 57). In pointing to disaffection, Mitropoulos raises the question of the myriad ways in which attachments otherwise may form, without any prescribed direction for how they should. This provides a useful framing for the three iterations of affective ambivalence I look at below: social ambivalence, ambivalence against management, and technological ambivalence. Each example provides an insight into the tensions characteristic of the affective composition of class.

6.1 *Social Ambivalence*

Amplified during the experience of the pandemic, there has been a growing dissonance expressed between the expectations to demonstrate motivation and commitment to and on the job, while often feeling exhausted, anxious, burnt out, and disaffected with work. As Sarah Jaffe argues, the affective regime of work has begun to break under the weight of wage stagnation, overwork, and the unfulfilled promise of existential reward (2021). The conditions of this breakdown lead to new articulations of long entrenched social contradictions and conflicts. In terms of the antagonism of affective compositions between labour and capital, the general tension between motivation and disaffection is one of its primary characteristics. Underpinning this process, at least in part, is the proliferation of jobs in the low-end service sector. While the definition of services is notoriously unwieldy (Smith, 2020), it remains notable that, for example in the US,

> blue-collar manual (manufacturing, mining, construction) has steadily lost ground to the booming low-wage service sector, which comprises everything from retail and sales to food service, nursing assistance, and home health care.
>
> COOPER, 2024:109

Similar trends, with fastest job growth in healthcare and related services, are evident in Australia (Kaplan, 2024), while the broadly defined service sector continues to grow in China, UK and elsewhere. The following examples of affective contestation, indicating what we might hypothesise as new elements of refusal and class behaviours, have been expressed primarily in the low-wages service sector or immaterial white-collar sectors.

The most popular expressions of an affective politics of refusal had a viral life on social media, while also reflecting real and specific antagonisms and practices. In response to the pressures of work and reproduction in China, famously called the 996-work regime, the Tang Ping (Lying Flat) manifesto became very popular. The 996-work week indicates a six-day, twelve-hour day week, which saw popular criticism on Chinese social media. The critique of 996 resonated among "tech company employees in 2019" exposing the reality of "simmering discontent among young Chinese professional employees over the toxic work culture involving long working hours" (Wen, 2023: np). Related to the critiques of 996, was the notion of *neijuan*, or involution. *Neijuan* is a "term that the metropolitan Chinese use to describe the ills of their modern lives, their sense of frantically treading water in a hyper-competitive society" (Wildcat, 2021: np). The critique of involution marked a connection between the individual and collective experience of stagnation, even though it may not have resulted in collective acts of rebellion.

Other expressions of refusal also found popular expressions in China as well. Tang Ping, or lying-flat, reflected an active-passive reclamation of time in the context of involution, the structure of ever-declining returns on effort given to a system that only ever demands more of you. The Tang Ping Manifesto, described as an anti-work movement (Wen, 2023: np), embraced the refusal of motivation and work, seeking to articulate the collective, refusal to go to school, to work, to have children, and to have a family, and so it naturally has the potential to link a whole generation of people who are mostly oppressed under the current order. It tries to contact all those who refuse coercion and obedience, men and women, workers and the unemployed, citizens, farmers and nomads, hooligans, students and intellectuals, heterosexuals, homosexuals and other queer people, vagrants and pensioners ... what other idea could quietly build the secret affinities to set the stage for a general strike?

ANONYMOUS TANG PINGIST, 2021: np

While often seen as a middle-class phenomenon, in which "middle-class or educated groups were becoming more and more desperate with regard to the prospects for upward mobility and the accumulation of wealth", the material underpinnings of this withdrawal in wage stagnation and declining hopes in the future were shared across sectors (Zuoyue, 2023: np). A commonality in refusal was expressed in "discourses ranging from 'corporate slavery' to 'involution', from 'lying flat' to 'runology'... all revealing an ever-greater loss of faith in the political-economic system" (Zuoyue, 2023: np).[4] Wen speculates on these elements of popular expression marking the behaviours of a new cycle of struggle, constituting a "rudimentary form of class consciousness, insofar as people have begun to recognize that their predicament transcends their individual experiences" (2023: np). While the outcomes and directions of these types of activity, and how they register at the individual and collective level can be difficult to read, it is worth considering the connection between these behaviours and the broader composition of class.

In the US, Australia, and elsewhere, the Great Resignation, Quiet Quitting, and a relative spike in strike activity illustrated, again, a contestation over work, and its affective regime of motivation and commitment. The refusal of motivation and commitment, this time expressed in the 'Great Resignation' and 'Quiet Quitting' has concerned managers and capital in recent years. As business and management scholar Alexander Serenko (2023; 2023a) has explored, both the 'Great Resignation' and 'Quiet Quitting', reflect deeper seeded issues in the contemporary landscape of work. The Great Resignation was primarily a phenomenon of the low-wage service industries, while quiet quitting was pronounced among the white-collared labour force (Baker, 2023). The 'Great Resignation' refers to the increase in voluntary quits, across a range of sectors of the economy. Between May and July of 2021, 11.5 million people

---

4 'Runology' referes to the desire to leave China amidst worsening economic prospects. It was an online phenomenon during the years of pandemic lockdown in China.

quit their jobs in the US (Dirnbach, 2021). While primarily a US phenomenon, and owing to a range of causes and conditions, it had global iterations. 'Quiet Quitting', in part an informal work-to-rule approach to doing no more than one's job description, often tended to involve a disidentification with work as well. These phenomena arise from factors related to motivation, stress, and antagonism to bosses. Serenko states that "people were not extrinsically motivated to put additional time and effort into their jobs" and were sick of unpaid overtime (2023: 31). Workers also felt the need to "take care of their mental health, reduce stress, eliminate pressure, avoid further burnout and achieve a work-life balance". Other reasons for quitting, quietly or not, included the fact that employees "held grudges against their managers or their entire organisation" (Serenko, 2023: 31–32). With some caution, it is possible to entertain the idea that these practices express latent antagonisms not yet collectively expressed.

It is important not to overstate the Great Resignation and Quiet Quitting beyond their immediate contexts of the pandemic economy and labour market, or as constituting a resurgence of class organisation and conflict. Arguably, the general practice of quitting, whether in the form of leaving a job or in the refusal to do any more than the bare essential, manifests primarily as individual action. While an uptick in strike activity also shaped labour-capital relations in recent years, these are not historic heights in numbers of industrial actions, numbers of workers involved, and have not bucked the trend of declining strike activity (Smith, 2021). At the same time, these phenomena are part of an interesting story when placed in the historical context of slow growth and service economy expansion since at least 2008 (Smith, 2021; Benanav, 2021; Gittleman, 2022). Indeed, Erik Baker (2023) notes that if one was to trace the contemporary disenchantment with work, the narrative would have to begin with the 2008 economic crisis, while quit rates have been increasing in the US since 2013 (Dirnbach, 2021). From this vantage point, the popular expressions of detachment and disengagement from work expressed during the pandemic, mark a continuation of trends. The pandemic crisis inaugurated the first services recession then crisis, and a social expression of affective ambivalence. While the widespread social articulation of disaffection in work looks for its collective expression, the affective cadence of it remains telling – oriented not to an expression of the dignity of labour in employment, but against the indignities and impoverishment of work.

6.2   *Ambivalence against Affective Management*

The popular expressions of disengagement help to see a subjective iteration of ambivalence in relation to the affective regime of capital. But it is worth considering further examples of how forms of affective ambivalence manifest.

Articulations of affective ambivalence can be found in workplace organising practices that cultivate and deploy affective politics as a practice of solidarity or resistance. As indicated earlier in this chapter, the affective composition of labour incorporates the fears, hopes, pain and so on in relation to work (Read, 2024), as well as the management of labour through affect. Affective arrangements were also presented as means through which the work team facilitates affective management (Slaby et al., 2019). Affective management is thus not only about job attitudes, but as we saw in Chapter 5, centres the dynamics of affective relations as the terrain of work intensification and intervention. The question of ambivalence thus manifests in the subversion of this terrain.

The affective modes of management can have specific impacts on workers, such that a feeling of emotional or affective drain or burnout arises from the conditions of work (Roemmich et al., 2023). Specific forms of burnout or dissonance have led to a reconsideration of the concept of alienation within affective production. Indeed, an emphasis on alienation resonates with Jamie Woodcock's experience working in a call centre (2017: 54). For Woodcock, the "affective package that workers are required to perform during the labour process is demanding" (2017: 53). This leads to an "emotional dissonance [as] a specific alienating effect derived from the form of affective labour" (Woodcock, 2017: 54). While Woodcock discusses alienation as a specific experience of affective labour, he also emphasises the realities of exploitation, and the persistence of conflict as workers confront their own labour objectified within the production process. Importantly, these are linked to forms of workplace resistance.

Woodcock provides a useful discussion of informal work resistance in call centre work, drawing from Kate Mulholland's (2004) important analysis of workplace contestation. Mulholland's study itself provides fascinating insights into "the formation of informal workplace collective attitudes and practices among Irish call centre workers" and argues "that this is a neglected and important aspect of workplace resistance" (2004: 709). Moreover, Mulholland's study demonstrates that informal, collective action by workers undermines the claims of management theorists that see an alignment between individual worker subjectivity and company goals (2004: 718). Widening the scope of what can be considered workplace resistance, both Mulholland (2004) and Woodcock (2017), press upon the need to include often hard to see forms of worker resistance. One example provided by Woodcock, in which motivational sessions are turned into a means to reduce work time stands out here in terms of affective ambivalence. As Woodcock puts it,

> At the start of each three-and-a-half hour shift there was a buzz session with the supervisors. These played a motivational role as well as providing

> an opportunity for management to inculcate workers with the various
> rules of the workplace.
>
> 2017: 105

Buzz sessions functioned like a Q&A session, but the length of these sessions was never defined. Woodcock outlines how workers could ask questions in such a way as to extend the session and reduce the time on the phones (2017: 106). He argues that "a successful extension involved a careful balancing act of feigning interest, posing questions and stimulating discussion" and that a "collective approach emerged around this" to best extend the session. According to Woodcock, practices involved subtle forms of cooperation that saw a "balancing act of feigning interest, posing questions and stimulating discussion" that could extend the session, that is reduce time on the phones, by up to 45 minutes (Woodcock, 2017: 105). I draw attention to this example, because it illustrates how a managerial activity and group practice geared toward employee motivation is subverted through an example of counter-cooperation into a form of collective work refusal.

Informal practices of resisting affective management such as the above, can also find a more direct expression. Mulholland identifies the concept of the "collective worker" to name "the manner in which work groups evolve and form defensive alliances through their experience of workplace relations" (2004: 708–709). Insofar as affective management situates motivation, engagement, commitment, and workplace relations as the terrain of intervention, the collective worker can come to act on this same terrain. Subverting the affective field of management thus falls into the informal practices of affective resistance. The use of moral pressure and emotional actions are a way to subvert and express the ambivalence of affective politics in the workplace (Recomposition, 2011). 'Moral pressure' and 'emotional action' are tactical methods for exerting force within a workplace, a form of "direct action grievance ... [in which] workers will *collectively* confront whatever problem they may be having" (Recomposition, 2011: np). This method first identifies affective management as a terrain of intervention, and then acts to leverage this terrain against management, affective and otherwise. For example,

> management training courses encourage supervisors to be aware of the emotional state of the staff. Shop-level managers are told to 'be a friend' to their employees. This way when workers disobey a rule, not only are they breaking company policy, they are letting down a friend. However, just as managers use emotional pressure to influence their workers, workers can do the same to them.
>
> RECOMPOSITION, 2011: np

As articulated by the Industrial Workers of the World (IWW), "emotional action is when we offer our boss a choice: make work less of a headache for us or we will make work more of a headache for the boss", exercised when "workers, as a group, consistently confront a manager on inappropriate behaviour" (Recomposition, 2011: np). As an example, the IWW give the following:

> workers at a restaurant may say, 'It's not right that the company keeps our tips; we have bills to pay. I'm not interested in speaking to someone who helps steal my money. Perhaps we can talk when you stop asking for my tip money at the end of my shift'.
>
> RECOMPOSITION, 2011: np

A related example of action that can subvert the affective politics and power relations within a workplace arrangement is a 'march on the boss'. A march on the boss "is when a group of workers spring a meeting on an owner or someone in management. The workers give a testimony about their working conditions, present a demand and then exit" (Industrial Workers of the World, 2019). While modest, these examples of an informal, direct-action grievance mobilise the significance of affective politics within a workplace, but counter to the objectives of management. In this mode of action, a form of counter-cooperation is practiced to effect change in the interests of labour.

The above examples illustrate measures through which the affective regime of capital as expressed in particular workplaces becomes the material of subversion. The cooperative practices the animate the examples are not given in the labour processes involved, but rather reflect a counter-cooperation formed in worker self-organisation. None of these examples are of the scale of the strike or a mass withdrawal of labour, but nonetheless form elements of a practice of resistance that illustrate how the affective terrain of management can be subverted and repurposed.

6.3   *Ambivalence against Affective Technology*

The integration of the affective sciences into the technical composition of class and capital provides further insights into affective ambivalence and contestation at work. Affective technologies have been implemented in workplaces in forms that modulate the articulation of affective labour, as well as monitoring, measuring and collecting data about worker moods, activity, and disposition (Lopez et al., 2018; Cecchinato and Cox, 2017). As we saw in Chapter 6, examples of affective technologies in the workplace include speech and facial recognition technologies, as well as technologies associated with the quantified self (Moore, 2018). While often posited in dystopian terms of disempowerment, the implementation of these affective technologies creates unique points of encounter between labour and capital that are subject to contestation, and which in some instances provide a basis for a practice of ambivalence. Where affective technologies are implemented to modulate labour, elements of refusal in the form affective labour withdrawal tend to emerge. In the context of mood and disposition monitoring in the workplace, the repurposing of data usage may indicate areas of contestation articulated through the use of affective AI by workers.

The monitoring and tracking of workers in various iterations of surveillance is a long-established practice. These include things like GPS tracking of delivery drivers and facial recognition to document workplace attendance. The incorporation of affective technologies within the gamut of monitoring measures expands the scope of what is monitored, measured and how. As Kat Roemmich et al. describe, "the use of emotion AI in the workplace generates *emotion data* about workers – inferences of workers' emotions, moods, affects, and other interior states and traits". These data are then used to "inform organisational strategy, drive workforce decisions, and manage employees more precisely" (2023: np). While surveillance of workers is not new, the dynamics of increasing affective monitoring poses new challenges for combatting the negative impacts of monitoring. Nonetheless, examples of existing forms of resistance to digital productivity monitoring may indicate where similar practices can emerge in relation to affective technology.

The proliferation of monitoring and tracking devices in the workplace has generated useful discussion on mechanisms workers can use to protect privacy, collectively respond to monitoring, and build new structures of governance (Bodie, 2023). One significant example of resistance takes the form of sousveillance. Sousveillance can be framed as a form of practical resistance in the interests of workers, defined as "an activity where the observer becomes the observed using digital technologies" and functions as an "an inverted form of surveillance or bottom-up observation" (Taylor and Dobbins, 2021). Practices that have been employed by workers to resist digital surveillance have been widespread and documented. Digital platform workers provide some examples, as Ho et al. outline, in results from

> digital labor platform surveys, workers commonly report using encryption tools like VPNs, obscuring or withholding personal identifying information, turning off or physically covering web cameras, or downloading anti-tracking software.
>
> 2024: np

These are all measures that can inhibit the capacities of 'Bossware' technologies to monitor workers. Ho et al. also point to other informal measures to counter surveillance in the gig economy, noting that workers often "use sousveillance methods such as taking 'progress report' screenshots, recording dash cam footage, and saving chatlogs with requesters" (2024: np). These examples of sousveillance align with the practices of digital labour ambivalence outlined by Leonardi et al. (2019) and mentioned earlier in the chapter.

Phoebe Moore (2018), in her extensive work on the agile workplace and the quantified self, theorises and analyses examples of sousveillance in relation to affective labour. Moore asks the question,

> what is stopping workers from using data generated from self-tracking devices to justify our outputs and activities in the appraisal scenario or however our employability or hireability is determined? Could cross-tabulated data help us to prove that we are more stressed when we have too much work and provide a defense against work intensification.
>
> 2018: 16–17

Moore thus outlines where this type of sousveillance could take on a strategic workplace orientation as a form of countermeasure. Such activities could, and indeed do, manifest as "sousveillance where people 'watch the watcher' by using their own methods to gain access to information they do not normally have" and hacking and sharing information (2019: 121). This reflects similar practices noted by Ho et al., where "researchers collaborated with Amazon Turk workers to create We Are Dynamo, a tool that crowd-sources workers' reviews of requesters", indicating which requesters are worse than others (2024: np). Ho et al. add that "these tools have been shown to alleviate the detriments of surveillance and provide benefits such as reducing wage theft and highlighting workers' unpaid, invisible labour" (2024: np). Developing practices that employ affective sousveillance indicate one direction the subversion of affective AI in the workplace could develop.

Marta Cecchinato et al. (2021) have already indicated where these directions could be taken. Drawing from the work of Phoebe Moore (2018), Cecchinato et al. argue that affective technologies of self-tracking are "used by management to dominate workers but can also be used by those same workers to organise around and negotiate improvements" in their working conditions (2021: 133). In this instance, as Cecchinato et al. (2021) argue, the practice of affective sousveillance, sharing and documenting the experiences of work, its affective impacts among workers, socialising the individualised measures taken by workplace monitoring, could form the basis for challenging the disciplinary character of tracking devices. Such a practice would invert the use of this data from the perspective of labour. Cecchinato et al. point to the

> potential for new collective practices of shared aggregation and curation
> of individual data that enrich our understanding of work and hold the
> possibility of undergirding coordinated responses to contemporary soci-
> etal and industrial challenges.
>
> 2021: 128

In turn, this could lead not only to a "greater understanding of the physical and affective impacts of contemporary work but a framework of bargaining over the terms under which that work is performed and remunerated" (2021: 128). Developing further inquiry into these possibilities in repurposing the use of affective technologies will prove an important field for co-research and organisation going forward.

The above considerations of ambivalence in relation to social expression, management, and technology, are offered as indications as to how an affective politics within and against work might take shape. A critical engagement and refusal of the affective articulations of capital and its work order characterises the disaffection, emotional action, and countermeasures employed in the above forms of action. It is true that these are a long way from revolution or even strikes and collective revolt, instead constituting minor expressions of "struggles against capital's everyday forms of barbarism" (Best, 2024: 140). Nonetheless, moving towards a co-articulation of the minor and major scales of revolt will draw from the forms of collectivity developed in everyday struggles within and against work.

7   Conclusion

The internalisation of affective relations by capital, in terms of managerial technique and technologies of work, generates a condition of sharp contestation over the affective politics that characterise our lives. When approached through the lens of class composition and ambivalence, affective production cannot be understood as characterised by an autonomous mode of cooperation. The internalisation of affect means that the labour producing affect remains internal to, that is, remains a mode of expression of capital. As Read writes, "the affective composition of labour combine[s] the structural conditions of the economy with the specific articulation of a given workspace" (2024: 64). Woven through management, technological forms, the commodity, and cooperative practices, capital gives expression to an affective politics geared toward accumulation. But the knots entangling the production of affect as a component of capital become clear points of potential subversion and resistance. As the concept of ambivalence articulates, accumulation and management are not the only ends to which an affective politics can be bent. Rather, affective politics can be mobilised as a form of counter-cooperation from within the workplace or outside of it, to subvert and challenge the logic of accumulation.

The categories of class composition developed by the *operaisti* provided an initial entry point into the critique of affective capital and labour. Building on the analyses of the previous two chapters, that explored the forms of affective management and affective technologies in the workplace, the current chapter emphasised the need to bring affect within the critique of the technical composition of class and capital. The analysis of the technical composition of class illuminates where affect as a mode of capital can be challenged and subverted. However, identifying affect as a component of capital only tells part of the story; to develop the concept of affective politics further, the chapter explored the ideas of the affective and social compositions of labour. Drawing the concept of affective politics into dialogue with the categories of class composition and ambivalence provided a perspective through which affective politics can be dissected and viewed as both an object of critique and a basis of political activity.

Furthermore, looking at the ambivalence of affective composition helps to frame how a politics of disaffection and disidentification might come to inform a wider, collective expression of class composition. Finally, the chapter explored specific ways through which the idea of ambivalence can be used to explore contemporary affective politics. From call centres to delivery riders, to care work, the examples explored above offer contexts for how ambivalence can be valorised in the interests of labour. Importantly, the illustrations of affective ambivalence emerge from within and against the labour processes in which the labour is located, and as such demonstrate the counter-cooperation and repurposing of affect towards the interests of labour. As such, the analysis provided above gives an indication of where research and practice can be explored to develop the concept of affective ambivalence further. Finally, the chapter has established a basis upon which the critique of affective production can move beyond the limitations of the postworkerist theorisation of immaterial and affective labour.

CHAPTER 8

Conclusion

The analysis developed throughout *Motivations for Refusal* takes the contestation of capitalist social relations to be inherent to class society, expressed in the visible, invisible, formal and informal practices of insubordination. One of the key axes along which antagonism is articulated is the labour-capital relation. Antagonism is not reducible to the institutions of labour, the state, or law and can emerge anywhere labour encounters capital, or anywhere the rule of private property seeks to assert itself. However, the articulation of antagonism takes place through material structures and social relations that are historically configured and open to transformation. The compositions of these structures and relations are thus significant for the analysis and critique of the forms of rule that we encounter, the ways in which labour and time are organised, and how we might confront and transform them. How we understand work and develop the critique of it, therefore, needs to be a key point of attention for contemporary, critical social science.

Throughout this book, I have taken debates about contemporary arrangements of work in its affective modes as an entry point from which to better understand the contours and dynamics of social contestation. Work and the organisation of labour are foundations for capital's abstract and concrete forms of rule, while also constituting a terrain from which a radical refusal of domination can be expressed. Work also provides an insight into the tension between continuity and change in terms of both class rule and resistance. In developing my analysis of work and its social contestation, I have sought to engage with and update the critique of immaterial and affective modes of labour. *Motivations for Refusal* has offered this critique by developing a novel perspective on class composition analysis.

Theorisations of affective production mark an important contribution to grappling with the challenges posed by deindustrialisation and the growth of service economies. However, I have shown the ontological turn of affect limits the critical purchase of these theories in developing a critique of labour in the present. In contrast to the ontologies of affective production, this book has developed a critique of labour and affect as expressions of capital, while also exploring affect as a component of contestation, refusal, and class movement. In doing so, this book has sought to explore the character of affective politics at the heart of contemporary forms of political and social contestation emerging from the dynamics of work in late capitalism.

Motivations for Refusal has built a counter-reading of affective production and politics to that proposed by postworkerism. The argument has been developed through four primary points of analysis. The first element of critique drew upon value-form theory to illustrate that the critique of capitalist social relations implies the critique of labour, and that this perspective is missing from contemporary postworkerism. The second point was articulated through a direct critical engagement with postworkerism, focused upon how the production of affect is integrated into contemporary modes of labour as an element of commodity production. The third element of critique analysed the formations of affective capital that have taken shape via the integration of the affective sciences into management and workplace technologies. And the final dimension of critique explored how the contradictions between affective labour, and affective management and technological mediation, produce specific forms of affective politics and struggle.

The primary contributions of *Motivations for Refusal* can be summarised and grouped in the following areas: the theorisation and critique of value; the contribution to contemporary class composition analysis through the critique of the affective sciences as a mode of capital; the theorisation of affective composition and politics, and in advancing the critique of affective modes of ambivalence. I will briefly outline the implications of these contributions for further research.

Motivations for Refusal makes two contributions to advance the theorisation and critique of value. First, to demonstrate the persistence of the internalisation of labour to capital even in its immaterial modes, and thus the need to retain a critique of labour and value. And second, *Motivations for Refusal* illustrates that while the critique of abstract labour and the value form is necessary, so too is an attention to the contours of antagonism as they emerge in production processes in their affective and immaterial modes. Throughout the first three chapters *Motivations for Refusal*, draws together the critique of value with the analysis of the technical composition of class to explain the dynamics of affective production today. One of the important implications of the argument developed in the book is the destabilisation of the ontological turn that has characterised not only some fields of labour studies, but also social and cultural studies. The ontological turn can be summarised in arguments regarding the functional collapse between labour and life. As *Motivations for Refusal* has demonstrated, arguments built on the tenets of this alleged collapse are limited in their capacity to make a critique of labour and value, while tending to misdiagnose the sites from which refusal takes place.

The theorisation of value remains highly contentious within Marxian theory and beyond. *Motivations for Refusal* develops a critique of value as the historically specific form of mediation and domination that marks capitalist social relations. The book has retraced key articulations of labour theories of value to critique the historical iterations of foundational value grounded in specific forms of labour. The point of this is to demonstrate the political implications arising from foundational theories of value. This analysis shows that theories of foundational value tend toward a political orientation that valorises the particular form of labour identified as productive, and this blunts the critique of the historical specificity of abstract labour as value. This is precisely the limit reached in the postworkerist perspective on labour and value, grounded in their conception of affective production.

In Part 1, we saw that *operaismo* was characterised by an ambivalence that oscillated between negationist and affirmationist tendencies. On the one hand, *operaismo* called for the radical negativity of work refusal, and on the other hand, it articulated an affirmationist valorisation of working-class subjectivities. Mario Tronti once wrote, "in order to struggle against capital the working class must struggle against itself inasmuch as it is capital" (1966: 260). Later, Negri would write "proletarian self-valorisation is the strength to withdraw from exchange value and the capacity to base itself on use values ... proletarian self-valorisation is wholly innovative" (2005 [1977]: 241). The tension at the centre of these tendencies can produce a dynamic process of political composition and critique, if an articulation of each tendency is maintained. However, the distance between these two perspectives is also significant, and the trajectory of those that would go on to theorise postworkerism, have come to see contemporary modes of immaterial production as already withdrawn from exchange-value. Such a perspective loses sight of the degree to which the ambivalence of labour persists. Labour is internal to the labour-capital relation but imbued with the capacity to negate this condition. Exploring the character of this ambivalence in conditions of affective production has provoked important debates about the forms of work today, as well as the prospects for a radically different future.

Postworkerism, as illustrated particularly in Chapters 3 and 4, has contributed significantly to thinking labour in conditions of immaterial and affective production. The fundamental strength of postworkerism, retained in modified form from the original tenets of *operaismo*, is its insistence upon the creativity of the proletariat, or multitude, in struggle. Beginning with the initiative and creativity of labour to act in its own interests, postworkerism has consistently refused the narrative that our lives, relationships, and forms of collectivity, occur only upon the terms and terrain of capital. At its most compelling, postworkerism challenges us to continually ask anew what the shifting arrangements of labour and reproduction in the present moment are, and to seek to identify the emerging trends of antagonism and their forms of organisation. As a perspective, it challenges us to look to how the desires and practices of social and class struggles exceed the limits imposed upon them by the objectives of capital accumulation. The insistence upon an inherent, lived antagonism that is not only the harbinger of a distant future society, but is actively shaping the world in which we live, can be a welcome breath of fresh air in times prone to despair.

Postworkerism has articulated the politics of affective labour as an immediate autonomy from capital. In this formulation, the affective character of production creates a separation between labour and capital: labour is a self-organised form of production that confronts a parasitic mode of capital that profits through the extraction of the common capacities of labour. The foundation that articulates the autonomy of labour is said to be the cooperative capacities inherent to immaterial and affective production. The disarticulation of labour and capital, from the postworkerist perspective, reflects the socialisation of labour, now unmediated by value, and immediately social in its character. Postworkerism has been genuinely innovative in its orientation to theory and practice, and highly productive in terms of generating concepts and lines of inquiry into the dynamics of late capitalism. However, this ongoing pursuit of the new leads to the peculiar political impasse that characterises postworkerism today. At the foundation of the postworkerist perspective is a specific articulation of affective politics rooted in production that proves incapable of developing a critique of the condition of labour today. The argument pursued throughout this book challenges the postworkerist formulation of production and its foundational ontology of labour-value-affect.

The proliferation of service work and the production of intangible outputs, in particular, have challenged theories based in embodied notions of value. As a result, in the contemporary debates regarding service work, immaterial and affective production, it has become commonplace that the theory of value no longer holds or is at least fundamentally challenged by the intangibility of outputs. As demonstrated particularly in Chapter 4, this perspective tends to be based on an understanding that sees the organisation of concrete labour as the determinate factor in the consideration of value. For the postworkerists, they simultaneously break with theories of value that rely on embodied value in tangible objects, while reinscribing a new ontological foundation in the construct of labour-value-affect. This affirmationist ontology of labour-value-affect leads to a productivist notion of immaterial production. The claim of postworkerism that affective production is expressed as an autonomous form of cooperation separate from capital highlights the inability of postworkerism to critique labour in the present. This limitation emerges from the productivist, foundational theory of value anchored in labour-value-affect.

In contrast, *Motivations for Refusal* demonstrates that the condition of immaterial and affective production remains, in part at least, internal to the labour-capital relation. As such, it remains articulated through and mediated by value. Moreover, the specific conditions of cooperation that animate imma-terial production are also in part articulated by capital. It is thus necessary to retain a critique of value as a form of mediation and domination that emerges in the labour capital relation. Retracing Marx's consideration of the value-form and abstract labour allows for the critique of labour as a mode of expression of capital, even in labour's affective and immaterial forms.

Chapters 5 and 6 developed a critique of how the tensions between the epis-temologies of affect are reflected in their implementation in the workplace and the labour-capital relation more broadly. Specifically, the affective sciences, grounded in various iterations of biological and psychological concepts of affect, have informed the development of affective forms of management and technologies. This contrasts with the Spinozist concept of affect typically asso-ciated with theories of affective labour. The concepts of affect as articulated in the affective sciences are physiologically inscribed and quantifiable. New approaches to management which have developed around the ideas of moti-vation and engagement have relied upon the affective sciences in developing the standards of measure. Chapter 5 outlined the theoretical foundations of this turn in management, critiqued its implementation in the workplace, and situated the emergence of this form of management as a component of the technical composition of class in late capitalism.

Chapter 6 critically analysed a second component of the integration of the affective sciences into the technical composition of class and capital. The use of affective technologies, informed by the affective sciences, in the workplace illustrates the technological mediation of affect and labour. The critique devel-oped throughout Chapter 6 focused upon two related elements of the use of affective technologies at work. One element is the production of the indexes of affect in datasets against which affective labour is measured and moni-tored. In this iteration of affective technologies, affects are fixed within the technologies as index of measure. The second aspect explored in Chapter 6 demonstrated that the encounter between living labour and affective technol-ogies manifests as the modulation of affective labour. As such, the articulation of affective labour is in part mediated through the technological nexus of affect. The critical consideration of affective production in the present must grapple with these issues.

The internalisation of affect to the labour-capital relation was demonstrated through the analysis of the integration of the affective sciences into the practices of management and the technological modulations of affective labour. Repurposing the concepts of technical and political composition of class, via the critical reading of the affective sciences at work, establishes a critical foundation from which to begin developing a political framework adequate to the challenges of the service economy. But to note the internalisation of affect to the labour-capital relation is not dismiss the contestation of work and capital. Rather, it opens the possibility to consider the ambivalent character of affective politics through the lens of class composition. *Motivations for Refusal* develops the concepts of affective politics and affective composition to explore this final point.

It is important to emphasise that the point of the analysis offered in *Motivations for Refusal* is political in nature. The ongoing entanglement of forms of affective production within the labour-capital relation has consequences for how the critique of capitalist production is articulated. *Motivations for Refusal* demonstrates through the critique of value that immaterial labour has not shattered the forms of abstract labour and domination. As a result, rather than a political perspective that takes for granted the social and cooperative character of affective production, we must work to identify those moments and conditions of affect's internalisation to the labour capital relation, such that these can become the object of critique. To do so introduces a fundamental condition of ambivalence and contestation to affective production, such that affective capital be approached from a negationist perspective. Approaching this question through the lens of class composition analysis clarifies the terms of ambivalence.

Motivations for Refusal updates and expands the consideration of class composition analysis in conditions of affective production. The contributions of *Motivations for Refusal* in class composition analysis relate to the critique of the technical composition of class, considerations of the political composition of class, and the theorisation of the affective composition of class. First, the analysis developed in the book expands and updates the analysis of the technical composition of class. The original contribution of *Motivations for Refusal* identifies the integration of the affective sciences into the technical composition of class. Tracing the integration of the affective sciences into both managerial technique and the technological mediation of labour charts new territory in the critique of affective modes of labour.

Motivations for Refusal demonstrates the means through which affective production is internalised to the labour-capital relation and clarifies how modes of affective refusal might take shape in those contexts. To emphasise

the dynamics of affective production as articulated through the technical composition of class and capital, is not to limit forms of social, political, and class
movement to the formalised terrain of capital, employment, and work. Indeed,
the contestation of capital is not reducible to the condition of one's internality
to the capital relation: refusal and movement emerge within and against the
direct commodification of labour, and beyond that condition as well. As economic, social, political, and climate crises deepen across the globe, struggles
over the character of the social organisation of our lives assume ever greater
significance. The political and affective compositions of these movements will
continue to emerge from across the entire social terrain. The co-articulation
of struggles against capital's exploitation and appropriation of labour and
resources, and movements for a different future, will remain an ongoing organisational question to be posed anew across the cycles of struggle. Much can
be learned from the past, and much will be learned through the inquiries into
emerging compositions across the multiple axes of antagonism.

Motivations for Refusal has sought to make clear the fact that the conditions
of affective production are not immediately social, cooperative, or beyond
capital. Far from this condition undermining the capacities of refusal and
class antagonism, grasping affect as a component of capital will allow us to
clarify the terms of refusal and negation. Understanding affect in work and
labour processes will help us to better comprehend where the production of
affect bound to the imperatives of accumulation takes place, what the terms
of refusal might be, and where the counter-production of communistic affects
might proliferate.

Bibliography

Adkins, Lisa. 1995. *Gendered Work*. Buckingham: Open University Press.

Adkins, Lisa. 2005. 'The New Economy, Property and Personhood.' *Theory, Culture and Society* 22(1): 111–130.

Adkins, Lisa. 2008. 'From Retroactivation to Futurity: The End of the Sexual Contract?' *NORA: Nordic Journal of Feminist and Gender Research* 16(3): 182–201.

Adkins, Lisa. 2012. 'Out of Work or Out of Time? Rethinking Labour After the Financial Crisis.' *South Atlantic Quarterly* 111(4): 621–642.

Adkins, Lisa. 2013. 'What do Wages Do? Feminist Theory for Austere Times.' Paper presented at Rethinking Money, Australian Working Group on Financialisation workshop, Sydney, November 4–5.

Adkins, Lisa and Celia Lury. 2012. 'Introduction: Special Measures.' *The Sociological Review* 59(2): 5–23.

Adorno, Theodore W. 2007 [1966]. *Negative Dialectics*. New York: Continuum.

Affective Capitalism Symposium. 2014. University of Turku, Finland, June 5–6. Retrieved July 2, 2024. (http://affectivecapitalism.wordpress.com/).

Alessandrini, Donatella. 2012. 'Immaterial Labour and Alternative Valorisation Processes in Italian Feminist Debates: (Re)exploring the Commons of Reproduction.' *Feminists@law*, 1(2): 1–28.

Alquati, Romano. 2001. *Nella società industriale d'oggi*, Working Paper, non-publ., Torino, 2000–2003.

Alquati, Romano. 2013 [1961]. 'Organic Composition of Capital and Labour-Power at Olivetti.' *Viewpoint Magazine*, September 27. Retrieved August 1, 2024 (http://viewpointmag.com/2013/09/27/organic-composition-of-capital-and-labor-power-at-olivetti-1961/).

Alquati, Romano. 2013 [1964]. 'Struggle at Fiat.' *Viewpoint Magazine*, September 26. Retrieved August 1, 2024. (http://viewpointmag.com/2013/09/26/struggle-at-fiat-1964/).

Alquati, Romano. 2013 [1967]. 'Outline of a Pamphlet on FIAT.' *Viewpoint Magazine*, September 26. Retrieved August 1, 2024. (http://viewpointmag.com/2013/09/26/outline-of-a-pamphlet-on-fiat-1967/).

Alvesson, Mats and Hugh Willmott. 1992. 'Critical Theory and Management Studies: An Introduction.' Pp. 1–20 in *Critical Management Studies*, edited by Mats Alvesson and Hugh Willmott. London: Sage.

Alvesson, Mats, Todd Bridgman and Hugh Willmott. 2009. 'Introduction.' Pp. 1–26 in *The Oxford Handbook of Critical Management Studies*, edited by M. Alvesson, T. Bridgman and H. Willmott. Oxford: Oxford University Press.

Andrews, Gavin J. and Cameron Duff. 2020. 'Enrolling Bodies, Feasting on Space: How Wellbeing Serves the Forms and Flows of a New Capitalism.' *Wellbeing and Society* 1: 1–10.

Angry Workers. 2019. *Class Power on Zero Hours*. London: PM Press.

Anonymous Tangpingist. 2021. *Tangpingist Manifesto: Tangpingists of the World, Unite!* Retrieved July 31, 2024. (https://theanarchistlibrary.org/library/anonymous -tangpingist-manifesto).

Armano, Emiliana, Andrea Cavazzini, and Rosanna Maccarone. 2024. 'Enhancement or Impoverishment? Algorithmic Management and "Distance" Education During the Pandemic: Theoretical and Interpretive Hypotheses.' *Work Organisation, Labour, and Globalisation* 18(1): 31–43.

Armano, Emiliana and Annalisa Murgia. 2017. 'Hybrid Areas of Work in Italy.' Pp. 47–59 in *Mapping Precariousness, Labour Insecurity and Uncertain Livelihoods: Subjectivities and Resistance*, edited by Emiliana Armano, Arianna Bove and Annalisa Murgia. London: Routledge.

Armano, Emiliana and Devi Sacchetto. 2009. La conricerca contro l'industrializzazione dell'umano *Breve nota sul convegno: "Romano Alquati. Immagini e percorsi soggettivi e collettivi di una ricercar."* Archivo Primo Moroni. Retrieved August 1, 2024. (https://www.inventati.org/apm/index.php?step=alquati).

Arthur, Chris. 1979. 'Dialectic of the Value-Form'. Pp. 67–81 in *Value: The Representation of Labour in Capitalism: essays*, edited by Diane Elson. London: CSE Books.

Arvidsson, Adam. 2012. 'General Sentiment: How Value and Affect Converge in the Information Economy.' *The Sociological Review* 59(2): 39–59.

Ashkanasy, Neal M. and Catherine Daus. 2001. 'Emotion in the Workplace: The New Challenge for Managers.' *Academy of Management Executive* 16(1): 76–86.

Ashton-James, Claire E. and Neal M. Ashkanasy. 2008. 'Affective Events Theory: A Strategic Perspective.' Pp. 1–34 in *Emotions, Ethics and Decision-Making (Research on Emotion in Organizations, Vol. 4)* edited by W.J. Zerbe, C.E.J. Hartel and Neal Ashkanasy. Leeds: Emerald Group Publishing.

Athanasiou, Anthea, Pothiti Hantzaroula and Kostas Yannakopoulos. 2008. 'Towards a New Epistemology: The "Affective Turn".' *Historein* 8: 5–16.

Backhaus, Hans Georg. 1980. 'On the Dialectics of the Value-Form.' *Thesis Eleven* 1: 99–120.

Backhaus, Hans George. 1992. 'Between Philosophy and Science: Marxian Social Economy as Critical Theory.' Pp. 54–92 in *Open Marxism: vol 1 Dialectics and History*, edited by Werner Bonefeld, Richard Gunn and Kosmas Psychopedis. London: Pluto Press.

Baker, Erik. 2023. 'The Age of the Crisis of Work: What is the Sound of Quiet Quitting?' *Harper's Magazine*. May 2023.

Balestrini, Nanni and Primo Moroni. 2021 [1997]. *The Golden Horde: Revolutionary Italy 1960–1977*. London: Seagull Books.

Barbagallo, Camille and Silvia Federici. 2012. *The Commoner*, 15.

Barber, Larissa K., and Xinyu Hu. 2020. 'Implications of Technological Work Practices for Employee Affect.' Pp. 497–510 in *The Cambridge Handbook of Workplace Affect*, edited by Liu-Qin Yang, Russel Cropanzo, Catherine S. Daus and Vincente Martinez-Tur. Cambridge: Cambridge University Press.

Barca, Stefania. 2024. *Workers of the Earth: Labour, Ecology and Reproduction in the Age of Climate Change*. London: Pluto Press.

Bargetz, Brigitte. 2015. 'The Distribution of Emotions: Affective Politics of Emancipation.' *Hypatia* 30(3): 580–596.

Bastani, Aaron. 2019. *Fully Automated Luxury Communism: A Manifesto*. London: Verso.

Bates, Joseph. 1994. 'Believable Agents.' *Communications of the ACM*, 37(7): 122–125.

Baumeler, Carmen. 2008. 'Technologies of the Emotional Self: Affective Computing and the "Enhanced Second Skin" for Flexible Employees.' Pp. 179–190 in *Sexualised Brains: Scientific Modelling of Emotional Intelligence from a Cultural Perspective*, edited by Nicole Karafyllis and Gotlind Ulshofer. Cambridge, Mass.: MIT Press.

Bechtoldt, Myriam N., Bianca Beersma, Sonja Rohrmann and Jeffrey Sanchez-Burks. 2013. 'A Gift That Takes its Toll: Emotion Recognition and Conflict Appraisal'. *European Journal of Work and Organizational Psychology* 22(1): 56–66.

Bélanger, Jacques and Paul Edwards. 2013. 'The Nature of Front-Line Service Work: Distinctive Features and Continuity in the Employment Relationship'. *Work, Employment and Society* 27(3): 433–450.

Bell, Daniel. 2008 [1973]. *The Coming of Post-Industrial Society: A Venture in Social Forecasting*. New York: Basic Books.

Bellet, Clement S., Jan-Emmanuelle de Neve and George Ward. 2024. 'Does Employee Happiness Have an Impact on Productivity?' *Management Science* 70(3): 16561679.

Bellofiore, Riccardo. 2006. 'Between Panzieri and Negri: Mario Tronti and the workerism of the 1960s and 1970s.' Paper presented at Historical Materialism, London.

Bellofiore, Riccardo. 2009. 'A Ghost Turning into a Vampire: The Concept of Capital and Living Labour.' Pp. 178–194 in *Re-reading Marx: New Perspectives After the Critical Edition*, edited by Riccardo Bellofiore and Roberto Fineschi. New York: Palgrave Macmillan.

Benanav, Aaron. 2021. 'Service Work in the Pandemic Economy.' *International Labour and Working Class History* 99: 66–74.

Benanav, Aaron. 2020. *Automation and the Future of Work*, New York: Verso.

Benjamin, Walter. 2007. *Illuminations*. New York: Schocken Books.

Berardi, Franco Bifo. 2007. 'Anatomy of Autonomy.' Pp. 148–171 in *Autonomia: Post-Political Politics*, edited by Sylvere Lotringer and Christian Marazzi. Los Angeles: Semiotext(e).

Berardi, Franco Bifo. 2008. *Felix Guattari: Thought, Friendship and Visionary Cartography*. Hampshire: Palgrave Macmillan.

Berardi, Franco Bifo. 2009. *Precarious Rhapsody: Semiocapitalism and the Pathologies of the Post-Alpha Generation*. London: Minor Compositions.

Berardi, Franco Bifo. 2009a. *The Soul at Work: From Alienation to Autonomy*. Los Angeles: Semiotext(e).

Berardi, Franco Bifo. 2011. *After the Future*. Edinburgh: AK Press.

Berardi, Franco Bifo. 2011a. 'Repression, Expression, Depression.' Pp. 186–204 in *The Guatarri Effect*, edited by Eric Alliez and Andrew Goffey. London: Continuum International Publishing Group.

Berardi, Franco Bifo. 2012. *The Uprising: On Poetry and Finance*. Los Angeles: Semiotext(e).

Berardi, Franco Bifo. 2022. 'Resign.' *E-flux: notes* 124, February. Retrieved October 30, 2024. https://www.e-flux.com/journal/124/443422/resign/.

Berlant, Lauren. 2011. *Cruel Optimism*. Durham: Duke University Press.

Berlant, Lauren. 2011a. 'A Properly Political Conception of Love: Three Approaches in Ten Pages.' *Cultural Anthropology* 26(4): 683–691.

Bertelsen, Lone and Andrew Murphy. 2010. 'An Ethics of Everyday Infinities and Powers: Felix Guattari on Affect and the Refrain.' Pp. 138–157 in *The Affect Theory Reader*, edited by Melissa Gregg and Gregory J. Seigworth. Durham: Duke University Press.

Best, Beverley. 2011. '"Frederic Jameson Notwithstanding": The Dialectic of Affect.' *Rethinking Marxism* 23(1): 60–82.

Best, Beverley. 2021. 'Wages for Housework Redux: Social Reproduction and the Utopian Dialectic of the Value-Form.' *Theory and Event* 24(4): 896–921.

Best, Beverley. 2024. *The Automatic Fetish: The Law of Value in Marx's Capital*. London: Verso.

Bianchi, Pietro. 2011. 'The Word and the Flesh.' *Angelaki: Journal of the Theoretical Humanities* 16(3): 39–51.

Bidet, Jacques. 2005. *Exploring Marx's Capital: Philosophical, Economic and Political Dimensions*. Chicago: Haymarket Books.

Bindl, U.K. and S.K. Parker. 2012. 'Affect and Employee Proactivity: A Goal-Regulatory Perspective.' Pp. 225–256 in *Experiencing and Managing Emotions in the Workplace: Research on Emotions in Organizations*, edited by N. Ashkanasy, C. Hartel and W. Zerbe. Bingley: Emerald Group Publishing.

Bjerg, Helle and Dorthe Staunaes. 2011. 'Self-Management Through Shame – Uniting Governmentality Studies and the "Affective Turn."' *Ephemera* 11(2): 138–156.

Blanc, Eric. 2019. *Red State Revolt: The Teachers' Strikes and Working-Class Politics.* London: Verso.

Bloois, Joost de, Monica Jansen and Frans Willem Korsten. 2014. 'Introduction: From Autonomism to Post-*Autonomia*, From Class Composition to a New Political Anthropology?' *Rethinking Marxism: A Journal of Economics, Culture and Society* 26(2): 163–177.

Bodie, Matthew. 2023. 'Beyond Privacy: Changing the Data Power Dynamics in the Workplace.' *Law and Political Economy Project.* February 7. Retrieved August 1, 2024. (https://lpeproject.org/blog/beyond-privacy-changing-the-data-power-dynamics -in-the-workplace/).

Boehner, Kirsten, Rogerio DePaula, Paul Dourish and Phoebe Sengers. 2005. 'Affect: From Information to Interaction.' Pp. 59–68 in proceedings of *4th Decennial Conference on Critical Computing: Between Sense and Sensibility.*

Bohm, Steffen and Chris Land. 2012. 'The New "Hidden Abode": Reflections on Value and Labour in the New Economy.' *The Sociological Review* 60(2): 217–240.

Bologna, Sergio. 1972. 'Class composition and Theory of the Party at the Origins of the Workers' Council Movement.' *Telos* 13: 3–27.

Bologna, Sergio. 1977. 'Eight Theses on Militant Historiography.' *Primo Maggio* 11. Retrieved July 25, 2024. (http://libcom.org/library/eight-theses-militant-historio graphy).

Bologna, Sergio. 1993a [1973]. 'Money and Crisis: Marx's Correspondent of the New York Daily Tribune 1856–57 part I.' *Common Sense* 13: 29–53.

Bologna, Sergio. 1993b [1973]. 'Money and Crisis: Marx's Correspondent of the New York Daily Tribune 1856–57 part II.' *Common Sense* 14: 63–89.

Bologna, Sergio. 2004. 'The Social Pattern of Knowledge Workers: Myth and Reality.' Paper presented at Humanities Conference, Prato, July 20–22.

Bologna, Sergio. 2005. 'Negri's Proletarians and the State: A Critique' Pp. 38–47 in *The Philosophy of Antonio Negri: Resistance in Practice*, edited by Timothy S. Murphy and Abdul-Karim Mustapha. London: Pluto Press.

Bologna, Sergio. 2007. 'Tribe of Moles.' Pp. 36–61 in *Autonomia: Post-Political Politics*, edited by Sylvere Lotringer and Christian Marazzi. Los Angeles: Semiotext(e).

Bologna, Sergio. 2010 [2007]. 'The Sense of Coalition.' Pp. 167–219, in *Post-Fordism and its Discontents*, edited by Gal Kirn. Retrieved July 16, 2024. (http://tinyurl.com/lgdw6a8).

Boltanski, Luc and Eve Chiapello. 2005 [1999]. *The New Spirit of Capitalism.* London: Verso.

Bonefeld, Werner. 2004. 'On Postone's Courageous but Unsuccessful Attempt to Banish the Class Antagonism from the Critique of Political Economy.' *Historical Materialism* 12(3): 103–124.

Bosworth, Kai. 2022. *Pipeline Populism: Grassroots Environmentalism in the Twenty-First Century*. Minneapolis: University of Minnesota Press.

Boyd, Karen L., and Nazanin Andalibi. 2023. 'Automated Emotion Recognition in the Workplace: How Proposed Technologies Reveal Potential Futures of Work.' *PACM on Human-Computer Interaction*, 5(1) Article 95.

Brennan, Eugene. 2021. 'Mapping Logistical Capitalism.' *Theory, Culture and Society* 38(4): 135–146.

Brief, Arthur P., and Howard M. Weiss. 2002. 'Organisational Behaviour: Affect in the Workplace.' *Annual Review of Psychology*, 53: 279–307.

Bromuri, Stefano, Alexander P. Henkel, Deniz Iren and Visara Urovi. 2021. 'Using AI to Predict Service Agent Stress from Emotion Patterns in Service Interactions.' *Journal of Service Management*, 32(4): 581–611.

Brotheridge, Celeste M. and Alicia A. Grandey. 2002. 'Emotional Labor and Burnout: Comparing Two Perspectives of "People Work."' *Journal of Vocational Behaviour* 60(1): 17–39.

Brown, Alexander. 2012. 'Precarious Time: The Revolutionary Temporality of the Present.' Pp. 175–186 in *Movements in Time: Revolution, Social Justice, and Times of Change*, edited by Cecile Lawrence and Natalie Churn. Newcastle Upon Tyne: Cambridge Scholars Publishing.

Bryan, Dick. 1990. '"Natural" and "Improved" Land in Marx's Theory of Rent.' *Land Economics* 66(2): 176–181.

Bryan, Dick, Randy Martin and Mike Rafferty. 2009. 'Financialisaton and Marx: Giving Labour and Capital a Financial Make Over.' *Review of Radical Political Economics* 41(4): 458–472.

Bulan, Heather Ferguson, Rebecca J. Erickson and Amy S. Wharton. 1997. 'Doing for Others on the Job: The Affective Requirements of Service Work, Gender, and Emotional Well-Being'. *Social Problems* 44(2): 235–256.

Byron, Kristin, Sophia Terranova and Stephen Nowicki Jr. 2007. 'Nonverbal Emotion Recognition and Salespersons: Linking Ability to Perceived and Actual Success.' *Journal of Applied Social Psychology* 37(11): 2600–2619.

Caffentzis, George. 1987. 'Review: Marx beyond Marx: Lesson on the *Grundrisse*.' *New German Critique* 41: 186–192.

Caffentzis, George. 2003 [1998]. 'The End of Work or the Renaissance of Slavery? A critique of Rifkin and Negri.' Pp. 115–134 in *Revolutionary Writing: Common Sense Essays in Post-Political Politics*, edited by Werner Bonefeld. Brooklyn: Autonomedia.

Caffentzis, George C. 2011. 'How Savage was Spinoza? Spinoza and the Economic Life of Seventeenth-Century Holland.' Pp. 193–214 in *Reading Negri: Marxism in the Age of Empire*, edited by Pierra Lamarche, Max Rosenkrantz, and David Sherman. Chicago: Carus Publishing Company.

Caffentzis, George C. 2011a. 'Immeasurable Value? An essay on Marx's legacy.' Pp. 101–126 in *Reading Negri: Marxism in the Age of Empire*, edited by Pierra Lamarche, Max Rosenkrantz, and David Sherman. Chicago: Carus Publishing Company.

Caffentzis, George. 2011b. 'A Critique of "Cognitive Capitalism."' Pp. 23–56 in *Cognitive Capitalism, Education and Digital Labor*, edited by Michael A. Peters and Ergin Bulut. New York: Peter Lang Publishing.

Callahan, Jamie E. and Eric E. McMollum. 2002. 'Obscured Variability: The Distinction Between Emotion Work and Emotional Labour.' Pp. 219–231 in *Managing Emotions in the Workplace*, edited by N.M. Ashkansy, W.J. Zerbe and C.E.J. Hartel. London: Routledge.

Cant, Callum. 2019. *Riding for Deliveroo: Resistance in the New Economy*, Polity Press.

Casarino, Cesare and Antonio Negri. 2008. *In Praise of the Common: A Conversation on Philosophy and Politics*. Minneapolis: University of Minnesota.

Casas-Cortes, Maribel. 2014. 'A Genealogy of Precarity: A Toolbox for Rearticulating Fragmented Social Realities In and Out of the Workplace.' *Rethinking Marxism: A Journal of Economics, Culture and Society* 26(2): 206–226.

Cecchinato, Marta, Sandy J.J. Gould and Frederick Harry Pitts. 2021. 'Self-Tracking and Sousveillance at Work: Insights from Human-Computer Interaction and Social Science.' Pp. 127–137 in *Augmented Exploitation: Artificial Intelligence, Automation and Work*, edited by Phoebe Moore, and Jamie Woodcock. London: Pluto Press.

Cecchinato, Marta E. and Anna L. Cox. 2017. 'Smartwatches: Digital Handcuffs or Magic Bracelets?' *Computer Magazine* 50: 106–109.

Chaudhary, Ajay Singh. 2024. *The Exhausted of the Earth: Politics in a Burning World*. London: Repeater Books.

Chong, Patricia. 2009. 'Servitude with a Smile: An Anti-Oppression Analysis of Emotional Labour.' *Global Labour University*. Retrieved July 22, 2024 (http://tinyurl.com/leuzglz).

Christensen, Scott S., Barbara L. Wilson and Shaun Duane Hansen. 2022. 'Using Affective Events Theory to Conceptualise Nurses' Emotional Behaviour: A Scoping Review.' *Collegian* 30: 147–153.

Christiaens, Tim. 2022. *Digital Working Lives: Worker Autonomy and the Gig Economy*. Maryland: Rowman and Littlefield.

Christophers, Brett. 2020. *Rentier Capitalism: Who Owns the Economy and Who Pays for it?* London: Verso.

Chuang. 2021. *Social Contagion and Other Materials on Microbiological Class War in China*. Chicago: Charles H. Kerr.

Cleaver, Harry. 1979. *Reading 'Capital' Politically*. Brighton: Harvester Press.

Cleaver, Harry. 1992. 'The Inversion of Class Perspective in Marxian Theory: From Valorisation to Self-Valorisation.' Pp. 106–144 in *Open Marxism: Vol 2 Theory and*

Practice, edited by Werner Bonefeld, Richard Gunn and Kosmas Psychopedis. London: Pluto Press.

Clegg, Stewart, Martin Kornberger, Chris Carter and Carl Rhodes. 2006. 'For Management?' *Management Learning* 37(1): 7–27.

Clough, Patricia Ticineto. 2007. 'Introduction.' Pp. 1–33 in *The Affective Turn: Theorising the Social*, edited by Patricia Ticineto and Jean Halley. Durham: Duke University Press.

Clough, Patricia T. 2010. 'The Affective Turn: Political Economy, Biomedia and Bodies.' Pp. 206–225 in *The Affect Theory Reader*, edited by Melissa Gregg and Gregory J. Seigworth. Durham. London: Duke University Press.

Clough, Patricia Ticineto, Greg Goldberg, Rachel Schiff, Aaron Weeks and Craig Willse. 2007. 'Notes Towards a Theory of Affect-Itself.' *Ephemera* 7(1): 60–77.

Colbert, Amy, Nick Yee and Gerard George. 2016. 'The Digital Workforce and the Workplace of the Future.' *Academy of Management Journal* 59(3): 731–739.

Control Engineering. 2007. 'Omron Facial Recognition Software Now Measures Smiling Faces' in *Control engineering Asia magazine*. Retrieved August 10, 2014 (http://www.ceasiamag.com/article/omron-facial-recognition-software-now-measures-smiling-faces/3241).

Cooper, Melinda. 2002. 'The Living and the Dead: Variations on de Anima.' *Angelaki: Journal of the Theoretical Humanities* 7(3): 81–104.

Cooper, Melinda. 2011. 'Complexity Theory After the Financial Crisis.' *Journal of Cultural Economy* 4(4): 371–385.

Cooper, Melinda. 2011a. 'Marx beyond Marx, Marx before Marx: Negri's Lucretian Critique of the Hegelian Marx.' Pp. 127–148 in *Reading Negri: Marxism in the Age of Empire*, edited by Pierra Lamarche, Max Rosenkrantz, and David Sherman. Chicago: Carus Publishing Company.

Cooper, Melinda. 2012. 'Workfare, Familyfare, Godfare: Transforming Contingency into Necessity.' *South Atlantic Quarterly* 111(4): 643–662.

Cooper, Melinda. 2013. 'Why I Am Not a Postsecularist.' *Boundary 2* 40(1): 21–40.

Cooper, Melinda. 2015. 'Shadow Money and the Shadow Workforce: Rethinking Labour and Liquidity.' *South Atlantic Quarterly* 114 (2): 395–423.

Cooper, Melinda. 2017. *Family Values: Between Neoliberalism and the New Social Conservatism*. New York: Zone Books.

Cooper, Melinda. 2024. *Counterrevolution: Extravagance and Austerity in Public Finance*. New York: Zone Books.

Cooper, Melinda and Catherine Waldby. 2014. *Clinical Labor: Tissue Donors and Research Subjects in the Global Bioeconomy*. Durham: Duke University Press.

Crawford, Kate. 2021: *Atlas of AI*. Yale: Yale University Press.

Cristofaro, Matteo. 2020. 'I Feel and Think, Therefore I Am: An Affect-Cognitive Theory of Management Decisions.' *European Management Journal* 38: 344–355.

Cropanzo, Russell, Stefanie K. Johnson and Brittany K. Lambert. 2020. 'Leadership, Affect, and Emotion.' Pp. 229243 in *The Cambridge Handbook of Workplace Affect*, edited by Liu-Qin Yang, Russel Cropanzo, Catherine S. Daus and Vincente Martinez-Tur. Cambridge: Cambridge University Press.

Cunninghame, Patrick. 2008. 'Italian Feminism, Workerism and Autonomy in the 1970s.' *Amnis*. September 1. Retrieved July 1, 2024. (http://amnis.revues.org/575).

Dalla Costa, Maria Rosa. 2012. 'Mariarosa Dalla Costa Statement on "Women and the Subversion of the Community" and Her Cooperation with Selma James.' Retrieved July 22, 2024. (http://tinyurl.com/ocux84s).

Dalla Costa, Maria Rosa and Selma James. 1975 [1972]. *The Power of Women and the Subversion of the Community*. Bristol: Falling Wall Press.

Dalla Costa, Maria Rosa. 2007. 'The Diffused Intellectual: Women's Autonomy and the Labour of Reproduction.' Pp. 145–162 in *Utopian Pedagogy: Radical Experiments against Neoliberal Globalisation*, edited by Mark Cote, Richard J.F. Day and Greig de Peuter. Toronto: University of Toronto Press.

Dashtipour, Parisa. 2014. 'Freedom Through Work: The Psychosocial, Affect and Work.' Pp. 104–125 in *The Psychosocial and Organization Studied: Affect at Work*, edited by Kate Kenny and Marianna Fotaki. New York: Palgrave MacMillan.

Daus, Catherine S., Russell Cropanzo, Vicente Martinez-Tur and Liu-Qin Yang. 2020. 'Emotion at Work: From the Leaner Years to the Affective Revolution.' Pp. 3–14 in *The Cambridge Handbook of Workplace Affect*, edited by Liu-Qin Yang, Russel Cropanzo, Catherine S. Daus and Vincente Martinez-Tur. Cambridge: Cambridge University Press.

De Angelis, Massimo. 1995. 'Beyond the Technological and the Social Paradigms: A Political Reading of Abstract Labour as the Substance of Value.' *Capital and Class* 19(3): 107–134.

De Angelis, Massimo. 2007. *The Beginning of History: Value Struggles and Global Capital*. London: Pluto Press.

De Angelis, Massimo. 2000. *Keynesianism, Social Conflict and Political Economy*. London: Macmillan Press.

De Angelis, Massimo and David Harvie. 2007. 'Cognitive Capitalism and the Rat Race: How Capital Measures Immaterial Labour in British Universities.' *Historical Materialism* 17(3): 3–30.

Dean, Jodi and Paul A. Passavant (eds). 2004. *Empire's New Clothes: Reading Hardt and Negri*. New York: Routledge.

Dejours, Christophe and Jean-Philippe Deranty. 2010. 'The Centrality of Work.' *Critical Horizons* 11(2): 167–180.

Deleuze, Gilles. 1988 [1970]. *Spinoza: Practical Philosophy*. San Francisco: City Lights Books.

Deleuze, Gilles. 1990. 'In Conversation with Antonio Negri.' Retrieved August 20, 2014. (http://www.uib.no/sites/w3.uib.no/files/attachments/6._deleuze-control_and _becoming.pdf).

Deleuze, Gilles. 2005 [1968]. *Expressionism in Philosophy: Spinoza*. New York: Zone Books.

Deleuze, Gilles. 2006 [1986]. *Foucault*. New York: Continuum.

Deleuze, Gilles and Felix Guattari. 2004. *A Thousand Plateaus: Capitalism and Schizophrenia*. London: Continuum.

Deleuze, Gilles and Felix Guattari. 2009 [1977]. *Anti-Oedipus: Capitalism and Schizophrenia*. London: Penguin Books.

Deleuze, Gilles and Claire Parnett. 1987 [1977]. *Dialogues II*. London: Continuum.

Dellaert, Frank, Thomas Polzin and Alex Waibel. 1996. 'Recognising Emotion in Speech.' *Proceeding of Fourth International Conference on Spoken Language Processing. ICSLP '96, October 3–6, 1996*. New York.

Del Re, Alisa. 1996. 'Women and Welfare: Where is Jocasta?' Pp. 99–114 in *Radical Thought in Italy: A Potential Politics*, edited by Paolo Virno and Michael Hardt. Minneapolis: University of Minnesota Press.

Del Re, Alisa. 2005. 'Feminism and Autonomy: Itinerary of Struggle.' Pp. 48–72 in *The philosophy of Antonio Negri: Resistance in Practice*, edited by Timothy S. Murphy and Abdul-Karim Mustapha. London: Pluto Press.

Desai, Radhika. 2011. 'The New Communists of the Commons: 21st Century Proudhonists.' *International Journal of Critical Thought* 1(2): 204–223.

Diefenbach, Katja. 2010. 'Living Labor, Form Giving Fire: The Postworkerist Reading of Marx and the Concept of Biopolitical Labour.' Pp. 63–95 in *Post-Fordism and its Discontents*, edited by Gal Kirn. Retrieved July 16, 2024. (http://tinyurl.com/lgdw6a8).

Diefenbach, Katja. 2011. 'Im/Potential Politics: Political Ontologies in Negri, Agamben and Deleuze.' European Institute for Progressive Cultural Politics. Retrieved August 1, 2024. (http://eipcp.net/transversal/0811/diefenbach/en).

Diefenbach, Katja. 'The Paradoxes of Politics: On the Postworkerist Reading of Marx.' Retrieved July 24, 2024. (http://www.after1968.org/app/webroot/uploads/Living laborx%281%29.pdf).

Dinerstein, Ana Cecilia and Frederick Harry Pitts. 2021. *A World Beyond Work: Labour, Money and the Capitalist State Between Crisis and Utopia*, Bingley: Emerald Publishing.

Dirnbach, Eric. 2021. 'Millions of Workers are Quitting but Should Organise Instead.' *Organizing Work*. Retrieved July 29, 2024. (https://organizing.work/2021/09/millions -of-workers-are-quitting-but-should-organize-instead/).

Do, Kimberley, Maya De Los Santos, Michael Muller, and Saiph Savage. 2024. 'Designing Gig Worker Sousveillance Tools'. *Proceedings of the CHI Conference on Human Factors in Computing Systems (CHI '24)*, May 11–16, 2024, Honolulu, HI, USA. ACM, New York.

Dooley, Peter C. 2005. *The Labour Theory of Value*. London: Routledge.

Dosse, Francois. 2010 [2007]. *Gilles Deleuze and Felix Guattari: Intersecting Lives*. New York: Columbia University Press.

Douthat, Ross. 2013. 'A World Without Work.' *New York Times*, February 23.

Dowling, Emma. 2007. 'Producing the Dining Experience: Measure, Subjectivity and the Affective Worker,' *Ephemera* 7(1): 117–132.

Dowling, Emma. 2021. *The Care Crisis: What Caused It and How Can We End It?* London: Verso.

Dror, Otniel E. 2001. 'Counting the Affects: Discoursing in Numbers.' *Social Research* 68(2): 357–378.

Ducey, Ariel. 2007. 'More Than a Job: Meaning, Affect, and Training Health Care Workers.' Pp. 187–208 in *The Affective Turn: Theorising the Social*, edited by Patricia Ticineto Clough and Jean Halley. Durham: Duke University Press.

Ducey, Ariel. 2010. 'Technologies of Caring Labour: From Objects to Affects.' Pp. 18–32 in *Intimate Labours: Cultures, Technologies and the Politics of Care*, edited by Eileen Boris and Rhacel Salazar Parreñas, Stanford: Stanford University Press.

Dyer-Witheford, Nick. 1999. *Cyber-Marx: Cycles and Circuits of Struggles in High Technology Capitalism*. Urbana and Chicago: University of Illinois Press.

Dyer-Witheford, Nick. 2005. 'Cyber-Negri: The General Intellect and Immaterial Labor'. Pp. 136–162 in *The Philosophy of Antonio Negri: Resistance in Practice*, edited by Timothy S. Murphy and Abdul-Karim Mustapha. London: Pluto Press.

Dyer-Witheford, Nick. 2008. 'For a Compositional Analysis of the Multitude.' Pp. 247–266 in *Subverting the Present, Imagining the Future: Insurrection, Movement, Commons*, edited by Werner Bonefeld. New York: Autonomedia.

Dyer-Witheford, Nick. 2015. *Cyber-Proletariat*. London: Pluto Press.

Dyer-Witheford, Nick, Atle Mikkola Kjosen and James Steinhoff. 2019. *Inhuman Power: Artificial Intelligence and the Future of Capitalism*. London: Pluto Press.

Eden, Dave. 2012. 'Angels of Love in the Unhappiness Factory,' *Subjectivity* 5: 15–35.

Eden, Dave. 2012. *Autonomy: Capitalism Class and Politics*. Surrey: Ashgate.

Ekman, Paul. 1992. 'An Argument for Basic Emotions.' *Cognition and Emotion*, 6(3): 169–200.

Ekman, Paul and Richard J. Davidson. 1994. 'Affective Science: A Research Agenda.' Pp. 411–430 in *The Nature of Emotion*, edited by P. Ekman and R. Davidson. Oxford: Oxford University Press.

Elbe, Ingo. 2013. 'Between Marx, Marxism, and Marxisms – Ways of Reading Marx's Theory.' *Viewpoint Magazine*, October 21. Retrieved August 1, 2024. (http://viewpointmag.com/2013/10/21/between-marx-marxism-and-marxisms-ways-of-reading-marxs-theory/).

Elson, Diane. 1979. 'The Value Theory of Labour.' Pp. 115–180 in *Value: The Representation of Labour in Capitalism: Essays*, edited by Diane Elson. London: CSE Books.

Endnotes Collective. 2008. *Endnotes 1: Preliminary Materials for a Balance Sheet of the 20th Century*. London: Endnotes.

Endnotes Collective. 2010. *Endnotes 2: Misery and the Value Form*. London: Endnotes.

Endnotes Collective. 2010a. 'Communisation and Value-Form Theory.' Pp. 68–105 in *Endnotes 2*. London: Endnotes.

Endnotes Collective. 2013. *Endnotes 3: Gender, Class, Race and Other Misfortunes*. London: Endnotes.

Endnotes Collective. 2013. 'The Logic of Gender.' Pp. 56–91 in *Endnotes 3: Gender, Class, Race and Other Misfortunes*. London: Endnotes.

Endnotes Collective and Aaron Benanav. 2010. 'Misery and Debt: On the Logic and History of Surplus Populations and Surplus Capital.' Pp. 21–51 in *Endnotes 2*. London: Endnotes.

Enxuga, Shay. 2013. 'Queer Struggles Are Class Struggles: Halifax Queer and Trans Workers at Forefront of Service Worker and Barista Movement.' *Halifax Media Co-op: News from Nova Scotia's Grassroots*. Retrieved August 1, 2024. (http://tinyurl.com/k84ab3x).

Federici, Silvia. 2008 [2006]. 'Precarious Labor: A Feminist Viewpoint.' Paper presented at This is Forever: From Inquiry to Refusal Discussion Series. New York, October 28. Retrieved August 1, 2024. (http://tinyurl.com/kynx72l).

Federici, Silvia. 2011. 'On Affective Labour.' Pp. 57–74 in *Cognitive Capitalism, Education and Digital Labor*, edited by Michael A. Peters and Ergin Bulut. New York: Peter Lang Publishing.

Federici, Silvia. 2012 [1975]. 'Wages Against Housework.' Pp. 15–22 in Silvia Federici *Revolution at Point Zero: Housework, Reproduction, and Feminist Struggle*. Brooklyn: PM Press.

Federici, Silvia. 2012. *Revolution at Point Zero: Housework, Reproduction, and Feminist Struggle*. Brooklyn: PM Press.

Feher, Michel. 2009. 'Self-Appreciation; Or, the Aspirations of Human Capital.' *Public Culture* 21(1): 21–41.

Ferguson Bulan, Heather, Rebecca J. Erickson and Amy S. Wharton. 1997. 'Doing for Others on the Job: The Affective Requirements of Service Work, Gender and Emotional Well-Being.' *Social Problems* 44(2): 235–256.

Fine, Ben. 1986. 'Introduction.' Pp. 1–17 in *The Value Dimension: Marx Versus Sraffa*, edited by Ben Fine. London: Routledge.

Fine, Ben and Alfredo Saad-Filho. 2009. 'Twixt Ricardo and Rubin: Debating Kincaid Once More.' *Historical Materialism* 17(3): 192–207.

Fineman, Stephen. 2001. 'Emotions and Organizational Control.' Pp. 219–237 in *Emotions at Work: Theory, Research and Applications in Management*, edited by Roy L. Payne and Cary L. Cooper. Chichester: John Wiley & Sons.

Fisher, Samuel. 2024. 'Abstract Models, Concrete Frictions: On Mau's Mute Compulsion.' *Spectre Journal* July. Retrieved July 28. (https://spectrejournal.com/abstract-models-concrete-frictions/).

Fisher, V.E. and Joseph V Hanna. 1931. *The Dissatisfied Worker*. New York: The MacMillan Company.

Fleming, Peter and Matteo Mandarini. 2009. 'Towards a Workers' Society? New Perspectives on Work and Emancipation.' Pp. 328–344 in *The Oxford Handbook of Critical Management Studies*, edited by M. Alvesson, T. Bridgman and H. Willmott. Oxford: Oxford University Press.

Fleming, Peter. 2014. *Resisting Work: The Corporatisation of Life and its Discontents*. Philadelphia: Temple University Press.

Fleming, Peter. 2015. *The Mythology of Work: How Capitalism Persists Despite Itself*. London: Pluto Press.

Fletcher, Keaton A., Ruth Kanfer and Corey Tatel. 2020. 'Workplace Emotions and Motivation: Toward a Unified Approach.' Pp. 52–63 in *The Cambridge Handbook of Workplace Affect*, edited by Liu-Qin Yang, Russel Cropanzo, Catherine S. Daus and Vincente Martinez-Tur. Cambridge: Cambridge University Press.

Fortunati, Leopoldina. 1981. *The Arcane of Reproduction: Housework, Prostitution, Labour and Capital*. New York: Autonomedia.

Fotaki, Marianna, Kate Kenny and Sheena J. Vachhani. 2017. 'Thinking Critically About Affect in Organisation Studies: Why It Matters.' *Organization* 24(1): 3–17.

Foucault, Michel. 2007. *Security, Territory and Population: Lectures at the College de France 1977–1978*. New York: Palgrave Macmillan.

Frenkel, Steve. 2009. 'Critical Reflections on Labor Process Theory, Work, and Management.' Pp. 525–535 in *The Oxford Handbook of Critical Management Studies*, edited by M. Alvesson, T. Bridgman and H. Willmott. Oxford: Oxford University Press.

Fritsch, Jonas. 2009. 'Understanding Affective Engagement as a Resource in Interaction Design', in proceedings of *Engaging Artefacts, Nordic Design Research Conference*.

Fumagalli, Andrea. 2010. 'The Global Economic Crisis and Socioeconomic Governance.' Pp. 61–84 in *Crisis in the Global Economy: Financial Markets, Social Struggle, and New Political Scenarios*, edited by Andrea Fumagalli and Sandro Mendrazza. Los Angeles: Semiotext(e).

Fumagalli, Andrea. 2011. 'Twenty Theses on Contemporary Capitalism (Cognitive Biocapitalism)'. *Angelaki: Journal of the Theoretical Humanities* 16(3): 7–17.

Gabin, Nancy. 1982. '"They Have Placed a Cost on Womanhood": The Protest Actions of Women Auto-Workers in Detroit-Area UAW Locals 1954–1947.' *Feminist Studies*, 8(2): 373–398.

Gawne, Mark. 2012. "The Modulation and Ordering of Affect: From Emotion Recognition Technology to the Critique of Class Composition." *Fibreculture*, 21.

Gawne, Mark. 2020. 'Love Is a Battlefield: on the Affective Politics of Crisis.' Pp. 76–79 in *Love: Art, Ideas, Music, Politics*, edited by The Love Collective. Wollongong: Kembla Books.

Gerstein, Ira. 1986. 'Production, Circulation and Value.' Pp. 45–93 in *The Value Dimension: Marx Versus Sraffa*, edited by Ben Fine. London and New York: Routledge and Keegan Paul.

Girardi, Daniela, Filippo Lanubile, Nicole Novielli and Alexander Serebrenik. 2021. 'Emotions and Perceived Productivity of Software Designers at the Workplace.' *IEEE Transactions on Software Engineering* 48(9) doi: 10.1109/TSE.2021.3087906.

Gittleman, Maury. 2022. 'The Great Resignation in Perspective.' *Monthly Labor Review*, U.S. Bureau of Labor Statistics, July 2022, Retrieved August 1, 2024. https://doi.org/10.21916/mlr.2022.20.

Goddard, Michael. 2011. 'From the Multitudo to the Multitude: The Place of Spinoza in the Political Philosophy of Antonio Negri.' Pp. 171–192 in *Reading Negri: Marxism in the Age of Empire*, edited by Pierra Lamarche, Max Rosenkrantz, and David Sherman. Chicago: Carus Publishing Company.

Goette, Lorenz and David Huffman. 2005. Affect as a Source of Motivation in the Workplace: A New Model of Labor Supply, and New Field Evidence on Income Targeting and the Goal Gradient. IZA Discussion Paper No. 1890, December. Retrieved August 1, 2024. (http://tinyurl.com/md7ezp7).

Goldberg, Michelle. 2013. 'A Generation of Intellectuals Shaped by the 2008 Crash Rescues Marx from History's Dustbin.' *Tablet Magazine*. Retrieved July 14, 2023. (http://tinyurl.com/kzvnges).

Gordon, Kristyn. 2007. 'Theorising Emotion and Affect: Feminist Engagements.' *Feminist Theory* 8(3): 333–348.

Graeber, David. 2012. *Debt: The First 5000 Years*. Brooklyn: Melville House.

Graeber, David. 2013. 'On the Phenomenon of Bullshit Jobs'. *Strike Magazine*. August 1, 2024. (http://tinyurl.com/od4oldf).

Grandey, Alicia A., Katelyn E. England and Louis Boermerman. 2020. 'Emotional Labour: Display Rules and Emotion Regulation at Work.' Pp. 146–159 in *The Cambridge Handbook of Workplace Affect*, edited by Liu-Qin Yang, Russel Cropanzo, Catherine S. Daus and Vincente Martinez-Tur. Cambridge: Cambridge University Press.

Gray, Nick. 2010. 'Abstraction, Universality, Money and Capital: The Capital-Theory of Value.' Paper presented at Marx and Philosophical Society annual conference, London, June.

Gray, Neil. 2011. 'In Exchange with Marina Vishmidt: The Economy of Abolition/Abolition of the Economy.' *Variant* 42: 7–11.

Gregg, Melissa. 2011. *Work's Intimacy*. Cambridge: Polity Press.

Gregg, Melissa. 2018. *Counterproductive: Time Management in the Knowledge Economy*. Durham: Duke University Press.

Gregg, Melissa and Seigworth, Gregory J. 2010. 'An Inventory of Shimmers.' Pp. 1–25 in *The Affect Theory Reader*, edited by Melissa Gregg and Gregory J. Seigworth. Durham: Duke University Press.

Grimm, Sabine and Klaus Ronneburger. 2007. 'An Invisible History of Work: Interview with Sergio Bologna.' *Springerin* 1(7). Retrieved August 1, 2024. (https://metropolitan factory.wordpress.com/wp-content/uploads/2012/07/an-invisible-history-of-work .pdf).

Guattari, Felix and Antonio Negri. 2010. *New Lines of Alliance, New Spaces of Liberty*. Brooklyn: Autonomedia.

Guattari, Félix. 1995. *Chaosmosis: An Ethico-Aesthetic Paradigm*. Sydney: Power Publications.

Guattari, Felix. 2011 [1979]. *Machinic Unconscious: Essays in Schizoanalysis*. Los Angeles: Semiotext(e).

Gunes, Hatice, Massimo Piccardi and Tony Jan. 2004. 'Face and Body Gesture Recognition for a Vision-Based Multimodal Analyser', *The Pan-Sydney Area Workshop on Visual Information Processing (VIP2003)* 36, Sydney: Conferences in Research and Practice in Information Technology.

Gunn, Richard. 1992. 'Against Historical Materialism: Marxism as First-Order Discourse.' Pp. 1–45 in *Open Marxism: Vol 2 Theory and Practice*, edited by Werner Bonefeld, Richard Gunn and Kosmas Psychopedis. London: Pluto Press.

Gutiérrez-Rodríguez, Encarnación. 2010. *Migration, Domestic Work and Affect: A Decolonial Approach on Value and the Feminization of Labor*. New York: Routledge.

Hanlon, Gerard. 2007. 'HRM Is Redundant?: Professions, Immaterial Labour and the Future of Work.' Pp. 263–280 in *Searching for the Human in Human Resource Management: Theory, Practice and Workplace Contexts*, edited by Sharon Bolton and Maeve Houlihan. New York: Bloomsbury Publishing.

Hanlon, Gerard. 2016. *The Dark Side of Management: A Secret History of Management Theory*. London and New York: Routledge.

Hanlon, Gerard. 2017. 'Digging Deeper Towards Capricious Management: "Personal Traits Become Part of the Means of Production."' *Human Relations* 70(2): 168–184.

Hardt, Michael. 1993. *Gilles Deleuze: An Apprenticeship in Philosophy*. Minneapolis: University of Minnesota Press.

Hardt, Michael. 1999. 'Affective Labour.' *Boundary 2* 26(2): 89–100.

Hardt, Michael. 2005. 'Into the Factory: Negri's Lenin and the Subjective Caesura (1968–73).' Pp. 7–37 in *The Philosophy of Antonio Negri: Resistance in Practice*, edited by Timothy S. Murphy and Abdul-Karim Mustapha. London: Pluto Press.

Hardt, Michael. 2007. 'Foreword: What Affects Are Good For.' Pp. ix–xiii in *The Affective Turn: Theorising the Social*, edited by Patricia Ticineto Clough and Jean Halley. Durham: Duke University Press.

Hardt, Michael. 2010. 'The Common in Communism.' *Rethinking Marxism: A Journal of Economics, Culture and Society* 22(3): 346–356.

Hardt, Michael. 2011. 'For Love or Money?' *Cultural Anthropology* 26(4): 676–682.

Hardt, Michael. 2012. 'Falsify the Currency.' *The South Atlantic Quarterly* 111(2): 359–379.

Hardt, Michael and Antonio Negri. 1994. *Labor of Dionysus: A Critique of the State Form* Minneapolis: University of Minnesota Press.

Hardt, Michael and Antonio Negri. 2000. *Empire.* Cambridge: Harvard University Press.

Hardt, Michael and Antonio Negri. 2004. *Multitude: War and Democracy in the Age of Empire.* London: Hamish Hamilton.

Hardt, Michael and Antonio Negri. 2009. *Commonwealth.* Cambridge: Harvard University Press.

Hardt, Michael and Antonio Negri. 2012. *Declaration.* New York: Melanie Jackson Agency.

Hardt, Michael and Antonio Negri. 2017. *Assembly.* Oxford: Oxford University Press.

Harney, Stefano. 2005. 'Management Cliché.' *Critical Perspectives on Accounting* 16: 579–591.

Harney, Stefano. 2006. 'Management and Self-Activity: Accounting for the Crisis and Profit Taking.' *Critical Perspectives on Accounting* 17: 935–946.

Harney, Stefano. 2006a. 'Programming Immaterial Labour.' *Social Semiotics* 16(1): 75–87.

Harney, Stefano and Fred Moten. 2013. *Undercommons: Fugitive Planning and Black Study.* Wivenhoe: Minor Compositions.

Hatton, Erin. 2011. *The Temp Economy: From Kelly Girls to Permatemps in Postwar America.* Philadelphia: Temple University Press.

Haug, Wolfgang Fritz and Joseph Fraccia. 2009. 'Historical-Critical Dictionary of Marxism: Immaterial Labour'. *Historical Materialism* 17(4): 177–185.

Hauptmann, Deborah and Warren Neidich (eds). 2010. *Cognitive Architecture. From Bio-Politics to Noo-Politics: Architecture & Mind in the Age of Communication and Information.* Rotterdam: 010 Publishers.

Heinrich, Michael. 2005. 'Invaders from Marx: On the Uses of Marxian Theory, and The Difficulties of a Contemporary Reading.' Retrieved August 1, 2024. (http://www.oekonomiekritik.de/205Invaders.htm).

Heinrich, Michael. 2012. *An Introduction to the Three Volumes of Karl Marx's Capital.* New York: Monthly Review Press.

Heinrich, Michael. 2013. 'The "Fragment on Machines" a Marxian Misconception in the *Grundrisse* and its Overcoming in *Capital.*' Pp. 197–212 in *In Marx's Laboratory: Critical Interpretations of the Grundrisse,* edited by Riccardo Bellofiore, Guido Starosta and Peter D. Thomas. Leiden: Brill.

Helms, Gesa. 2011. 'The Presence of Precarity: Self-Employment as Contemporary Form'. *Variant* 41: 39–42.

Helms, Gesa, Marina Vishmidt and Lauren Berlant. 2010. 'Affect & the Politics of Austerity: An interview exchange with Lauren Berlant.' *Variant* 39/40: 3–6.

Hemmings, Clare. 2005. 'Invoking Affect: Cultural Theory and the Ontological Turn.' *Cultural Studies* 19(5): 548–567.

Henkel, Alexander P., Stefano Bromuri, Deniz Iren and Visara Urovi. 2020. 'Half Human, Half Machine: Augmenting Service Employees with AI for Interpersonal Emotion Regulation.' *Journal of Service Management* 31(2): 247–265.

Henwood, Doug. 2003. *After the New Economy.* New York: New Press.

Herriot, Peter. 2001. 'Future Work and Its Emotional Implications.' Pp. 307–325 in *Emotions at Work: Theory, Research and Applications in Management,* edited by Roy L. Payne and Cary L. Cooper. Chichester: John Wiley & Sons.

Hersey, Rexford B. 1932. *Workers' Emotions in Shop and Home: A Study of Individual Workers from the Psychological and Physiological Standpoint.* Philadelphia: University of Pennsylvania Press.

Hester, Helen and Nick Srnicek. 2023. *After Work: A History of the Home and the Fight for Free Time.* London: Verso.

Hochschild, Arlie. 2000. 'Global Care Chains and Emotional Surplus Value.' Pp. 130–146 in *On the Edge: Globalization and the New Millennium,* edited by Tony Giddens and Will Hutton. London: Sage Publishers.

Hochschild, Arlie. 2003. *The Managed Heart: Commercialisation of Human Feeling.* Berkeley, Los Angeles and London: University of California Press.

Holloway, John. 1992. 'Crisis, Fetishism, Class Composition.' Pp. 145–169 in *Open Marxism: Vol 2 Theory and Practice,* edited by Werner Bonefeld, Richard Gunn and Kosmas Psychopedis. London: Pluto Press.

Holloway, John. 2010. *Crack Capitalism.* New York: Pluto Press.

Holttinen, Heli. 2010. 'Social Practices as Units of Value Creation: Theoretical Underpinnings and Implications.' *International Journal of Quality and Service Sciences* 2(1): 95–112.

Hudlicka, Eva. 2003. 'To Feel or Not to Feel: The Role of Affect in Human-Computer Interaction.' *International Journal of Human-Computer Studies* 59: 1–32.

Hunter, Carolyn and Nina Kinaven. 2022. *Affect in Organization and Management.* New York: Routledge.

Iedema, Rick, Carl Rhodes and Hermine Scheeres. 2005. 'Presencing Identity: Organisational Change and Immaterial Labour.' *Journal of Organisational Change Management* 18(4): 327–337.

Iedema, Rick, Carl Rhodes and Hermine Scheeres. 2006. 'Surveillance, Resistance, Observance: Exploring the Teleo-Affective Volatility of Workplace Interaction.' *Organisation Studies* 27(8): 1111–1130.

Industrial Workers of the World. 2019 [2008]. 'Deep Cuts: Emotional Pressure and Organisation Building.' *Industrial Worker.* Retrieved August 1, 2024. (https://indus trialworker.org/deep-cuts-emotional-pressure-and-organization-building/).

Industrial Workers of the World. 2022. 'March on the Boss.' *Industrial Worker*. Retrieved August 1, 2024. (https://industrialworker.org/march-on-the-boss/).

Institute for Precarious Consciousness. 2014. 'We Are All Very Anxious: Six Theses on Anxiety and Why It Is Effectively Preventing Militancy, and One Possible Strategy for Overcoming It.' Retrieved August 1, 2024. (http://tinyurl.com/l2sz5gg).

Itzkovich, Yariv, Sibylle Heilbrunn and Niva Dolev. 2022. 'Drivers of Intrapreneurship: An Affective Events Theory Viewpoint.' *Personnel Review* 51(4): 1149–1170.

Ives, Peter. 2011. 'Book reviews: Christian Marazzi Capital and Language: From the New Economy to the War Economy.' *Capital and Class* 35(1): 154–156.

Jabour, Bridie. 2014. 'Australia's "Unsustainable" Welfare System to be Overhauled, Says Minister.' *The Guardian*, January 21. Retrieved August 2, 2024. (http://tinyurl.com /p8eopgs).

Jackson, Sarah. 2023. 'A millionaire CEO is rooting for higher unemployment, saying it's time to "remind people that they work for the employer, not the other way around."' *Business Insider*, September 14.

Jaffe, Sarah. 2021. *Work Won't Love You Back: How Devotion to Our Jobs Keeps Us Exploited, Exhausted, and Alone*. London: Hurst & Co.

Jaimes, Alejandro, and Sebe, Nicu. 2007. 'Multi-Modal Human-Computer Interaction: A Survey,' *Computer Vision and Image Understanding* 108: 116–134.

James, Nicky. 1992. 'Care = Organisation + Physical Labour + Emotional Labour.' *Sociology of Health and Illness* 14(4): 488–509.

James, Selma. 2012 [1972]. 'Women, the Unions, and Work, or What is Not to be Done?' Pp. 60–75 in *Sex, Race and Class, The Perspective of Winning, a Selection of Writings 1952–2011*, edited by Selma James. Oakland: PM Press.

James, Selma. 2012 [1974]. 'Sex, Race and Class.' Pp. 92–101 in *Sex, Race and Class, The Perspective of Winning, a Selection of Writings 1952–2011*, edited by Selma James. Oakland: PM Press.

Jenkins, Sarah, Rick Delbridge and Ashley Roberts. 2010. 'Emotional Management in a Mass Customised Call Centre: Examining Skill and Knowledgeability in Interactive Service Work.' *Work, Employment and Society* 24(3): 546–564.

Johnson, Hazel-Anne M. and Paul E. Spector. 2007. 'Service with a Smile: Do Emotional Intelligence, Gender, and Autonomy Moderate the Emotional Labour Process?' *Journal of Occupational Health Psychology* 12(4): 319–333.

Johnston, Alannah and Jörgen Sandberg. 2008. 'Controlling Service Work: An Ambiguous Accomplishment Between Employees, Management and Customers.' *Journal of Consumer Culture* 8(3): 389–417.

Judge, Timothy A., Howard M. Weiss, John D. Kammeyer-Mueller and Charles L. Hulin. 2017. 'Job Attitudes, Job Satisfaction, and Job Affect: A Century of Continuity and Change.' *Journal of Applied Psychology* 102(3): 356–374.

Junca-Silva, Ana and Eunice Lopes. 2023. 'Testing the Affective Events Theory in Hospitality Management: A Multi-Sample Approach.' *Sustainability* 15: 1–13.

Junge, Martin and Rainer Reisenzein. 2013. 'Indirect Scaling Methods for Testing Quantitative Emotion Theories.' *Cognition and Emotion* 27(7): 1247–1275.

Kanfer, Ruth and Richard J. Klimosji. 2002. 'Affect and Work: Looking Back to the Future.' Pp. 473–490 in *Emotions in the Workplace: Understanding the Structure and Role of Emotions in Organisational Behaviour*, edited by Robert G. Lord, Richard J. Klimoski and Rith Kanfer. San Francisco: Wiley.

Kang, Edward B. 2023. 'On the Praxes and Politics of AI Speech Emotion Recognition.' *ACM Conference on Fairness, Accountability, and Transparency (FAccT '23)*, June 12–15, 2023, Chicago, IL, USA. ACM, New York.

Kanto, Jodi and Sam Hodson. 2014. 'Working Anything But 9–5: Scheduling Technology Leaves Low Income Parents with Hours of Chaos.' *New York Times*. August 1, 2024. (http://tinyurl.com/k2urq6r).

Karpi, Tero, Lotta Kahkonen, Mona Manevuo, Mari Pajala and Tanja Sivonen (eds). 2016. 'Affective Capitalism', *Ephemera: Theory and Politics in Organisation*, 16(4).

Kay, Joseph. 2013. 'Capital Can't Be Reasoned With: The Importance Affective Politics.' Retrieved August 1, 2024. (http://tinyurl.com/lb793nx).

Kelly, Lauren Kate. 2024. 'Why Woolworths Workers Can't Sleep at Night: Inside the Supermarket Giant's Controversial Framework.' *The Conversation*. October 24, 2024.

Kenny, Kate, Marianna Fotaki. 2014. 'Introduction.' Pp. 18–22 in *The Psychosocial and Organization Studied: Affect at Work*, edited by Kate Kenny and Marianna Fotaki. New York: Palgrave MacMillan.

Kicillof, Axel and Guido Starosta. 2007. 'Value Form and Class Struggle: A Critique of the Autonomist Theory of Value.' *Capital and Class* 92: 13–40.

Kicillof, Axel and Guido Starosta. 2007a. 'On Materiality and Social Form: A Political Critique of Rubin's Value-Form Theory.' *Historical Materialism* 15: 9–43.

Kincaid, Jim. 2009. 'The Logical Construction of Value-Theory: More on Fine and Saad-Filho.' *Historical Materialism* 17(3): 208–220.

King, M.G. 2001. 'Emotions in the Workplace: Biological Correlates.' Pp. 85–106 in *Emotions at Work: Theory, Research and Applications in Management*, edited by Roy L. Payne and Cary L. Cooper. Chichester: John Wiley & Sons.

Kison, Markus. 2009. *Touched Echoe*. Art installation, Osnabrück, Germany, April 22– October 4. Retrieved August 1, 2014. (http://www.markuskison.de/index.html# touched_echo).

Knafo, Sam. 2007. 'Political Marxism and Value Theory: Bridging the Gap Between Theory and History.' *Historical Materialism* 15: 75–104.

Knights, Davis and Hugh Willmott. 1990. 'Introduction.' Pp. 1–45 in *Labour Process Theory*, edited by David Knights and HughWillmott. London: MacMillan.

Knowing Machines Project. https://knowingmachines.org/ Retrieved August 1, 2024.

Koivunen, Anu. 2009. 'An Affective Turn? Reimagining the Subject of Feminist Theory.' Pp. 8–28 in *Working with Affect in Feminist Studies: Disturbing Differences*, edited by Marianne Liljestrom and Susanna Paasonen, London: Routledge.

Kurz, Robert. 1991. 'The Lost Honour of Labour'. Retrieved August 1, 2024. (http://tinyurl.com/kncylqf).

LaborInArt. 2014. 'Running Along Disaster: A Conversation with Franco Bifo Berardi.' *E-flux*. August 1, 2024. (http://tinyurl.com/nucx4gl).

La Caze, Marguerite, and Henry Martyn Lloyd. 2011. 'Editor's Introduction: Philosophy and the Affective Turn.' *Parrhesia*, 13: 1–13.

Lane, Dorian. 2021. 'Revisiting the Impact of Goals on Affect and Effort.' *Accounting Perspectives* 20(4): 617–651.

Lao, Shihong and Masato Kawade. 2004. 'Vision-Based Understanding Technologies and Their Applications.' Pp. 339–348 in *Sinobiometrics*, edited by S.Z. Li, Berlin: Springer-Verlag.

Larsen, Neil, Mathias Nilges, Josh Robinson and Nicholas Brown. 2014. *Marxism and the Value Critique*. Chicago: MCM Publishing.

Latham, Gary. 2007. *Work Motivation: History, Theory, Research*. California: Sage Publications.

Latham, Gary P. And Craig C. Pinder. 2005. 'Work Motivation Theory and Research at the Dawn of the Twenty-First Century.' *Annual Review of Psychology* 56: 485–516.

Lazzarato, Maurizio. 1996. 'Immaterial labor.' Pp. 133–150 in *Radical Thought in Italy: A Potential Politics*, edited by Paolo Virno and Michael Hardt. Minneapolis: University of Minnesota Press.

Lazzarato, Maurizio. 2006. 'The Concepts of Life and the Living in the Societies of Control.' Pp. 171–190 in *Deleuze and the Social*, edited by Martin Fuglsang, Bent Meier Sørensen. Edinburgh: Edinburgh University Press.

Lazzarato, Maurizio. 2006a. 'From Biopower to Biopolitics.' *Tailoring Biotechnologies* 2(2): 11–20.

Lazzarato, Maurizio. 2007. 'Strategies of the Political Entrepreneur.' *SubStance* 36(1): 87–97.

Lazzarato, Maurizio. 2010. 'Multiplicity, Totality and Politics.' *Parrhesia* 9: 23–30.

Lazzarato, Maurizio. 2012. *The Making of the Indebted Man*. Los Angeles: Semiotext(e).

Lazzarato, Maurizio. 2014. *Signs and Machines: Capitalism and the Production of Subjectivity*. Los Angeles: Semiotext(e).

Lazzarato, Maurizio. 2023. *The Intolerable Present, The Urgency of Revolution: Minorities and Classes*. South Pasadena: Semiotext(e).

Lazzarato, Maurizio and Toni Negri. 1991. 'Travail Immaterial and Subjectivite.' *Futur Anterieur* 6: 1993.

Lebowitz, Michael. 2003. *Beyond Capital: Marx's Political Economy of the Working Class.* New York: Palgrave Macmillan.

Lee, Hangwoo. 2023. *Affective Capitalism: For a Critique of the Political Economy of Affect.* Singapore: Palgrave MacMillan.

Lemke, Thomas. 2011. *Biopolitics: An Advanced Introduction.* New York: New York University Press.

Leonard, Andrew. 2014. 'Robots are Stealing Your Job: How Technology Threatens to Wipe Out the Middle Class.' *Salon,* January 17. Retrieved August 1, 2024. (http://tiny url.com/kqlkcav).

Leonardi, Daniela, Annalisa Murgia, Marco Briziarelli and Emiliana Armano. 2019. 'The Ambivalence of Logistical Connectivity: A Co-Research with Foodora Riders.' *Work Organisation, Labour and Globalisation* 13(1): 155–171.

Leys, Ruth. 2011. 'The Turn to Affect: A Critique.' *Critical Inquiry* 37: 434–472.

Li, Wen-Dong, Xin Zhang, Zhaoli Song and Yating Wang. 2020. 'Behavioural Genetics and Affect at Work: A Review and Directions for Future Research.' Pp. 64–75 in *The Cambridge Handbook of Workplace Affect,* edited by Liu-Qin Yang, Russel Cropanzo, Catherine S. Daus and Vincente Martinez-Tur. Cambridge: Cambridge University Press.

Locke, Edwin A. and Gary P. Latham. 2019. 'The Development of Goal Setting Theory: A Half Century Retrospective.' *Motivation Science* 5(2): 93–105.

Lopes, Paulo N., Daisy Grewal, Jessica Kadis, Michelle Gall and Peter Salovey. 2006. 'Evidence That Emotional Intelligence is Related to Job Performance and Affect and Attitudes to Work.' *Psicothema* 18: 132–138.

Lopez, Franci Suni, Nelly Condori-Fernandez and Alejandro Catala. 2018. 'Towards Real Time Automatic Stress Detection for Office Workplaces.' *Information Management and Big Data 5th International Conference,* Lima, Peru, September 3–5, 2018, Proceedings. https://doi.org/10.1007/978-3-030-11680-4_27.

Lopez, Steven H. 2006. 'Emotional Labor and Organized Emotional Care: Conceptualizing Nursing Home Care Work.' *Work and Occupations* 33(2): 133–160.

Lordon, Frederic. 2014. *Willing Slaves of Capital: Spinoza and Marx on Desire.* London: Verso.

Loyall, A. Bryan. 1997. *Believable Agents: Building Interactive Personalities.* Unpublished PhD Thesis. School of Computer Science, Stanford University.

Lucarelli, Stefano. 2010. 'Financialization as Biopower.' Pp. 119–138 in *Crisis in the Global Economy: Financial Markets, Social Struggle, and New Political Scenarios,* edited by Andrea Fumagalli and Sandro Mendrazza. Los Angeles: Semiotext(e).

Macdonald, Cameron Lynne and David Merrill. 2009. 'Intersectionality in the Emotional Proletariat.' Pp. 113–134 in *Service Work: Critical Perspectives,* edited by M. Korczynski and C. Macdonald. New York: Routledge.

Maggenti, Maria. 2003. 'Interview.' *Act-Up Oral History Project*. Retrieved July 20 2024. (http://www.actuporalhistory.org/beta/interviews/images/maggenti.pdf).

Malabou, Catherine. 2008. *What Should We Do with Our Brain?* New York: Fordham University Press.

Mann, Geoff. 2010. 'Value after Lehman.' *Historical Materialism* 18: 172–188.

Mantello, Peter and Manh-Tung Ho. 2023. 'Emotional AI and the Future of Wellbeing in the Workplace.' *AI and Society* Open Forum. https://doi.org/10.1007/s00146-023 -01639-8.

Marazzi, Christian. 1977. 'Money and the World Crisis.' *Zerowork* 2: 91–111.

Marazzi, Christian. 2008 [2002]. *Capital and Language*. London: Semiotext(e).

Marazzi, Christian. 2011 [1994]. *Capital and Affects: The Politics of the Language Economy*. Los Angeles: Semiotext(e).

Marazzi, Christian. 2011a. *The Violence of Financial Capitalism*. Los Angeles: Semiotext(e).

Marazzi, Christian. 2014. 'Money and Financial Capital: The Return of the Substance of Value.' Pp. 27–39 in *Post-Crisis Perspectives: The Common and Its Powers*, edited by Oscar Garcia Agustin and Christian Ydesen. New York: Peter Lang.

Marazzi, Christian. 2014a. *The Linguistic Nature of Money and Finance*. Los Angeles: Semiotext(e).

Martin, Randy. 2012. *Under New Management: Universities, Administrative Labor, and the Professional Turn*. Philadelphia: Temple University Press.

Martin, Randy, Michael Rafferty and Dick Bryan. 2008. 'Financialisation, Risk and Labour.' *Competition and Change* 12(2): 120–132.

Martinez-Tur, Vicente. 2020. 'The Service Encounter.' Pp. 285–296 in *The Cambridge Handbook of Workplace Affect*, edited by Liu-Qin Yang, Russel Cropanzo, Catherine S. Daus and Vincente Martinez-Tur. Cambridge: Cambridge University Press.

Marx, Karl. 1864. Marx to Kugelmann in Hanover. Retrieved August 1, 2024. (https://www.marxists.org/archive/marx/works/1868/letters/68_07_11-abs.htm).

Marx, Karl. 1904 [1859]. *A Contribution to the Critique of Political Economy*. Chicago: Charles H. Kerr.

Marx, Karl. 1951. 'Wage Labour and Capital' in *Selected Works volume 1*, edited by Karl Marx and Frederick Engels. Moscow: Foreign Languages Publishing House.

Marx, Karl. 1972. *Theories of Surplus Value*. Vol 3. London: Lawrence and Wishart.

Marx, Karl. 1975. *Theories of Surplus Value*. Vol 1. Moscow: Progress Publishers.

Marx, Karl. 1975a. *Theories of Surplus Value*. Vol 2. Moscow: Progress Publishers.

Marx, Karl. 1990 [1867]. *Capital: A Critique of Political Economy*. Vol 1. London: Penguin.

Marx, Karl. 1992 [1885]. *Capital: A Critique of Political Economy*. Vol 2. London: Penguin.

Marx, Karl. 1992 [1894]. *Capital: A Critique of Political Economy*. Vol 3. London: Penguin.

Marx, Karl. 1993 [1939]. *Grundrisse*. London: Penguin.

Massaro, Sebastiano. 2020. 'The Organisational Neuroscience of Emotions.' Pp. 15–36 in *The Cambridge Handbook of Workplace Affect*, edited by Liu-Qin Yang, Russel Cropanzo, Catherine S. Daus and Vincente Martinez-Tur. Cambridge: Cambridge University Press.

Massumi, Brian. 2002. *Parables for the Virtual: Movement, Affect, Sensation.* Durham: Duke University Press.

Masterman-Smith, Helen and Barbara Pocock. 2008. *Living Low Paid: The Dark Side of Prosperous Australia.* Crows Nest, NSW: Allen & Unwin.

Mathy, Gabriel. 2020. 'The First Services Recession.' *Phenomenal World* March 25. Retrieved July 29, 2024. (https://www.phenomenalworld.org/analysis/the-first-ser vices-recession/).

Mattick, Paul. 2019. *Theory as Critique: Essays on Capital.* Chicago: Haymarket Books.

Mau, Soren. 2023. *Mute Compulsion: A Marxist Theory of the Economic Power of Capital.* London: Verso.

Mavridis, Nikolaos. 2022. 'How Gender is Intertwined with Robots and Affective Technologies: A Short Review' in Davide Cirillo, Silvina Catuara-Solarz, Emre Guney (eds) *Sex and Gender Bias in Technology and Artificial Intelligence.* Cambridge: Academic Press.

McCabe, Darren. 2007. *Power at Work: How Employees Reproduce the Corporate Machine.* New York: Routledge.

McRobbie, Angela. 2011. 'Reflections on Feminism, Immaterial Labour and the Post-Fordist Regime.' *New Formations* 70: 60–76.

Mears, Jane. 2004. 'Global Labour Markets: Care Work and "Chains of Caring."' in Proceedings of *Mobile Boundaries, Rigid Worlds.* Retrieved August 01, 2024. (http:// www.crsi.mq.edu.au/publications/conference_proceedings/).

Merlo, Kelsey L., Stefanie P. Shaughnessy and Howard M. Weiss. 2018. 'Affective Influences on Within-Person Changes in Work Performance as Mediated by Attentional Focus.' *European Journal of Work and Organizational Psychology* 27(1): 126–139.

Midnight Notes Collective. 1992 [1990]. 'The New Enclosures' Pp. 317–333 in *Midnight Oil: Work, Energy, War 1973–1992*, edited by Midnight Notes Collective. New York: Autonomedia.

Miller, Richard W. 1984. *Analyzing Marx: Morality, Power, and History.* Princeton: Princeton University Press.

Mirowski, Philip. 1999. *More Heat Than Light: Economics as Social Physics, Physics as Nature's Economics.* Cambridge: Cambridge University Press.

Mitropoulos, Angela. 2005. *Precari-Us?* Retrieved August 1, 2024. (http://tinyurl.com /q42elsb).

Mitropoulos, Angela. 2006. 'Autonomy, Recognition, Movement.' *The Commoner* 11: 5–14.

Mitropoulos, Angela. 2007. 'The Social Softwar', *Mute* 2(4). Retrieved August 1, 2024. (http://www.metamute.org/en/The-Social-SoftWar).

Mitropoulos, Angela. 2011. *From Precariousness to Risk Management*. Retrieved July 22, 2024. (http://tinyurl.com/lxgj666).

Mitropoulos, Angela. 2012. *Contract and Contagion: Biopolitics to Oikonomia*. New York: Minor Compositions.

Mitropoulos, Angela. 2012a. 'The Time of the Contract: Insurance, Contingency, and the Arrangement of Risk.' *South Atlantic Quarterly* 111(4): 763–782.

Mitropoulos, Angela. 2015. *Fascism, From Fordism to Trumpism*. Retrieved August 1, 2024.

Moore, Phoebe V. 2018. *The Quantified Self in Precarity: Work, Technology and What Counts*. London: Routledge.

Moore, Phoebe V. 2021. 'Agility of Affect in the Quantified Workplace.' Pp. 225–249 in *The Agile Imperative: Teams, Organizations and Society under Reconstruction?*, edited by Sabine Pfeiffer, Manuel Nicklich and Stefan Sauer. Springer International Publishing.

Moore, Phoebe V. 2022. 'Designing Work for Agility and Affect's Measure.' Pp. 185–196 in *Marx and the Robots: Networked Production, AI, and Human Labour*, edited by F. Butler and S. Nuss. London: Pluto Press.

Morfino, Vittorio. 2014. 'The Multitudo According to Negri: On the Disarticulation of Ontology and History.' *Rethinking Marxism: A Journal of Economics, Culture and Society* 26(2): 227–238.

Morini, Cristina and Andrea Fumugalli. 2007. 'Life Put to Work: Towards a Life Theory of Value.' *Ephemera* 10(3): 234–252.

Moulier Boutang, Yann. 2011. *Cognitive Capitalism*. Malden: Polity Press.

Mulholland, Kate. 2002. 'Gender, Emotional Labour and Teamworking in a Call Centre.' *Personnel Review* 31(3): 283–303.

Mulholland, Kate. 2004. 'Workplace resistance in an Irish call centre: slammin', scammin' smokin' an' leavin'.' *Work, Employment, and Society* 18(4): 709–724.

Murgia, Annalisa, Lara Maestripieri and Emiliana Armano. 2017. 'The Precariousness of Knowledge Workers Part 2: Forms and Critiques of Autonomy and Self-Representation.' *Work Organisation, Labour and Globalisation* 11(1): 1–9.

Murphy, Timothy S. 2001. 'Ontology, Deconstruction, and Empire.' *Rethinking Marxism* 13(3–4): 16–23.

Murphy, Timothy S. 2012. *Antonio Negri*. Cambridge: Polity Press.

Murray, Patrick. 1988. *Marx's Theory of Scientific Knowledge*. Atlantic Highlands, NJ: Humanities Press International.

Murray, Patrick. 2013. 'Unavoidable Crises: Reflections on Backhaus and the Development of Marx's Value-Form Theory in the *Grundrisse*.' Pp. 121–146 in *In Marx's*

Laboratory: Critical Interpretations of the Grundrisse, edited by Riccardo Bellofiore, Guido Starosta and Peter D. Thomas. Chicago: Haymarket Books.

Nadasen, Premilla. 2023, *Care: The Highest Stage of Capitalism*. Chicago: Haymarket Books.

Nappalos, Scott Nikolas. 2013. *Lines of Work: Stories of Jobs and Resistance*. Edmonton: Black Cat Press.

Nath, Vandana. 2011. 'Aesthetic and Emotional Labour Through Stigma: National Identity Management and Racial Abuse in Offshored Indian Call Centres.' *Work Employment Society* 25(4): 709–725.

Neel, Phil A. 2018. *Hinterland: America's New Landscape of Class and Conflict*. Chicago: Reaktion Books.

Negishi, Kaima. 2012. 'Smiling in the Post-Fordist Economy "Affective Economy."' *Transformations* 22. Retrieved August 1, 2024. (http://www.transformationsjournal.org/journal/issue_22/article_02.shtml).

Negishi, Kaima. 2013. 'From Surveillant Text to Surveilling Device: The Face in Urban Transit Spaces.' *Surveillance and Society* 11(3): 324–333.

Negri, Antonio. 1989. *The Politics of Subversion: A Manifesto for the Twenty-First Century*. Cambridge: Polity Press.

Negri, Antonio. 1991. *Marx Beyond Marx: Lessons on the Grundrisse*. Brooklyn: Autonomedia.

Negri, Antonio. 1992. 'Interpretation of the Class Situation Today: Methodological Aspects.' Pp. 69–105 in *Open Marxism: Vol 2 Theory and Practice*, edited by Werner Bonefeld, Richard Gunn and Kosmas Psychopedis. London: Pluto Press.

Negri, Antonio. 1999. 'Value and Affect.' *Boundary 2* 26: 77–88.

Negri, Antonio. 1999a. 'The Spectre's Smile.' Pp. 5–16 in *Ghostly Demarcations: A Symposium on Jacques Derrida's Spectres of Marx*, edited by Michael Sprinker. London: Verso.

Negri, Antonio. 2003. *Time for Revolution*. London: Continuum.

Negri, Antonio. 2004. *Negri on Negri: Antonio Negri in Conversation with Anne Dufourmantelle*. London: Routledge.

Negri, Antonio. 2005 [1971]. 'Crisis of the Planner-State: Communism and Revolutionary Organisation.' Pp. 1–50 in *Books for Burning: Between Civil War and Democracy in 1970s Italy*, edited by Timothy S. Murphy. London: Verso.

Negri, Antonio. 2005 [1977]. 'Domination and Sabotage: on the Marxist Method of Social Transformation.' Pp. 231–290 in *Books for Burning: Between Civil War and Democracy in 1970s Italy*, edited by Timothy S. Murphy. London: Verso.

Negri, Antonio. 2005 [1977a]. 'Toward a Critique of the Material Constitution.' Pp. 180–230 in *Books for Burning: Between Civil War and Democracy in 1970s Italy*, edited by Timothy S. Murphy. London: Verso.

Negri, Antonio. 2008. *The Porcelain Workshop: For a New Grammar of Politics*. Los Angeles: Semiotext(e).

Negri, Antonio. 2008 [1981]. *The Savage Anomaly: The Power of Spinoza's Metaphysics and Politics*. Minneapolis: University of Minnesota Press.

Negri, Antonio. 2008 [2003]. 'On Social Ontology: Material Labour, Immaterial Labour and Biopolitics.' Pp. 60–78 in *Reflections on Empire*. Cambridge: Polity Press.

Negri, Antonio. 2010. 'Postface.' Pp. 263–272 in *Crisis in the Global Economy: Financial Markets, Social Struggle and New Political Scenarios*, edited by Andrea Fumagalli and Sandro Mendrazza. Los Angeles: Semiotext(e).

Negri, Antonio. 2013 [1996]. *The Winter Is Over: Writings on Transformation Denied, 1989–1995*. Los Angeles: Semiotext(e).

Negri, Antonio. 2013a. *Spinoza for Our Time: Politics and Postmodernity*. New York: Colombia University Press.

Negri, Antonio. 2013b. 'Building Coalitions of the Multitude.' *Global Project*. Retrieved August 1, 2024. (http://tinyurl.com/k7mhf4l).

Negri, Antonio. 2014. 'Reflections on the "Manifesto for an Accelerationist Politics".' *E-flux Journal* 53. August 1, 2024. (http://tinyurl.com/lk7eqc6).

Negri, Antonio. 2022. *Marx in Movement: Operaismo in Context*. Cambridge: Polity Press.

Negri, Antonio. 2023. *The Common*. Cambridge: Polity Press.

Negri, Antonio and Raf Scelsi. 2008. *Goodbye Mr Socialism: Radical Politics for the 21st Century*. London: Seven Stories Press.

Negri, Antonio and Carlo Vercellone. 2022. 'The Capital-Labour Relationship in Cognitive Capitalism.' Pp. 100–110 in Antonio Negri, *Marx in Movement: Operaismo in Context*. Cambridge: Polity Press.

Negri, Toni. 1988 [1982]. 'Archaeology and Project: The Mass Worker and the Social Worker.' Pp. 199–228 in *Revolution Retrieved: Selected Writings on Marx, Keynes, Capitalist Crisis and New Social Subjects 1967–83*. London: Red Notes.

Nelson, Anitra. 1999. *Marx's Concept of Money: The God of Commodities*. London: Routledge.

New Tang Dynasty Television. 2009. 'Smile Training for Japanese workers.' Retrieved August 10, 2014. (http://www.youtube.com/watch?v=ReC86fy1pJQ).

Newman, Meredith A., Mary E. Guy, Sharon H. Mastracci. 2009. 'Beyond Cognition: Affective Leadership and Emotional Labor.' *Public Administration* 69(1): 6–20.

Notes from Below. 2018. 'What is Class Composition?' Retrieved August 1, 2024. (https://notesfrombelow.org/what-is-class-composition).

Noys, Benjamin. 2010. *The Persistence of the Negative: A Critique of Contemporary Continental Theory*. Edinburgh: Edinburgh University Press.

Nunes, Rodrigo. 2007. 'Forward Where, Forward How? (Post)Operaismo Beyond the Immaterial Labour Thesis.' *Ephemera* 7(1): 178–202.

O'Brien, M.E. 2023. *Family Abolition: Capitalism and the Communizing of Care*. London: Pluto Press.

O'Dwyer, Rachel and Linda Doyle. 2012. 'This is Not a Bit-Pipe: A Political Economy of the Substrate Network.' *Fibreculture* 20: 10–34.

OMRON. 2009. *OMRON: sensing tomorrow*. Annual Report.

Panzieri, Raniero. 1980. 'The Capitalist Use of Machinery: Marx Versus the Objectivists.' Pp. 44–68 in *Outlines for a Critique of Technology*, edited by Phil Slater. London: Ink Links.

Papoulias, Constantina and Felicity Callard. 2010. 'Biology's Gift: Interrogating the Turn to Affect.' *Body & Society* 16: 29–56.

Parke, Michael R. and Myeong-Gu Seo. 2017. 'The Role of Affect Climate in Organizational Effectiveness.' *Academy of Management Review* 42(2): 334–360.

Partala, Timo and Veikko Surakka. 2004. 'The Effects of Affective Interventions in Human-Computer Interaction.' *Interacting with Computers* 16: 295–309.

Pasquinelli, Matteo. 2011. 'Machinic Capitalism and Network Surplus Value: Notes on the Political Economy of the Turing Machine.' Retrieved August 1, 2024. (http://matteopasquinelli.com/docs/Pasquinelli_Machinic_Capitalism.pdf).

Pasquinelli, Matteo. 2014. 'To Anticipate and Accelerate: Italian Operaismo and Reading Marx's Notion of the Organic Composition of Capital.' *Rethinking Marxism: A Journal of Economics, Culture and Society* 26(2): 178–192.

Pasquinelli, Matteo. 2023. *The Eye of the Master: A Social History of Artificial Intelligence*. London: Verso.

Passavant, Paul A. and Jodi Dean (eds). 2004. *Empire's New Clothes: Reading Hardt and Negri*. London: Routledge.

Patrick, Warren Stanley, Munish Thakur and Jatinder Kumar Jha. 2023. 'Attachment and Attractiveness Towards Organizations: Reinforcing the Intention to Stay Amidst the "Great Resignation."' *Evidenced Based HRM: A Forum for Empirical Scholarship* 12(3): 611–629.

Payne, Roy. 2001. 'Measuring Emotions at Work.' Pp. 107–129 in *Emotions at Work: Theory, Research and Applications in Management*, edited by Roy L. Payne and Cary L. Cooper. Chichester: John Wiley & Sons.

Peck, Jamie and Nik Theodore. 2012. 'Politicizing Contingent Work: Countering Neoliberal Labor Market Regulation ... From the Bottom Up?' *South Atlantic Quarterly* 111(4): 741–762.

Perrotta, Cosimo. 2018. *Unproductive Labour in Political Economy: The History of an Idea*, New York: Routledge.

Picard, Rosalind. 1999. 'Affective Computing for HCI.' in Proceedings of *8th International Conference on Human-Computer Interaction: Ergonomics and User Interfaces* 1.

Picard, Rosalind W. 2000. *Affective Computing*. Cambridge: MIT Press.

Piccone, Paul. 1972. 'Introduction to Mario Tronti's Workers and Capital.' *Telos* 14: 23–24.

Pilling, Geoffrey. 1986. 'The Law of Value in Marx and Ricardo.' Pp. 18–44 in *The Value Dimension: Marx versus Sraffa*, edited by Ben Fine, London and New York: Routledge and Keegan Paul.

Pitts, Frederick Harry. 2022. 'Measuring and Managing Creative Labour: Value Struggles and Billable Hours in the Creative Industries.' *Organization*, 29(6): 1081–1098.

Pitts, Frederick Harry. 2023. *Marx in Management: Rethinking Value, Labour and Class Struggles*. New York: Routledge.

Plemmons, Stefanie A. and Howard M. Weiss. 2012. 'Goals and Affect.' Pp. 117–132 in *New Developments in Goal Setting and Task Performance*, edited by Edwin A. Locke and Gary P. Latham. New York: Routledge.

Postone, Moishe. 1993. *Time, Labour and Social Domination: A Reinterpretation of Marx's Critical Theory*. Cambridge: Cambridge University Press.

Postone, Moishe. 2012. 'Thinking the Global Crisis.' *South Atlantic Quarterly* 111(2): 227–249.

Prentice, Catherine, Sergio Dominique Lopes, and Xuequn Wang. 2019. 'Emotional intelligence or artificial intelligence: an employee perspective.' *Journal of Hospitality Marketing and Management* 29(4): 1–27.

Qiu, Jack Linchuan, Melissa Gregg and Kate Crawford. 2014. 'Circuits of Labor: A Labor Theory of the iPhone Era.' *TripleC*. Retrieved August 1, 2024. (http://tinyurl .com/ohc86fo).

Raskin, Jef. 2000. *The Human Interface: New Directions for Designing Interactive Systems*. Reading: Addison-Wesley.

Read, Jason. 2011. '*The Affective Composition of Labor.*' Unemployed Negativity. May 17. Retrieved August 1, 2024. (http://www.unemployednegativity.com/2011/05 /affective-composition-of-labor.html).

Read, Jason. 2024. *The Double Shift: Spinoza and Marx on the Politics of Work*, London: Verso.

Reber, Dierdra. 2012. 'Headless Capitalism: Affect as Free-Market Episteme.' *Differences: A Journal of Feminist Cultural Studies*. 25(1): 63–100.

Recomposition Collective. 2011. 'Direct Unionism: A Discussion Paper.' Retrieved August 1, 2024. (http://recomposition.info/direct-unionism/).

Records, Hal, Nancy Records, Richard Glass, Robert Behling, and Janet Prichard. 2007. 'The Potential Impact of Speech Recognition Technology on Workplace Productivity.' *Issues in Information Systems* 8(2): 541–546.

Red Notes. 1978. *Italy 1977–78: Living with an Earthquake*. London: Publications Distribution Cooperative.

Redding, Paul. 1999. *The Logic of Affect*. Melbourne: Melbourne University Press.

Ricardo, David. 1949 [1817]. *The Principles of Political Economy and Taxation*. London: Dent.

Richardson, Sharon. 2020. 'Affective Computing in the Modern Workplace.' *Business Information Review* 37(2): 78–85.

Richelt, Helmut. 1982. 'From the Frankfurt School to Value-Form Analysis.' *Thesis Eleven* 4: 166–169.

Richelt, Helmut. 1993. 'Some Notes on Jacques Bidet's Structuralist Interpretation of Marx's *Capital.*' *Common Sense* 13: 68–75.

Richelt, Helmut. 1995. 'Why did Marx Conceal His Dialectical Method?' Pp. 40–83 in *Emancipating Marx: Open Marxism 3*, edited by Werner Bonefeld, Richard Gunn, John Holloway and Kosmas Psychopedis. London: Pluto Press.

Roberts, Ariel, Paul E. Levy, Catalina Flores and Gina Thoebes. 2020. 'Performance Management and Workplace Affect.' Pp. 339–349 in *The Cambridge Handbook of Workplace Affect*, edited by Liu-Qin Yang, Russel Cropanzo, Catherine S. Daus and Vincente Martinez-Tur. Cambridge: Cambridge University Press.

Roemmich, Kat, Florian Schaub, and Nazanin Andalibi. 2023. 'Emotion AI at Work: Implications for Workplace Surveillance, Emotional Labour, and Emotional Privacy.' *CHI '23: ACM Conference on Human Factors in Computing Systems*, April 23–28 2023, Hamburg Germany. ACM, New York.

Roggero, Gigi. 2011. *The Production of Living Knowledge: The Crisis of the University and the Transformation of Labour in Europe and North America*. Philadelphia: Temple University Press.

Roggero, Gigi. 2014. 'Notes of Framing and Reinventing Co-Research.' *Ephemera: Theory and Politics in Organization* 14(3): 515–523.

Roggero, Gigi. 2020. 'To Avoid the Farce of the Common.' *Praktyka Teoretyczna* 4(38): 161–168.

Roggero, Gigi. 2023. *Italian Operaismo: History, Genealogy, Method.* Massachusetts: MIT Press.

Rowlinson, Michael, Roy Stager Jacques and Charles Booth. 2009. 'Critical Management and Organizational History.' Pp. 286–303 in *The Oxford Handbook of Critical Management Studies*, edited by M. Alvesson, T. Bridgman and H. Willmott. Oxford: Oxford University Press.

Rubin, I.I. 1990 [1928] *Essays on Marx's Theory of Value.* Montreal: Black Rose Books.

Rubin, I.I. 1978 [1927] 'Archive: Abstract Labour and Value in Marx's System.' *Capital and Class* 5: 107–139.

Rubin, Isaak Ilyich. 1989 [1929]. *A History of Economic Thought.* London: Pluto Press.

Ruddick, Susan. 2010. 'The Politics of Affect: Spinoza in the Work of Negri and Deleuze.' *Theory, Culture and Society* 27(4): 21–45.

Ruel, Huub and Esther Njoku. 2021. 'AI Redefining the Hospitality Industry.' *Journal of Tourism Futures* 7(1): 53–66.

Sacchetto, Devi, Emiliana Armano and Steve Wright. 2013. 'Co-research and Counter-Research: Romano Alquati's Itinerary Within and Beyond Italian Radical Political Thought.' *Viewpoint Magazine*, September 27. Retrieved August 1, 2024. (https://viewpointmag.com/2013/09/27/coresearch-and-counter-research-romano-alquatis-itinerary-within-and-beyond-italian-radical-political-thought/).

Salmenniemi, Suvi. 2022. *Affect, Alienation and Politics in Therapeutic Culture: Capitalism on the Skin*. Cham: Palgrave MacMillan.

Sampson, Tony D. 2012. *Virality: Contagion Theory in the Age of Network*. Minneapolis: University of Minnesota Press.

Sawaf, Ayman, Harold H. Bloomfield and Jared Rosen. 2001. 'Inner Technology: Emotions in the New Millennium.' Pp. 327–342 in *Emotions at Work: Theory, Research and Applications in Management*, edited by Roy L. Payne and Cary L. Cooper. Chichester: John Wiley & Sons.

Schaefer, Donovan O. 2019. *The Evolution of Affect Theory: The Humanities, Science, and the Study of Power*. Oxford: Oxford University Press.

Schmitt, Antje. 2020. 'Benefits of Negative Affects at Work.' Pp. 200–213 in *The Cambridge Handbook of Workplace Affect*, edited by Liu-Qin Yang, Russel Cropanzo, Catherine S. Daus and Vincente Martinez-Tur. Cambridge: Cambridge University Press.

Schultz, Susanne. 2006. 'Dissolved Boundaries and "Affective Labour": On the Disappearance of Reproductive Labour and Feminist Critique in *Empire.' Capitalism, Nature, Socialism* 17(1): 77–82.

Schweingruber, David and Nancy Berns. 2005. 'Shaping the Selves of Young Salespeople through Emotion Management.' *Journal of Contemporary Ethnography* 34(6): 679–706.

Sedgwick, Eve Kosofsky. 2007. 'Melanie Klein and the Difference Affect Makes.' *South Atlantic Quarterly* 106(3): 625–642.

Sedgwick, Eve Kosofsky and Adam Frank. 1995. 'Shame in the Cybernetic Fold: Reading Silvan Tomkins.' Pp. 1–29 in *Shame and its Sisters: A Silvan Tomkins Reader*, edited by Eve Kosofsky Sedgwick and Adam Frank. Durham: Duke University Press.

Sedgwick, Eve Kosofsky and Adam Frank. 1995a. *Shame and Its Sisters: A Silvan Tomkins Reader*. Durham: Duke University Press.

Sengers, Pheobe, Rainer Liesendahl, Werner Magar, Christoph Seibert, Boris Muller, Thorsten Joachims and Weidong Geng. 2002. 'The Enigmatics of Affect.' in Proceedings of *4th Conference on Designing Interactive Systems: Processes, Practices, Methods, and Techniques; Symposium on Designing Interactive Systems*, London, 25–26 June.

Seo, Myeong-Gu, Jean M. Bartunek and Lisa Feldman Barrett. 2004. 'The Role of Affective Experience in Work Motivation.' *Academy of Management Review* 29(3): 423–439.

Seo, Myeong-Gu, Jean M. Bartunek and Lisa Feldman Barrett. 2010. 'The Role of Affective Experience in Work Motivation: Test of a Conceptual Model.' *Journal of Organizational Behavior* 31: 951–968.

Serenko, Alexander. 2023. 'The Human Capital Management Perspective on Quiet Quitting: Recommendations for Employees, Managers, and National Policy Makers.' *Journal of Knowledge Management* 28(1): 27–43.

Serenko, Alexander. 2023a. 'The Great Resignation: The Great Exodus or the Onset of the Great Knowledge Revolution.' *Journal of Knowledge Management* 27(4): 1042–1055.

Shaviro, Steven. 2010. 'Post-Cinematic Affect: On Grace Jones, *Boarding Gate*, and *Southland Tales*.' *Film Philosophy* 14(1): 1–102.

Shukaitis, Stevphen. 2009. *Internal Machines: Autonomy and Self-Organization in the Revolutions of Everyday Life*. London: Minor Compositions.

Shukaitis, Stevphen. 2011. *The Wisdom to Make Worlds: Strategic Reality and the Art of the Undercommons*. Retrieved July 20 2024. (http://eipcp.net/transversal/0311/shukaitis/en).

Shukaitis, Stevphen. 2014. 'Learning Not to Labour.' *Rethinking Marxism: A Journal of Economics, Culture and Society* 26(2): 193–205.

Sic. 2011. *Sic 1: International Journal for Communisation*. London: Sic.

Slaby, Jan, Rainer Mulhoff and Philip Wuschner. 2019. 'Affective Arrangements.' *Emotions Review* 11(1): 3–12.

Smith, Adam. 1937 [1776]. *The Wealth of Nations*. New York: The Modern Library.

Smith, Adam. 2002. *The Theory of Moral Sentiments*. Cambridge: Cambridge University Press.

Smith, Jason E. 2020. *Smart Machines and Service Work: Automation in the Age of Stagnation*. Chicago: Reaktion Books.

Smith, Jason E. 2021. 'Striketober and Labor's Long Downturn.' *The Brooklyn Rail*, December 2021–January 2022.

Smith, Tony. 2000. *Technology and Capital in the Age of Lean Production: A Marxian Critique of the New Economy*. New York: State University of New York Press.

Smith, Tony. 2013. '"General Intellect" in the *Grundrisse* and Beyond'. Pp. 213–231, in *In Marx's Laboratory: Critical Interpretations of the Grundrisse*, edited by Riccardo Bellofiore, Guido Starosta and Peter D. Thomas. Leiden: Brill.

Southall, Nicholas. 2010. *A Multitude of Possibilities: The Strategic Vision of Antonio Negri and Michael Hardt*. Doctor of Philosophy Thesis, University of Wollongong.

Southall, Nick. 2024. *Disaster Communism and Anarchy in the Streets*. Wollongong: Kembla Books.

Spector, Paul E. 2020. 'Emotion and Various Forms of Job Performance.' Pp. 120–130 in *The Cambridge Handbook of Workplace Affect*, edited by Liu-Qin Yang, Russel Cropanzo, Catherine S. Daus and Vincente Martinez-Tur. Cambridge: Cambridge University Press.

Spinoza, Benedict de. 1951. *The Chief Works of Benedict de Spinoza*. New York: Dover Publications.

Spinoza, Benedict De. 1996. *Ethics*. London: Penguin.

Srnicek, Nick. 2017. *Platform Capitalism*. Cambridge: Cambridge University Press.

Stakeheimer, Kersten and Marina Vishmidt. 2016. *Reproducing Autonomy: Work, Money, Crisis and Contemporary Art*. Berlin: Mute.

Staples, David. 2007. 'Women's Work and the Ambivalent Gift of Entropy.' Pp. 119–150 in *The Affective Turn: Theorising the Social*, edited by Patricia Ticineto Clough and Jean Halley. Durham: Duke University Press.

Staples, David. 2007a. *No Place Like Home: Organising Home Based Labour in the Era of Structural Adjustment*. New York: Routledge.

Steiber, Nadia. 2013. 'Economic Crisis and Work Motivation.' Pp. 195–228 in *Economic Crisis, Quality of Work, and Social Integration: The European Experience*, edited by Duncan Gallie. Oxford: Oxford University Press.

Stitt, Greg. 2002. *Diverted to Delhi*. Sydney: Film Australia.

Sy, Thomas, Susanna Tram, Linda A. O'Hara. 2005. 'Relation of Employee and Manager Emotional Intelligence to Job Satisfaction and Performance.' *Journal of Vocational Behaviour* 68: 461–473.

Szadowski, Krystian. 2023. *Capital in Higher Education: A Critique of the Political Economy of the Sector*. Switzerland: Palgrave MacMillan.

Tadajewski, Mark, Pauline Maclaren, Elizabeth Parsons and Martin Parker. 2011. *Key Concepts in Critical Management Studies*. London: Sage.

Tadiar, Neferti X.M. 2012. 'Life-Times in Fate Playing.' *South Atlantic Quarterly* 111(4): 783–802.

Tao, Jianhua and Tienieu Tan. 2003. *Affective Information Processing*. London: Springer.

Taylor, Claire and Tony Dobbins. 2021. 'Social Media: A (New) Contested Terrain Between Sousveillance and Surveillance in the Digital Workplace.' *New Technology, Work and Employment* 36: 263–284.

Taylor, Steve and Melissa Tyler. 2000. 'Emotional Labour and Sexual Difference in the Airline Industry.' *Work, Employment and Society* 14(1): 77–95.

Terranova, Tiziana. 2014. 'Debt and Autonomy: Lazzarato and the Constituent Powers of the Social.' *The New Reader*. Retrieved August 1, 2024. (http://thenewreader .org/Issues/1/DebtAndAutonomy).

The Care Collective. 2020. *The Care Manifesto: The Politics of Interdependence*. London: Verso.

Thomas, James M. and Jennifer G. Correa. 2015. *Affective Labour: (Dis)Assembling, Distance and Difference*. Maryland: Rowman and Littlefield.

Thompson, Paul. 2005. 'Foundation and Empire: A Critique of Hardt and Negri.' *Capital & Class* 29: 73–98.

Thorne, Joe. 2011. 'The Workers Inquiry: What's the Point?' *The Commune*. Retrieved August 1, 2024. (https://libcom.org/article/workers-inquiry-whats-point).

Toffler, Alvin. 1984. *Future Shock*. New York: Bantam Books.

Tomba, Massimiliano. 2009. 'Historical Temporalities of Capital: An Anti-Historicist Perspective.' *Historical Materialism* 17(4): 44–65.

Tomba, Massimiliano. 2013. *Marx's Temporalities*. Chicago: Haymarket Books.

Tractinsky, Noam, Adi Shoval-Katz and Dror Ikar. 2000. 'What is Beautiful is Useable.' *Interacting with Computers* 13: 127–145.

Tronti, Mario. 1966. *Operai e Capitale.* Torino: Guilio Enualdi.

Tronti, Mario. 1972. 'Workers and Capital.' *Telos* 14: 25–62.

Tronti, Mario. 1973. 'Social Capital.' *Telos* 17: 98–121.

Tronti, Mario. 2007. 'The strategy of refusal.' Pp. 28–35 in *Autonomia: Post-political Politics*, edited by Sylvere Lotringer and Christian Marazzi. Los Angeles: Semiotext(e).

Tronti, Mario. 2008. 'Italy.' Pp. 229–235 in *Karl Marx's Grundrisse: Foundations of the Critique of Political Economy 150 Years Later*, edited by Marcello Musto. London: Routledge.

Tronti, Mario. 2012. 'Our Operaismo.' *New Left Review* 73. Retrieved August 1, 2024 (http://newleftreview.org/II/73/mario-tronti-our-operaismo).

Tronti, Mario. 2019 [1966]. *Workers and Capital.* London: Verso.

Trott, Ben. 2013. 'From the Precariat to the Multitude.' *Global Discourse: An Interdisciplinary Journal of Current Affairs and Applied Contemporary Thought* 3(3–4): 406–425.

Truong, Khiet P. 2010. 'Measuring Affective and Social Signals in Vocal Interaction', in proceedings of *Measuring Behaviour 2010*, Eindhoven, The Netherlands: August 24–27.

Udsen, Lars Erik & Anker Helms Jorgensen. 2005. 'The Aesthetic Turn: Unravelling Recent Aesthetic Approaches to Human-Computer Interaction.' *Digital Creativity* 16(4): 205–216.

Umemuro, Hiroyuki. 2009. 'Affective Technology, Affective Management, Towards Affective Society,' Pp. 683–692 in *Human-Computer-Interaction, Part III*, edited by J.A. Jacko. Berlin: Springer.

Uninomade. 2010. 'Nothing Will Ever Be The Same: Ten Theses on the Financial Crisis.' Pp. 237–262 in *Crisis in the Global Economy: Financial Markets, Social Struggle, and New Political Scenarios*, edited by Andrea Fumagalli and Sandro Mendrazza. Los Angeles: Semiotext(e).

Uppal, Anmol, Shweta Tyagi, Rishi Kumar and Seema Sharma. 2019. 'Emotion Recognition and Drowsiness Detection Using Python.' *9th International Conference on Cloud Computing, Data Science and Engineering (Confluence)*: 464–469.

Van Hoorebeke, Delphine. 2018. *The Management of Living Beings or Emo-Management.* London: ISTE Ltd.

Van Oort, Madison. 2023. *Worn Out: How Retailers Surveil and Exploit Workers in the Digital Age and How Workers Are Fighting Back.* Cambridge: The MIT Press.

Veldstra, Carolyn. 2020. 'Bad Feeling at Work: Emotional Labour, Precarity, and the Affective Economy' *Cultural Studies* 34(1): 1–24.

Venz, Laura, Anne Casper and Sabine Sonnentag. 2020. 'Affect, Stress, and Health: The Role of Work Characteristics and Work Events.' Pp. 105–119 in *The Cambridge*

Handbook of Workplace Affect, edited by Liu-Qin Yang, Russel Cropanzo, Catherine S. Daus and Vincente Martinez-Tur. Cambridge: Cambridge University Press.

Vercellone, Carlo. 1996. 'The Anomaly and Exemplariness of the Italian Welfare State.' Pp. 81–98 in *Radical Thought in Italy: A Potential Politics*, edited by Paolo Virno and Michael Hardt. Minneapolis: University of Minnesota Press.

Vercellone, Carlo. 2007. 'From Formal Subsumption to the General Intellect: Elements for a Marxist Reading of the Thesis of Cognitive Capitalism.' *Historical Materialism* 15: 13–36.

Vercellone, Carlo. 2010. 'The Crisis of the Law of Value and the Becoming-Rent of Profit.' Pp. 85–118 in *Crisis in the Global Economy: Financial Markets, Social Struggle, and New Political Scenario*, edited by Andrea Fumagalli and Sandro Mendrazza. Los Angeles: Semiotext(e).

Vercellone, Carlo and Stefano Dughera. 2019. 'Metamorphosis of the Theory of Value and Becoming-Rent of Profit: An Attempt to Clarify the Terms of a Debate.' Pp. 33–60 in *Cognitive Capitalism, Welfare and Labour: The Commonfare Hypothesis*, edited by Andrea Fumagalli, Alfonso Giuliani, Stefano Lucarelli and Carlo Vercellone. New York: Routledge.

Vercellone, Carlo and Alfonso Giuliani. 2019. 'An Introduction to Cognitive Capitalism: A Marxist Approach.' Pp. 10–32 in *Cognitive Capitalism, Welfare and Labour: The Commonfare Hypothesis*, edited by Andrea Fumagalli, Alfonso Giuliani, Stefano Lucarelli and Carlo Vercellone. New York: Routledge.

Vidal, Matt. 2022. *Management Divided: Contradictions of Labor Management*, Oxford University Press, Incorporated.

Vincent, Steven. 2011. 'The Emotional Labour Process: An Essay on the Economy of Feelings.' *Human Relations* 64(10): 1369–1392.

Virno, Paolo. 1996. 'Notes on the General Intellect'. Pp. 265–272 in *Marxism Beyond Marxism*, edited by Saree Makdisi, Cesare Casarino and Rebecca Karl, New York: Routledge.

Virno, Paolo. 1996a. 'The Ambivalence of Disenchantment.' Pp. 13–36 in *Radical Thought in Italy: A Potential Politics*, edited by Paolo Virno and Michael Hardt. Minneapolis: University of Minnesota Press.

Virno, Paolo. 1996b. 'Virtuosity and Revolution: The Political Theory of Exodus.' Pp. 189–212 in *Radical thought in Italy: A Potential Politics*, edited by Paolo Virno and Michael Hardt. Minneapolis: University of Minnesota Press.

Virno, Paolo. 1996c. 'Do You Remember Counter-Revolution?' Pp. 241–259 in *Radical Thought in Italy: A Potential Politics*, edited by Paolo Virno and Michael Hardt. Minneapolis: University of Minnesota Press.

Virno, Paolo. 2002. *General Intellect, Exodus, Multitude*. Retrieved July 20, 2024. (http://www.generation-online.org/p/fpvirno2.htm).

Virno, Paolo. 2004. *A Grammar of the Multitude*. Los Angeles: Semiotext(e).

Virno, Paolo. 2007. 'Dreams of a Successful Life.' Pp. 112–117 in *Autonomia: Post-Political Politics*, edited by Sylvere Lotringer and Christian Marazzi. Los Angeles: Semiotext(e).

Virno, Paolo. 2008. *Multitude: Between Innovation and Negation*. Los Angeles: Semiotext(e).

Virno, Paolo. 2009. 'Angels and the General Intellect: Individuation in Duns Scotus and Gilbert Simondon.' *Parrhesia* 7: 58–67.

Virtanen, Akseli. 2004. 'General Economy: The Entrance of Multitude into Production.' *Ephemera* 4(3): 209–232.

Vora, Kalindi. 2010. 'The Transmission of Care: Affective Economies in Indian Call Centers.' Pp. 33–48 in *Intimate Labours: Cultures, Technologies and the Politics of Care*, edited by Eileen Boris & Rhacel Salazar Parreñas, Stanford, CA: Stanford University Press.

Vora, Kalindi. 2013. 'Limits of "Labor": Accounting for Affect and the Biological in Transnational Surrogacy and Service Work.' *South Atlantic Quarterly* 111(4): 681–700.

Weeks, Jacquilyn. 2011. 'Un-/Re-productive Maternal Labour: Marxist Feminism and Chapter 15 of Marx's *Capital*.' *Rethinking Marxism* 23(1): 31–40.

Weeks, Kathi. 2011. *The Problem with Work: Feminism, Marxism, Antiwork Politics, and Postwork Imaginaries*. Durham: Duke University Press.

Weeks, Kathi. 2005. 'The Refusal of Work as Demand and Perspective' Pp. 109–135 in *The Philosophy of Antonio Negri: Resistance in Practice*, edited by Timothy S. Murphy and Abdul-Karim Mustapha. London: Pluto Press.

Wegge, Jurgen, Rolf van Dick, Gary K. Fisher, Michael A. West, Jeremy F. Dawson. 2006. 'A test of Basic Assumptions of Affective Events Theory (AET) in Call Centre Work.' *British Journal of Management* 17: 237–254.

Weiss, Howard M. and Kelsey L. Merlo. 2018. 'Affect, Attention, and Episodic Performance.' *Current Directions in Psychological Science* 29(5): 453–459.

Weiss, Howard M. 2002. 'Conceptual and Empirical Foundations for the Study of Affect at Work.' Pp. 20–63 in *Emotions in the Workplace: Understanding the Structure and Role of Emotions in Organisational Behaviour*, edited by Robert G. Lord, Richard J. Klimoski and Rith Kanfer. San Francisco: Wiley.

Weiss, Howard M. and Russell Cropanzano. 1996. 'Affective Events Theory: A Theoretical Discussion of the Structure, Causes and Consequences of Affective Experiences at Work'. *Research in Organisational Behaviour* 18: 1–74.

Weiss, Howard M. and Arthur P. Brief. 2001. 'Affect at Work: A Historical Perspective.' Pp. 133–171 in *Emotions at Work: Theory, Research and Applications in Management*, edited by Roy L. Payne and Cary L. Cooper. Chichester: John Wiley & Sons.

Wells, Robert. 2014. 'The Multitude: Ambivalence and Antagonism.' *Rethinking Marxism: A Journal of Economics, Culture and Society* 26(2): 239–251.

Wen. 2023. 'The End of an Era: Labor Activism in Early 21st Century China.' *Chuang*, April 24. Retrieved, July 26, 2024. (https://chuangcn.org/2023/04/the-end-of-an-era -labor-activism-in-early-21st-century-china/).

Wildcat. 2021. 'China: Neijuan.' *Wildcat* 107: np. Retrieved July 31 2024. (http://wildcat -www.de/en/wildcat/107/e_w107_china.html).

Williams, Evan Calder. 2013. 'Invisible Organisation: Reading Romano Alquati.' *Viewpoint Magazine*, September 26. Retrieved August 1, 2024. (https://viewpoint mag.com/2013/09/26/invisible-organization-reading-romano-alquati/).

Wilson, Elizabeth A. 2010. *Affect and Artificial Intelligence.* Seattle: University of Washington Press.

Winant, Gabriel. 2021. *The Next Shift: The Fall of Industry and the Rise of Health Care in Rust Belt America.* Cambridge: Harvard University Press.

Winner, Langdon. 2020. *The Whale and the Reactor: A Search for Limits in an Age of High Technology*, Chicago: University of Chicago Press.

Wissinger, Elizabeth. 2007. 'Modelling a Way of Life.' *Ephemera* 7(1): 250–269.

Wissinger, Elizabeth. 2007a. 'Always on Display: Affective Production in the Modelling industry.' Pp. 231–260 in *The Affective Turn: Theorising the Social*, edited by Patricia Ticineto Clough and Jean Halley. Durham: Duke University Press.

Wolfe, Charles T. 2007. 'Materialism and Temporality: on Antonio Negri's "Constitutive" Ontology.' Pp. 198–220 in *The Philosophy of Antonio Negri volume 2: Revolution in Theory*, edited by Timothy S. Murphy and Abdul-Karim Mustapha. London: Pluto Press.

Wolfe, Charles T. 2011. 'Antonio Negri's Ontology of Empire and Multitude.' *Ideas in History* 5(1–2): 109–135.

Woodcock, Jamie. 2017. *Working the Phones: Control and Resistance in Call Centres.* London: Pluto Press.

Woodcock, Jamie. 2019. 'Understanding Affective Labour.' Pp. 61–74 in *The Work Cure: Critical Essays on Work and Wellness*, edited by David Frayne. Monmouth: PCCS Books.

Wright, Steve. 1980. 'Intro to Italian Workerism.' *Journal of Australian Political Economy* 9: 73–85.

Wright, Steve. 2002. *Storming Heaven: Class Composition and Struggle in Italian Autonomist Marxism.* London: Pluto Press.

Wright, Steve. 2005. 'Reality Check: Are We Living in an Immaterial World?' *Metamute*, November 25. Retrieved August 1, 2024. (http://tinyurl.com/m5tkgqk).

Wright, Steve. 2005a. 'A Party of Autonomy?' Pp. 73–108 in *The Philosophy of Antonio Negri: Resistance in Practice*, edited by Timothy S. Murphy and Abdul-Karim Mustapha. London: Pluto Press.

Wright, Steve. 2011. 'Cattivi Maestri: Some Reflections on the Legacy of Guido Bianchini, Luciano Ferrari Bravo, and Primo Moroni.' Pp. 21–56 in *Reading Negri:*

Marxism in the Age of Empire, edited by Pierra Lamarche, Max Rosenkrantz, and David Sherman. Chicago: Carus Publishing Company.

Wright, Steve. 2013. 'Revolution from Above.' Pp. 369–394 in *Beyond Marx: Theorising the Global Labour Relations of the Twenty-First Century*, edited by Marcel van der Linden and Karl Heinz Roth. Leiden: Brill.

Wright, Steve. 2022. *The Weight of the Printed Word: Text, Context and Militancy in Operaismo*. Chicago: Haymarket Books.

Yang, Liu-Qin, Katharine McMahon and Jessie Fengmin Zhen. 2020. 'A Review of Quantitative Methods to Measure Workplace Affect,' Pp. 76–90 in *The Cambridge Handbook of Workplace Affect*, edited by Liu-Qin Yang, Russel Cropanzo, Catherine S. Daus and Vincente Martinez-Tur. Cambridge: Cambridge University Press.

Yeates, Nicola. 2004. 'A Dialogue With "Global Care Chain" Analysis: Nurse Migration in the Irish Context.' *Feminist Review* 77: 79–95.

Yeates, Nicola. 2005. 'A Global Political Economy of Care.' *Social Policy and Society* 4(2): 227–234.

Zapf, Dieter, M. Esther Garcia-Buades and Silvia Ortiz-Bonnin. 2020. 'Emotion Management and Emotion Work.' Pp. 298–309 in *The Cambridge Handbook of Workplace Affect*, edited by Liu-Qin Yang, Russel Cropanzo, Catherine S. Daus and Vincente Martinez-Tur. Cambridge: Cambridge University Press.

Zeng, Zhihong, Maja Pantic, Glenn I. Roisman, and Thomas S. Huang. 2007. 'A Survey of Affective Methods: Audio, Visual and Spontaneous Expressions', *ICMI '07* Nagoya, Japan: November 12–15. Retrieved August 1, 2024. (http://eprints.eemcs.utwente .nl/11644/01/ICMI07-ZengEtAl-FINAL.pdf).

Zerowork Collective. 1992 [1975]. 'Introduction to Zerowork I.' Pp. 109–114 in *Midnight Oil: Work, Energy, War 1973–1992*, edited by Midnight Notes Collective. New York: Autonomedia.

Zhao, Wen-Yi, Rama Chellappa, Jonathon P. Phillips, and Azriel Rosenfeld. 2003. 'Face Recognition: A Literature Survey.' *ACM Computing Surveys* 35(4): 399–458.

Zizek, Slavoj. 2009. *First as Tragedy, Then as Farce*. London: Verso.

Zoghbi-Manrique-De-Lara, Pablo and Maryamsadat Sharifiatashgah. 2020. 'An Affective Events Model of the Influence of the Physical Work Environment on Interpersonal Citizenship Behaviour.' *Journal of Work and Organizational Psychology* 36(1): 27–37.

Zuboff, Shoshana. 2019. *The Age of Surveillance Capitalism: The Fight for a Human Future at the New Frontier of Power*. New York: Public Affairs.

Zuoyue. 2023. 'Three Autumn Revolts: Breaking the Ice on China's "Anti-Lockdown Movement."' *Chuang* January 20, 2023. Retrieved July 31, 2024. (https://chuangcn .org/2023/01/three-autumn-revolts/).

Index